Britain's Desert War in
and Libya 1940–19

Britain's Desert War in Egypt and Libya 1940–1942

The End of the Beginning

By

D.W. Braddock, B.A.

with forewords by

Professor N.H. GIBBS, M.A., D.Phil.
(1964 Edition)

and

General Sir Nick Carter KCB CBE DSO ADC Gen
Chief of the Defence Staff (2019 Edition)

Pen & Sword

MILITARY

AN IMPRINT OF PEN & SWORD BOOKS LTD.
YORKSHIRE – PHILADELPHIA

First published in Great Britain in 1964 under the title *The Campaigns in Egypt and Libya 1940–1942* by Aldershot, Gale & Polden Ltd.
Republished in this format in 2019 by
Pen & Sword Military
An imprint of
Pen & Sword Books Ltd
Yorkshire – Philadelphia

ISBN 978 1 52675 978 8

A CIP catalogue record for this book is
available from the British Library.

Printed and bound in the UK by TJ International Ltd, Padstow, Cornwall.

Pen & Sword Books Limited incorporates the imprints of Atlas, Archaeology, Aviation, Discovery, Family History, Fiction, History, Maritime, Military, Military Classics, Politics, Select, Transport, True Crime, Air World, Frontline Publishing, Leo Cooper, Remember When, Seaforth Publishing, The Praetorian Press, Wharncliffe Local History, Wharncliffe Transport, Wharncliffe True Crime and White Owl.

For a complete list of Pen & Sword titles please contact

PEN & SWORD BOOKS LIMITED
47 Church Street, Barnsley, South Yorkshire, S70 2AS, England
E-mail: enquiries@pen-and-sword.co.uk
Website: www.pen-and-sword.co.uk

Or
PEN AND SWORD BOOKS
1950 Lawrence Rd, Havertown, PA 19083, USA
E-mail: Uspen-and-sword@casematepublishers.com
Website: www.penandswordbooks.com

Contents

Foreword

The campaigns in Egypt and Libya, 1940–42, are a most fruitful subject for the student of military history. Every aspect of war can be studied in them with interest and profit. At the grand strategy level they illustrate some of the fundamental problems Britain has had to face for generations past in the reconciliation of her island and world-wide interests. At the high command level, both British and German, there is rich material for the study of personalities and methods of command. Previous accounts of this aspect of these campaigns have, it is true, sometimes been distorted by bias. But the present author does not err in that respect. His own judgments are fair and he provides the serious student with ample material for the formation of independent conclusions. Again, the history of desert fighting offers not only the whole range of operations from small and often disjointed skirmishes to major set battles; it also provides a wealth of material for the study of the development of weapons and the impact which that development can have on the course of operations.

Finally, the desert fighting of these years saw the first genuine British inter-Service co-operation of the Second World War. Lessons were learned in Egypt and Libya which were of profound importance for the subsequent conduct of the war in Italy, in north-western Europe and in the Far East.

Mr. Braddock has written a scholarly and attractive study. His book provides officers (and others, too) with an excellent comprehensive account which should stimulate everyone who reads it to further reading.

Professor N.H. Gibbs, M.A., D.Phil.,
Chichele Professor of the History of War.

Foreword to 2019 Edition

I have always hugely enjoyed studying the campaigns in Egypt and Libya between 1940 and 1942. They are the source of a huge number of lessons for the student of military history, at all levels of command from the strategic to the tactical. Interestingly the outcome of the Campaign was in many ways determined by the science of supply. It is a truism that amateurs talk tactics and professionals talk logistics – but it was the combination of stuff and what fuelled it that was decisive.

The Campaign also teaches us much about the nature of the British Army at that time and its leadership. The hard-won lessons of World War One that had led to the very successful Hundred Day Campaign in the late summer of 1918 and the importance of combined Arms manoeuvre had regrettably not been applied as well as they might have been by this stage in World War Two. The arrival of Rommel ruthlessly exposed what the early battles against Italian opponents had not and it took a number of reverses for the British leadership to fix it.

Unlike the German Army the British Army lacked a war-fighting military doctrine and this was ruthlessly exploited by Rommel during the later battles of the Campaign. Indeed, he observed of the 8th Army's performance that "too often orders were the basis for discussion". And it was not until 1989 that this gap in the British Army's thinking was filled with the publication of 'The Design for Military Operations – the British Military Doctrine' which clearly laid out the hierarchy of Fighting Power - the Conceptual, the Moral and the Physical, and established the British Army's Command Philosophy.

As a young officer studying for the Staff College exam at that time, I was fortunate that the author was one of the academic instructors who patiently educated me in the tactics and techniques needed to out manoeuvre the examiners. Indeed, he helped me become a 'how to think thinker' rather than a 'what to think thinker'. His part in the development of much of the senior horsepower in the British Army has been huge. So, I commend this republished version of this excellent book to you. The analysis is as sound today as it was 55 years ago when it was first published.

General Sir Nick Carter KCB CBE DSO ADC Gen
Chief of the Defence Staff

List of Maps

Introduction

This book has been written with the intention of providing British Army officers who are studying for the Staff College and Promotion examinations with a short but reasonably comprehensive account in one volume of the principal events of the campaigns which were fought in the deserts of Egypt and Libya between June, 1940, and November, 1942. (It is regretted that lack of space has made it necessary to omit a description of the activities of the Long Range Desert Group.) At the same time, however, it is hoped that others who are interested in the study of war and generalship will find something of value in the description of campaigns which first brought into the public eye perhaps the most famous of all modern British armies, and some of the most notable of the British and German commanders of the 2nd World War.

The desert campaigns are still a subject for violent controversy and it has been the author's intention, so far as is possible, to describe the battles and then to let the facts speak for themselves. It is hoped that in this way readers can come to an honest and objective interpretation of the events of the war in the desert.

Military students should remember that this book is designed to serve as an introduction to a deeper study of these campaigns, and particular emphasis is laid on the need for them to make up their own minds on all controversial issues, and to examine very closely the validity of any criticisms and conclusions that may appear in the text.

The author takes full responsibility for any errors that may be present.

He also wishes to thank especially Major-General H. Essame, C.B.E., D.S.O., M.C., and Major-General E. K. G. Sixsmith, C.B., C.B.E., for their help and advice in the preparation of this book. They were kind enough to read the various manuscripts that were produced, and their criticisms and suggestions were invaluable in enabling the book to take its final form. Thanks are also due to Major H. C. H. Mead, M.A., who drew up the Chronology; Major- General R. M. P. Carver, C.B., C.B.E., D.S.O., M.C.; Brigadier A.W. Brown, C.B.E., D.S.O., M.C., of the Royal Armoured Corps

Tank Museum; Colonel E. F. Offord, D.S.O., M.B.E., of the School of Tank Technology; and Mr. A. Carson Clark, cartographer to the Geography Department in the University of Southampton.

It is also desired to acknowledge the generosity of Major-General I. S. O. Playfair and H.M.S.O. in allowing the chronological tables in the Official History to be used as a basis for those in this book, and the particular use that was made of the following works in the preparation of the present volume:

The Mediterranean and the Middle East, Vols. I–III (Official History) by Major-General I. S. O. Playfair. (H.M.S.O.)

The Sidi Resegh Battles and Crisis in the Desert by J. A. I. Agar-Hamilton and L. C. F. Turner. (O.U.P.)

Against Great Odds by Brigadier C. N. Barclay. (Sifton Praed and Co.)

The Desert Generals by Correlli Barnett. (Wm. Kimber.)

El Alamein (Batsford), and Articles in the Royal Armoured Corps Journal, 1949–51, by Major-General R. M. P. Carver.

Auchinleck by John Connell. (Cassell.)

The Rommel Papers (Collins), and The Tanks, Vol. II (Cassell) by Captain B. H. Liddell Hart.

El Alamein to the River Sangro (Hutchinson), and The Memoirs (Collins) by Field Marshal Viscount Montgomery of Alamein.

Finally, the author wishes to express his deep appreciation of the kindness of Professor Gibbs in consenting to write the Foreword to this book.

Chapter 1

The Strategic Background to The North African Campaigns, 1940–1942

Strategic Poker: Churchill's Royal Flush:
Great Britain, The Sea, The Air,
The Middle East, American Aid*

Ever since the time of Elizabeth I British strategic policy when engaged in war with the leading power of continental Europe has been to rely on the use of sea power to force the enemy to disperse his forces while the sea lanes are kept open and an army strong enough to deliver a decisive blow at a vital point is built up. Such a policy was necessary for a nation with limited resources of manpower which frequently found itself unprepared for war, and became increasingly important as the United Kingdom grew to rely more and more on supplies of food and raw materials from overseas to maintain her war production, and on foreign trade to keep her solvent.

Conversely her continental opponents strove to isolate her militarily by defeating her allies one by one, and to cripple her economically by cutting off her food supplies and trade. For all these enemies the physical subjugation of Britain was the ultimate objective, but in the end each suffered resounding defeat at the hands of the stubborn islanders who by keeping the seas clear gave themselves time to create the weapons and armies needed to destroy their continentally based enemies on their home ground.

This then was the basis for British strategy in the 1939–45 war and the context in which the fighting in the Mediterranean should be studied. The war there was essentially a struggle for the maintenance of communications for which control of the sea and air was indispensable, and neither of these could be achieved without the possession of Malta, Egypt, and the North African coast as far west as Tripoli.

• *See* Kennedy, "The Business of War", page 79.

Britain, already at war with Germany, began by hoping to keep Italy neutral and never contemplated a Mediterranean campaign without the help of France with her possessions of Algeria and Syria, but the fall of France and Italy's entry into the war brought about a radical change in the situation and after Dunkirk, when every effort was being directed towards the immediate defence of the British Isles the defence of the Mediterranean and Middle East was left in the hands of a tiny British force sandwiched between 500,000 Italians in Libya and Italian East Africa.

At the time the Axis powers controlled almost the whole of western Europe and with the Japanese beginning to show signs of entering the war on their side the Middle East became, if possible, even more important as the vital link between British interests in the eastern and western hemispheres.

In the Middle East lay Britain's chief sources of oil, and the Suez Canal, the key to her communications with India, the Far East, Australasia, and East Africa, and with the Red Sea, the only route by which war supplies from the USA could be safely carried to the British army in Egypt. If the Middle East were lost the empire would be split, vital oil resources lost to the enemy, and there would be no way of forcing the Axis powers to fight on two or more fronts simultaneously.

The importance of Greece and Turkey in this context was chiefly significant in terms of the defence of the northern flank of the Middle East but also because a failure by Britain to go to the help of an ally in her hour of need might well have had disastrous and world-wide repercussions. This in itself was ample justification for sending a force to Greece in 1941 when she was threatened with invasion by the Germans.

At the same time, although most of the Middle Eastern countries were well disposed towards Britain it was essential for military, logistic, economic, and political reasons that her presence and influence there should be firmly based, and the enemy prevented from gaining a foothold. It was for this reason and latterly so that help could be more easily given to Russia that Churchill insisted that Wavell, much against his will, and Auchinleck should use force to remove enemy influences from Syria and Iraq and Persia, and to consolidate allied influence in those countries. The East African campaigns in the winter of 1940–41 were mainly important because they removed the threat to the Red Sea routes to Egypt and ensured the safety of the overland air reinforcement route from Takoradi, but also because they guaranteed the security of the British colonies of Kenya, Uganda and Tanganyika, and liberated Ethiopia, the first of all the victims of Axis aggression.

The Germans at first were not very interested in the Mediterranean theatre and Hitler did not intervene in what had been agreed as an Italian sphere of influence until Mussolini's failures made it imperative for him to do so. Seeking the elimination of the British Isles as his prime objective he then failed to see the significance of the Middle East for British strategy. Even when Italian defeats in East Africa, the Western Desert, and Greece obliged him to take a hand in the Mediterranean the German dictator failed to realise how close he might come to an outstanding success there, perhaps because of his involvement with Russia after the 22nd June, 1941. Even that treacherous attack was related directly to his desire to smash the United Kingdom and her allies, or potential allies, one at a time after his attempts at a Blitzkreig victory in the Battle of Britain had failed. Before he attacked Russia he had also found it necessary to seize Greece in order to secure his southern flank after the Italians had been defeated in Albania, but though he recognized the opportunities this conquest gave him of attacking the British in the Middle East he preferred to concentrate on a continental war and continued to ignore the potential widespread power of his main adversary. In this he was like Napoleon and although in the spring of 1942 he conceived a strategy of converging attacks on the Middle East from north and west it was his obsession with the Russian campaign that prevented him from seeing that the oil prizes of Iraq and Persia might be more easily gained by a really powerful thrust from North Africa than by a difficult and costly drive through the Caucasus and Kurdistan.

Mussolini's decision to enter the war was a ghastly and tragic disaster for the Italian people and after the winter defeats of 1940–41 their country was chiefly important as a base for German operations, though the Italian fleet remained for a time an important factor in the naval situation in the Mediterranean. Russia, however, was more important. Before she was invaded she had posed a potential threat to the British in the Middle East, and afterwards there was the danger, at least until 1942, that the Germans might force their way into the Middle East via the Caucasus, or that Hitler might oblige Stalin to make a negotiated peace. These possibilities were constant sources of anxiety to Wavell and Auchinleck and it was the need to forestall such developments by putting pressure on the Germans elsewhere that, *inter alia*, led Churchill to urge early offensives upon both commanders in chief.

Even America's entry into the war brought its problems, first among them the need to convince the new ally and main source of supplies of the correctness of British policy in the theatre, not only towards the Axis but also

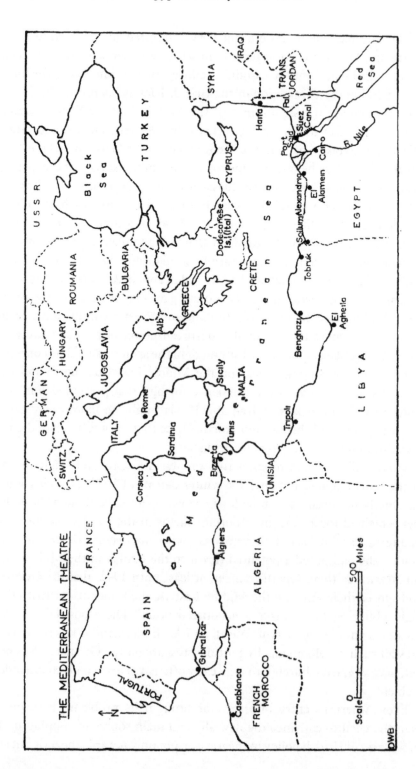

THE MEDITERRANEAN THEATRE

towards the USSR. Like the Russians, though for very different reasons, the Americans at first gave little support to Churchill's Mediterranean strategy of the Indirect Approach and it took a flat refusal by the Prime Minister to agree to a landing in France in 1942 before they were persuaded, and then with great reluctance, to agree to landings in French North Africa in the November of that year as an alternative.

For the British the whole theme of the Mediterranean war was to retain control of the sea lanes and it was for this reason, as well as to protect the Middle East that the desert campaigns were fought. With the sea in allied hands the enemy could be attacked at any suitable point along his southern front; without control of the air there could be no control of the sea; and air superiority in the theatre was impossible until the army had captured the airfields from the Egyptian border to Tripoli. These were the pre-requisites for the British strategy of the Indirect Approach although the need for a clear cut military victory was also extremely important for political reasons. Without a decisive victory in the field the United Kingdom could hardly hope to retain either a significant degree of influence over the conduct of the war, or her prestige, and as the only place where such a victory was possible at this time was in the desert, Montgomery's victory at El Alamein in October, 1942, was of more than ordinary importance.

The Royal Navy's contribution to victory in the Mediterranean cannot be overestimated. It was required to deal with the very powerful Italian fleet; to attack enemy supply routes; to supply and protect Malta; to safeguard convoys in the Eastern Mediterranean and Red Seas, and to support the army, all of which tasks it fulfilled, though not without heavy losses. It also prevented the Italians from reaching the Atlantic where their capital ships could have wreaked untold havoc in the British sea lanes. From time to time the navy lost control of the sea but always regained it, and Malta the key to the whole allied position in the Mediterranean, with all that that implied for future operations against Europe, remained in British hands.

The RAF also played a vital part in the Mediterranean at this period, chiefly by its attacks on enemy bases and supply routes, but also in the land battles where, after some early confusion, it gained experience and in the July fighting before Alamein may well have saved the army from further defeat. Like the army and navy the RAF had begun the war in the theatre by being weak and outnumbered but by the skill and determination of its members it overcame the disadvantages of often inferior equipment and established the superiority in the air that the army needed before it could defeat Rommel, and which was essential to the survival of Malta.

In North Africa the land battles themselves were never decisive in isolation as no battlefield victory there was capable of altering the whole balance of the war, but at the same time they had their own precise objects and played a vital part in the development of allied strategy. At different times they were important in helping Malta, taking pressure off the Russians, raising morale at home, enabling Churchill to retain control of the direction of the war, and maintaining British prestige, as well as fulfilling the army's primary role of destroying the enemy's power for battle and paving the way for future advances.

Chapter 2

The First British Offensive (1) Operation "Compass", the Battle of Sidi Barrani

The region in which the campaigns of 1940–1942 were fought, being essentially uninhabited, was strangely suited to the technical practice of war though the opposing commanders had to deal with great difficulties of terrain and climate.

In the 1,000 miles between Alexandria and El Agheila there was only one region, the Jebel Akdar, which was not desert, either sandy, as along most of the coastal plain, or more commonly, the rocky, stony, desert of the Libyan Plateau. The coastal plain between El Alamein and Gazala on the eastern edge of the Jebel varies in width from 25 miles to less than a mile at Solium and Maaten Baggush and is bordered on the south by the scarp of the Libyan Plateau which rises sharply to an average height of 500 feet OD (ordnance datum – a vertical datum used by ordnance survey for deriving altitudes on maps). This escarpment was of particular importance in the campaigns because west of Sofafi it was passable by vehicles in only a few places and at Sidi Resegh and El Duda commanded the Trigh Capuzzo, the main cross desert supply route.

The southern boundary of the desert known by the armies was marked by the oases at Siwa and Jarabub beyond which lay the impassable sand seas of Libya. North of these wastes movement in the desert was possible in any direction subject to the occasional existence of patches of soft sand, outcrops of rock, sudden hollows, and areas which became impassable for a period after heavy rain. The Qattara Depression, which marked the eastern boundary of the desert for military purposes, was simply a huge area of impossible going which extended from within 25 miles of the coast at El Alamein to the sand dunes of the Egyptian sand sea.

Water was extremely scarce, population almost non-existent, except in the tiny coastal settlements and in the Jebel, and the main lines of communication were ill-defined tracks like the Trigh Capuzzo and Trigh el Abd. The climate varies from the extremely hot in summer to the distinctly chilly in winter, there are great diurnal extremes, and rain when it comes can turn the desert into a sea of mud restricting the movement of vehicles and rendering airfields useless. Sand, which penetrated everywhere, and flies were other hazards of life in the desert but in general it was not an unhealthy region in which to live and fight, although the physical and mental strain on troops accustomed to more temperate climates was considerable.

For the commanders the desert's main characteristic was that it produced nothing for the support of armies and all that was required for operations and human survival had to be carried there from more favoured areas.

This then was the region in which the fighting war in the Mediterranean began, when, on 11th June, 1940, with the campaign in France nearly over, Italy declared war. On 22nd June France capitulated and Italy was left with only one enemy to face. At this time she had 215,000 men in North Africa forming the 5th and 10th Armies, the first in Tripolitania, and the other, of 10 divisions, deployed in Cyrenaica and along the Egyptian frontier. On the other hand the Italian heavy equipment was poor and there was a serious shortage of medium artillery. Training was bad, morale was low, and only in the 3 Blackshirt Divisions of the 10th Army was there any eagerness for war. Curiously the Italian Commander, Marshal Graziani did little to remedy these weaknesses though he was an experienced soldier and well aware of them.

The Italian Air Force in North Africa then consisted of 140 bombers and 101 fighters, many of which were modern, and enjoyed the use of numerous bases and airfields as well as the ability to reinforce quickly from the mainland of Europe, but its fighting power too was deeply suspect.

In such a region supply and maintenance were bound to be difficult but Graziani's problems were eased somewhat by the Via Balbia, a tarmac road which ran for 1,000 miles between Tripoli and the Egyptian frontier, and the presence of valuable ports at Benghazi, Tobruk, and Bardia.

To face this concentration of Italian military might Wavell had 36,000 British, Indian, and Dominion troops in Egypt and a further 14 infantry battalions and 2 Field Regiments of the Royal Artillery scattered variously about the rest of the Middle East. These figures, however, do not tell the whole story for not one of the formations in Egypt was at full strength. The 7th Armoured Division (Major-General M. O'Moore Creagh) had two instead of three regiments in its brigades, and even these were not fully equipped. The 4th Indian Division (Major-General N. de la P. Beresford-Peirse) consisted of two brigades only, and lacked much of its artillery; and General Freyberg was still waiting for two-thirds of his New Zealand Division to arrive. There was also a general shortage of guns, tanks, ammunition and transport. The RAF too was very weak in the numbers and quality of its aircraft. In Egypt and Palestine there were 96 elderly bombers, 75 Gladiator fighters, and 34 other aircraft, and the A.O.C.-in-C, Air Chief Marshal Sir Arthur Longmore, saw little prospect of early reinforcement.

Under Wavell, Lieutenant-General Sir Henry Maitland Wilson was the GOC British troops in Egypt, and Lieutenant-General R. N. O'Connor commanded the Western Desert Force, made up of the 7th Armoured and 4th Indian Divisions. Such aircraft as Longmore could provide for the desert were formed into 202 Group under the command of Air Commodore Collishaw, who set up his headquarters beside O'Connor's at Maaten Baggush.

The first large scale moves in the campaign were made by the Italians, when, between 13th and 16th September Graziani's forces advanced to Sidi Barrani, 60 miles inside the Egyptian frontier but still 80 miles west of the most advanced British position at Matruh. There Graziani halted and began to establish a supply base, to repair the road damaged by the retreating British, and to build a water pipe line up from the frontier.

Convinced that it would only be a matter of time before Mussolini joined forces with Hitler, Wavell had long decided that when war came he would make a large scale raid into Libya with the intention of persuading the Italians that the British strength was greater than it was, and for this purpose had deployed the 7th Armoured Division along the frontier. Longmore had meanwhile concentrated all his bombers on the forward airfields so that the RAF too could attack the enemy at the first opportunity.

These early attacks went well and Forts Capuzzo and Maddalena soon fell while armoured cars of the 11th Hussars cut the road between Tobruk and Bardia. The Italians then reacted fairly quickly and in the face of their growing strength the forts had to be given up, but small groups of British troops continued to attack enemy convoys, supply dumps and outposts until Graziani advanced in strength on 13th September. As a result the Italians became increasingly reluctant to venture far from the known roads and tracks while the British, as well as doing considerable damage and demoralising their opponents, learned how to fight in the desert. In the process they established a moral ascendency over the enemy which was not to be challenged until the arrival of Rommel the following summer.

These operations placed an intolerable strain on the British vehicles and in August Wavell withdrew the 4th Armoured Brigade while it was still serviceable and left only a strengthened Support Group to watch the frontier. When the enemy advanced in September this force withdrew, fighting hard but avoiding a full scale battle, and O'Connor, with 4th Armoured Brigade in hand, prepared to make a powerful counter-attack if and when Graziani reached the Matruh area. This eventuality did not arise however, and the army continued its harassing operations with great success while the navy and air force shelled and bombed the enemy's airfields and communications, doing severe damage to his equipment and morale.

Throughout this period the naval and air arms fought under great difficulties. The loss of the Sidi Barrani airfields sharply reduced the effectiveness of the bombers and the ability of the fighters to give satisfactory cover to the army and the fleet, deficiencies which could not be made good by reinforcements because of the need to replace the aircraft lost in the Battle of Britain. At the same time a lack of destroyers and of submarines capable of operating in the shallow waters of the Sicilian Narrows prevented the navy from disrupting the enemy's sea communications with Italy, and Graziani was able to build up his strength considerably.

Nevertheless the army's successes were real enough. 3,500 casualties were inflicted on the enemy for the loss of 150 British troops; the initiative was retained; and O'Connor's men gained experience of inestimable value in learning how the desert conditions could be turned to their own advantage.

Though forced by circumstances to adopt a defensive strategy Wavell had been looking since June for a chance to take the offensive against the Italians in the desert, and when the British Government decided in August to send the first of the Winston's Specials (W.S.) convoys to the Middle East the longed-for opportunity seemed to have arrived. This convoy, bringing with it 50 cruiser tanks, 52 light tanks, 48 anti-tank guns, 20 Bofors, and the 50 Infantry tanks (Matildas) of the 7th Royal Tank Regiment, was due to arrive at Suez on 24th September, and on the 11th the Commander-in-Chief ordered a study to be made of the difficulties likely to be encountered in the course of an offensive into Cyrenaica, with particular attention being given to problems of supply and maintenance. By this time too arrangements had been made for aircraft to be flown overland from Takoradi in Nigeria, and Wavell hoped that these reinforcements would be sufficient to give him air superiority over the likely battle area. He knew that an enemy attack could be expected before the end of the year but on the basis of his staff's reports and his new strength in armour he decided in October that given a suitable opportunity he could strike first, and he ordered plans to be made for a 4 to 5 day operation to be launched against the Italian positions in Egypt. He decided to impose this time limit because of the general shortage of stores and other equipment.

At first Wavell envisaged this operation in the form of simultaneous attacks against the enemy at Sidi Barrani and Sofafi with some exploitation northwards from Sofafi towards Buq Buq, but he subsequently accepted a plan put forward by O'Connor to whom he had assigned the task of carrying out the offensive. Thereafter, although he discussed his plans with Wavell, the conduct of operations was O'Connor's responsibility and to him must go much of the credit for the success of the campaign. He was a brilliant general and Wavell, who knew his outstanding qualities, backed him to the limit. It was as if the two men shared one mind and together they formed a team of exceptional talent and ability, Wavell controlling the strategy of the campaign and O'Connor making the tactical plans and carrying them out.

O'Connor considered that Wavel's original scheme involved an undesirable element of dispersion and for Operation "Compass" he now planned a battle in three stages. When Graziani halted at Sidi Barrani he placed a large part of his army in a series of fortified camps between Maktila on the coast and Sofafi some 50 miles inland, a deployment which invited disaster as the camps were incapable of supporting each other, and by placing his men in fixed positions the Italian commander deprived them of the ability to manoeuvre and maintain a coherent defensive front. O'Connor recognized this weakness and decided to exploit it, and in the first stage of his battle planned to send the 4th Indian Division and the infantry (I) tanks through the 15 mile gap which existed between the camps at Sofafi and Nibeiwa, after which they would swing north and assault the Nibeiwar and Tummar camps from the rear. In the meantime the 7th Armoured Division and the Matruh garrison would screen this movement and prevent the Italians at Sofafi and Buq Buq from going to the help of their fellows.

In the second stage the 4th Indian Division would move against Sidi Barrani while the armour advanced towards Buq Buq and prepared for the third stage, exploitation in strength by the 7th Armoured Division either north-westwards, or south in the direction of Sofafi.

The navy, which by its action at Taranto on 21st October had immobilized the Italian fleet in the East and Central Mediterranean, would help by bombarding the enemy at Maktila, Sidi Barrani, and Solium, while the RAF attacked ports, airfields, supply dumps, and coastal shipping throughout Cyrenaica with the aims of disrupting the Italians' supply system and reducing their numerical superiority in the air.

A very important part of the plan was the decision to place a mixed air component of fighters and army co-operation aircraft under O'Connor's direct command through a Special Air Liaison Officer at the headquarters of the Western Desert Force. The purpose of this arrangement was to ensure that the best possible results would be obtained from army/air co-operation, and it was the first practical application in the Middle East of the idea of a Tactical Air Force. For the first time too, the air force commander's headquarters were set up alongside those of the army commander where they were soon to be joined by a senior naval officer. The result was that inter-service co-operation in this campaign was outstandingly successful, particularly in comparison with some later campaigns when the respective headquarters were frequently undesirably far apart.

The plans for the tactical battle were only the first of the problems which Wavell and O'Connor had to resolve before their attack could begin. Somehow they had to overcome the enemy's advantage in numbers and the immense difficulties involved in supplying O'Connor's force as it advanced. Both knew that the Western Desert Force would be heavily outnumbered but were prepared to rely on surprise, and on the fitness, experience, good training, high morale, and fighting ability of their two regular divisions to overcome the enemy's greater numbers, the more so because Italian morale was known to be low, and as Wavell thought, liable to collapse completely under a heavy blow.

Wavell also knew, though he kept it from O'Connor, that soon after the battle had begun he would have to send the 4th Indian Division to the Sudan where Generals Platt and Cunningham were preparing to attack Eritrea, and that he might well lose some of his precious aircraft and anti-aircraft guns to the hard pressed Greeks who had been attacked by Mussolini on 28th October. The decision to send the Indian Division to the Sudan was confirmed on 2nd December when Wavell told Platt and Cunningham that it would leave the desert in mid-December by which time its part in O'Connor's offensive would have been completed. The Commander-in-Chief did not tell O'Connor of this decision as he had no wish to add to his worries, and perhaps in any case because he intended to replace the Indian Division with the 6th Australian Division. The divisional replacement, however, brought its own problems because the exchange was bound to take up valuable time and the Australians, though fit and hard, were neither fully trained nor a complete formation.

Shortages of equipment also worried Wavell for he did not dare to attack until he had many more 25-pounders for his field artillery, and he made the final decision to proceed with "Compass" on the assumption that 35 Hurricanes would be delivered by HMS *Furious* during the first week in December.

Surprise was an essential part of O'Connor's plan and a factor on which the success of the whole operation rested, and he set out to achieve it by a combination of good security and deception of the enemy. Only five very senior officers knew of the coming offensive and paper planning was cut to an irreducible minimum. The administrative preparations were advertised as defensive measures against an impending enemy attack; leave was stopped for the same reason; and rumours were spread in Cairo about plans to send more troops to Greece. At the same time the training of the army was intensified and in late November the whole operation was thoroughly rehearsed under the guise of training exercises. The troops were then told that these exercises would be repeated in early December, and so effective was the security that when the troops first moved out only commanding officers knew that it was a serious operation.

The RAF also played an important role in the deception plan, Longmore providing extra fighter squadrons so that complete air superiority could be guaranteed during the approach marches and over the assembly areas.

There remained the associated problems of supply and tactical mobility. The first objectives lay 80 miles beyond the railhead at Matruh, and O'Connor had to decide first how to arrange for the rapid approach march on which he relied for surprise, and secondly how to maintain his army in the ensuing battles, which were likely to be fought more than 100 miles from his main base. There were not enough vehicles to move the army forward and supply it, and it eventually took two nights to move the Indian Division to its assembly area. The problem was finally solved by the risky measure of setting up dumps in the open desert, stocking them with 5 days' supplies of food, fuel, and ammunition, and 2 days' supply of water, and leaving them camouflaged and defended only by patrols in the hope that they would not be discovered by the enemy. The Italians in fact were very bad at patrolling and preferred to huddle in their camps, so that the 11th Hussars were able to roam freely about the desert and cover the dumps without undue difficulty. Two such dumps, Field Supply Depots (FSD) 3 and 4, one for each division, were set up in the desert 40 miles west of Matruh between 11th November and 4th December, and were the forerunners of the many which were to serve the army throughout its conquest of Cyrenaica and in later campaigns.

Even after all these preparations had been made the success of "Compass" was still uncertain. In the first place the I tanks had never fought in the desert and their performance in those conditions was unknown. Secondly, no attacks had yet been made on a well-manned perimeter camp, and techniques for mine detection and ditch crossing had to be devised and practised, together with the tactics of assault, for a failure at Nibeiwa would wreck the whole enterprise. Fortunately O'Connor was an extremely good teacher, and under his direction the army trained hard and acquired a mastery of dispersed but controlled movement which was rarely apparent in later campaigns.

Thus the stage was set for the intended five-day offensive which was eventually to destroy the Italian 10th Army. Although Wavell had planned for a limited battle in the first instance because of material shortages he had however no intention of letting slip a chance to smash Graziani, and on 28th November he gave orders that the army was to be prepared "morally, mentally, and administratively" to use any such opportunity "to the fullest".

O'Connor issued his orders for the attack on 6th December and during the two following nights the army moved to its assembly areas between the Nibeiwa and Sofafi camps, while Colonel A. R. Selby, having placed a brigade of dummy tanks in the desert, took 1,800 men, all that the Matruh garrison could spare, to cover those at Maktila and Tummar.

The attack began at 7.15 a.m. on 9th December and three-and-a-half hours after the Matildas had broken through its rearward defences, Nibeiwa camp surrendered, yielding up 2,000 prisoners and valuable supplies of food and water. At noon Tummar West was attacked in a similar manner and four hours later also surrendered, though Tummar East held out until dark. Meanwhile the 7th Armoured Division had captured Azzizaya, and was across the Sidi Barrani–Buq Buq road and in full command of the area to the west of the 4th Indian Division. Selby, who had heard of the fall of Nibeiwa, then took his small force and made a daring attempt to cut the enemy's escape route from Maktila but was prevented from doing so by bad going and darkness.

O'Connor's next step was to send the 16th Infantry Brigade, Beresford-Peirse's divisional reserve, against Sidi Barrani, and by 1.30 p.m. on 10th December this brigade had closed the southern and western exits from the town. Beresford-Peirse promptly concentrated his 10 serviceable I tanks and all his divisional artillery for the assault, borrowed the 2nd Royal Tank Regiment from the 4th Armoured Brigade to cover his left flank, and at 4 p.m. moved in. By nightfall Sidi Barrani had fallen and Selby, coming up from Matruh, had accepted the surrender of two enemy divisions caught between his own troops and the town.

By that time the depleted 4th Armoured Brigade had reached Buq Buq, capturing men and supplies, and only the late arrival of an order prevented

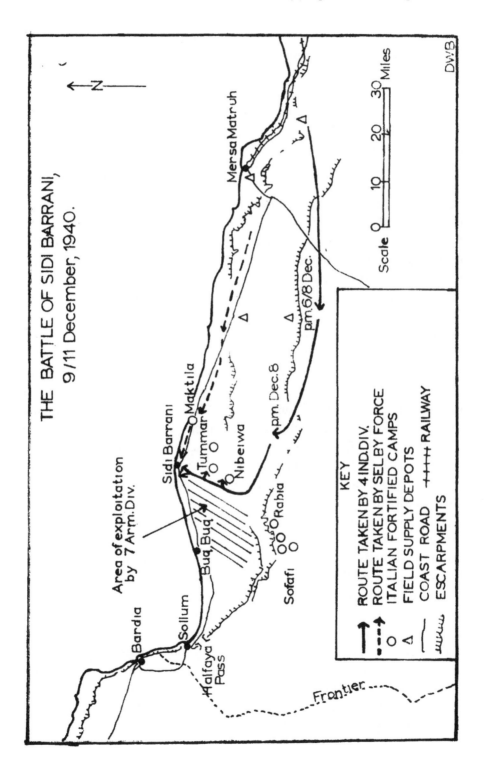

THE BATTLE OF SIDI BARRANI,
9/11 December, 1940.

KEY
➡ ROUTE TAKEN BY 4 IND.DIV.
⇢ ROUTE TAKEN BY SELBY FORCE
○ ITALIAN FORTIFIED CAMPS
△ FIELD SUPPLY DEPOTS
— COAST ROAD   +++ RAILWAY
ᴧᴧᴧ ESCARPMENTS

Scale
0 10 20 30 Miles

DwB

other elements of Creagh's division from cutting off the enemy's escape from the Sofafi group of camps as well.

O'Connor now decided to pursue the fleeing Italians, sending the 4th Armoured Brigade westwards above the escarpment and calling the 7th Armoured Brigade out of reserve to chase the enemy along the coast. The execution of these plans, however, was hampered by supply difficulties and especially by the absence of a harbour east of Solium as in the bad weather which now arose it was impossible to land supplies across the beaches. Even so the attempt was continued until a force sent to cut the road between Bardia and Tobruk had to be recalled on 12th December because of maintenance difficulties. It was then redirected on Sidi Omar, which, with Solium, fell on the 16th. The enemy by then had abandoned most of the frontier area and was holding Bardia on the coast and Siwa and Jarabub inland as his most easterly positions.

Operation "Compass", therefore, had been completely successful. O'Connor had made a daring and imaginative plan; had used his very limited resources to the utmost in order to inflict a crushing defeat on a numerically superior enemy; and had seen the measures taken to achieve strategic and tactical surprise succeed beyond all expectations. The Italian High Command had been warned that a British attack was likely and had seen the preparations for "Compass", but they were misled into thinking these were defensive measures and had then been caught unawares. In the battle itself O'Connor had gained complete tactical surprise by using new weapons, the I tanks, in an attack from an unexpected direction at an unexpected time, and well supported in the air and from the sea, had gained a splendid victory.

Between the 9th and 11th December the Italians had lost 38,300 prisoners, 237 guns, 73 tanks, and more than 1,000 vehicles, against a British loss of 624 killed, wounded, and missing. More serious, however, were the British losses in equipment, many tanks and aircraft having broken down in the harsh conditions of the desert.

Above all the victory reflected the remarkable precision of Wavell's strategic appreciation and the excellence of O'Connor's tactics and training. Wavell had taken great risks in denuding Egypt and the Sudan of aircraft and in deciding to attack a greatly superior enemy, but events had proved him right and his decision to back the quality of his small but highly experienced professional army against the quantity of the less skilled and more timid enemy was amply justified.

Chapter 3

The First British Offensive (2) The Development of the Campaign after the Battle of Sidi Barrani

he victory at Sidi Barrani saw the campaign enter an entirely new phase. Wavell had foreseen a three or four day battle around the camps and at Sidi Barrani but in two days O'Connor had destroyed the enemy in that area and was now bursting to follow up his success by driving the Italians deep into Cyrenaica. That such a move was possible was due to the extraordinary success of "Compass" and to O'Connor's flair for exploitation, two factors which led Wavell to change the concept of the offensive from that of a limited battle to one of pursuit and destruction.

Two difficulties had to be overcome, however, before O'Connor could develop his pursuit operations, the replacement of the 4th Indian Division by the 6th Australian Division, and the problems of supply and maintenance. The news that he was to lose Beresford-Peirse's division reached O'Connor on 11th December as a most unwelcome surprise, coming as it did at a time when he was already making plans to advance into Cyrenaica and was finding it extremely difficult to cope with the supply situation. Wavell, however, had decided on the 11th that the time had come for the Indians to go to the Sudan and the Australian division (Major-General I. G. Mackay) was ordered forward to replace them. The Commander-in-Chief was no less anxious than O'Connor to follow up the early victories but was equally determined that the pattern of his wider strategy should not be disturbed, and on 12th December the divisional exchange began with Mackay under orders to attack Bardia as soon as he was strong enough.

Naturally the exchange put an additional burden on O'Connor's administrative resources, already stretched to the limit by the need to maintain the army and deal with the huge numbers of prisoners, and although Solium was now open and captured enemy material was used whenever possible, Major-General N. McMicking, O'Connor's administrative chief, was still unable to satisfy all the demands that were made on him. Nevertheless plans for the capture of Bardia went ahead and on 19th December, while the 7th Armoured Division moved out to cover his left flank, Mackay deployed around the town and began to build up for a frontal assault, heavy naval and air bombardment having failed to induce the enemy to evacuate the fortress.

Unfortunately the supply problem grew with each mile's advance to the west and O'Connor now found that just as he was trying to build up for the attack on Bardia his vehicle strength was being rapidly reduced by the high rate of wear and tear always associated with desert fighting. The situation was eased somewhat by the arrival from Palestine of 50 heavy lorries and their crews, and by using captured trucks, though a shortage of crews prevented these from being used to the greatest advantage. By the end of the month a combination of old vehicles, and ceaseless use by tired drivers over bad country in difficult climatic conditions had led to 40 per cent wastage in vehicles, and there were no large repair workshops within easy reach.

The capture of Solium was a great help but the port had no equipment for handling heavy loads and the anchorage was exposed to the weather as well as to air attack and sporadic shelling from Bardia.

Another constant anxiety was the shortage of water and for some days the personal ration was cut to half a gallon a day for all purposes. The navy then brought up 3,500 tons from Alexandria, and though a great deal was lost by wastage, there being very few desert-worthy water carts, by the end of the month the situation had improved markedly, the Sidi Barrani and Buq Buq sources being again in use, and the Capuzzo tanks having been refilled by pumping from Solium.

Even so more general supplies were needed if the offensive was to continue, and with the 4th Armoured Brigade 170 miles from Matruh and 100 miles from its FSD new depots were essential. These were provided by establishing two chains of FSDs, one along the coast and the other above the escarpment. The depots in each were 50 miles apart, and as soon as a new one was opened its predecessor was eaten down and not restocked.

By this time the RAF too had outrun its established bases, and the forward airfields not only had no heavy equipment but were losing much of what they did possess by transfers to Greece. These difficulties were largely overcome by creating improvised Maintenance Units and Arms Stores, and by using captured weapons, but the sand, the greatest problem of all, remained. This made maintenance extremely difficult and frequently kept aircraft unserviceable for unusually long periods.

While these events were taking place Graziani, who well understood the significance of the pause in the British advance, sought permission to withdraw to Tobruk, where he could concentrate and wait for reinforcements to arrive from Italy. The Duce, however, in order to delay O'Connor's advance, ordered Bardia to be held and General Bergonzoli collected there inside a 17-mile perimeter protected by concrete strong points, mines, wire and an anti-tank ditch, a force of 45,000 men and 400 guns, the equivalent of 5 divisions.

O'Connor's force, which on 1st January, 1941, had become XIII Corps, then included the 7th Armoured and most of the 6th Australian Divisions; the 16th Infantry Brigade, left behind by the 4th Indian Division; the 23 serviceable I tanks of the 7th R.T.R.; two artillery regiments, and the 1st Battalion the Royal Northumberland Fusiliers. The assault was to be the first task of the Australian Division which though still incomplete was exceptionally tough and spoiling for a fight.

Mackay planned to attack from the west, thus achieving surprise by coming from an unexpected direction, and at the junction of two defensive sectors where a break-in would enable him to split the defence and isolate the Italian guns. O'Connor agreed, and in order to ensure that the I tanks would again be used to the best advantage, suggested that on this occasion the break-in should be made by the infantry, with the tanks following once the anti-tank obstacles had been cleared.

While the armoured division guarded the western and northern flanks the 16th Australian Brigade was ordered to break in on the west where the going was good, and then to sweep south towards the area where the 17th Australian Brigade would break in in its turn and attack the Italians' main artillery concentration. The navy and RAF were to help by carrying out their usual bombardments, this time reinforced by the 15in. guns of the battleships *Warspite*, *Barham*, and *Valiant*.

The attack was originally set for 2nd January but had to be postponed until the next day while stocks of ammunition were built up, the navy and air force filling in the gap. Then, at dawn on the 3rd, the 16th Brigade advanced and by 8.30 a.m. had taken most of its objectives, many weapons, and 8,000 prisoners at a low cost in men, although the tanks had been severely battered by the enemy artillery. The 17th Brigade's assault at 11.30 a.m. was less successful, and Italian resistance did not end until 1 p.m. on 5th January, although by that time the 16th Brigade had captured undamaged the harbour and the water supply plant.

Throughout the battle the RAF maintained absolute air superiority and for the loss of 645 men the Australians killed or captured the whole Italian garrison of 40,000 men, and took 400 guns, 130 tanks, and hundreds of

MT vehicles, thus completing the destruction in one month of 8 enemy divisions.

There was no pause in the British advance and even before Bardia had surrendered the 7th Armoured Division was working to cut off Tobruk. By 8th January this had been accomplished. The 16th and 19th Australian Brigades had moved up against the perimeter on the south and east while the 4th Armoured Brigade and the Support Group of the armoured division had completed the investment and cut the western exits from the town.

These moves were virtually unopposed, the Italian Air Force having lost its El Adem base and been so disorganized by the British land and air offensives that its power to interfere was negligible. By contrast 202 Group had moved its headquarters up to Solium and was well placed, except in numbers, to continue its support of the army.

Tobruk's value lay in the fact that possession of its port would enable most of the land communications with Alexandria to be dispensed with and a new administrative start to be made, based on seaborne supplies. Until Tobruk was taken, however, the old supply problems remained.

Both divisions had now outrun FSDs 8 and 9, and new depots FSDs 10 and 11 were formed, 35 miles east of Tobruk. These were intended to provide for the daily needs of the army, the build up for the attack on Tobruk, and to contain the reserves of material required to cover the period during which the port was being made operational once more. An immediate increase in the number of road convoys was thus unavoidable, and was almost impossibly difficult to work, sandstorms in particular upsetting all calculations of delivery dates.

Until this time the leap-frogging of FSDs, so that a division always had one within reach, had been very successful but the system was now beginning to fail in items which the troops could do without for a time, but of which a steady flow was essential if the fighting power and efficiency of the army was to be maintained. A fundamental difficulty lay in the problem of relating the bulk despatch of supplies from Alexandria to the needs of changing tactical situations, and as Bardia was no gain to the line of communications, Solium remained as the only effective sea head, great efforts being made to develop its capacity. By the end of January the port was handling more than 500 tons of stores each day, as well as prisoners and casualties, but road convoys from Matruh were still needed especially in emergencies, and on different occasions 120,000 gallons of fuel, and 16,000 rations had to be driven 200 miles up to the army in the desert.

Britain's Desert War in Egypt and Libya 1940–1942

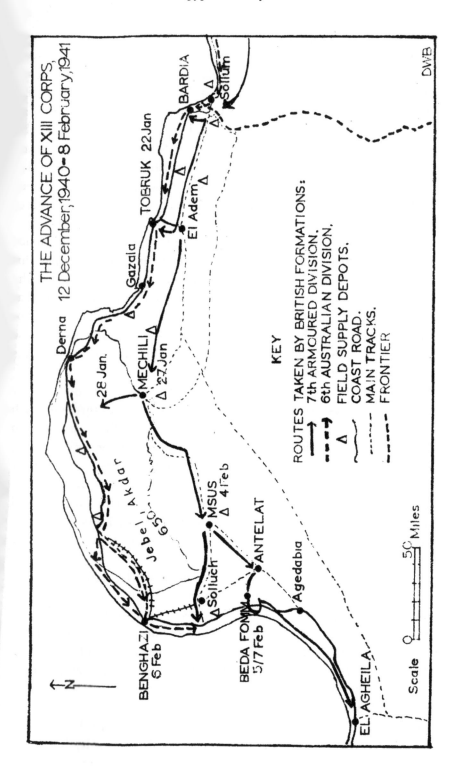

THE ADVANCE OF XIII CORPS, 12 December, 1940 – 8 February, 1941

KEY

ROUTES TAKEN BY BRITISH FORMATIONS:
7th ARMOURED DIVISION.
6th AUSTRALIAN DIVISION.
△ FIELD SUPPLY DEPOTS.
COAST ROAD.
MAIN TRACKS.
FRONTIER

Scale 0 ___ 50 Miles

DWB

A deliberate attack on Tobruk was inevitable, as altho
assault by the armoured division might have succeeded it wou
have ended that formation's value as a weapon of pursuit. B
division was reduced to 69 cruiser and 126 light tanks, and
strength was a cause of great concern to O'Connor. He did, in
the heavily damaged 8th Hussars and 6th R.T.R. and gave th
tanks to other regiments. Thus reorganized, the division, whi
kept intact as a formation, was ordered to advance to Derna a
soon as Tobruk fell. The particular importance of Mechili hac
O'Connor's notice and even before Tobruk fell he was to sen
forward to capture this vital route centre.

Once more it was Mackay's Australians who were to mak
and for the second time his chief problem was to find a way
remaining I tanks, now 12 in number, through the anti-tank ob
Tobruk defences were similar to those at Bardia but as the per
nearly twice as long, and there were only 20,000 men to defend
a quick success were high. Speed was particularly important as
there would be little chance of capturing the valuable port in
before they were sabotaged.

The plan was for a battalion of the 16th Brigade to break in on
front in the south-east sector before dawn and to make a gap throu
the I tanks and the rest of the brigade would pass. These forces w
push inwards to give the lodgment area depth, and also along the p
while the 17th Brigade and the Support Group mounted dive
attacks to the east and west of the town. Once again great care w
taken to neutralise the enemy artillery at the earliest opportunity. Tl
Navy and the RAF were to be asked to perform their usual bombar
and destroyers would wait offshore in case the old cruiser *San*
tried to escape.

The attack went in at 5.40 on the morning of 21st January
mid-afternoon next day Tobruk had been captured, together with
prisoners, 208 guns, and 87 tanks. XIII Corps had lost 400 men, nea
Australians. Fortunately the harbour had suffered little damage and a
the spoils were found 10,000 tons of water; refrigeration and distill
plants; bulk storage gear for petrol; 4,000 tons of coal; and a power st
Two days later the harbour had been swept of mines and was ready to re
the first supply ships.

Meanwhile O'Moore Creagh's armour pushed on and by nigh
on the 22nd the 4th Armoured Brigade had cut the tracks leading w

south, and south-east from Mechili, where there was a considerable Italian armoured force, and the 7th Armoured Brigade lay within 20 miles of Derna.

Benghazi was now the next major objective, the Defence Committee having decided on 21st January that its capture was to be regarded as a matter of the utmost importance. Ten days earlier the British Government had decided that all possible help should be given to the Greeks in order to ensure that they would meet the impending German invasion of their country with force, and Wavell was informed that after the fall of Tobruk the needs of the Greek campaign would have absolute priority in terms of men and supplies. He and Longmore objected strongly to the subsequent proposals to denude the forces in Libya, particularly since the build up of the Luftwaffe in Sicily boded ill for the future, but they were overridden by the Prime Minister and the Chiefs of Staff who, nevertheless, insisted that Benghazi should be taken and developed as a base for both navy and air force, seeing in the port a means of ending the army's dependence on an overland line of communication 600 miles long.

At this point XIII Corps was approaching a region vastly different from that of the desert. In the Derna-Benghazi-Solluch-Mechili quadrilateral rose the Jebel Akdar, an upland country, rising in places to 2,500 feet, whose good soil and ample rainfall had enabled it to become an important area of Italian colonisation. It was a settled region with good internal communications, including a railway and a good road from Derna to Benghazi, although minor roads were few, and after heavy rain usually impassable. Its capital was Benghazi, then a city with a population of 65,000 people.

In strategic terms the Jebel could be easily defended against attacks from the east or south, and become almost impossibly bad for wheeled or tracked vehicles, while on its southern flank the desert was huge in size, waterless, and included every variety of "going" down to the impassable.

At the end of January, 1941, the remains of the Italian 10th Army, in strength approaching two divisions, were disposed as follows. The bulk of the force was near Derna, presumably guarding the coast road, while an armoured group with some 160 tanks lay at Mechili. Not without reason the Italians seemed to have decided to leave the defence of their desert flank to the nature of the ground and to fight a holding campaign in the Jebel. Their air force, however, which was now standing on its last Cyrenaica airfields, was suffering greatly from maintenance difficulties and on 20th January could muster only 46 bombers and 36 fighters of the 380 aircraft with which it had started in December.

O'Connor saw in the Italian dispositions and the distance between Derna and Mechili a degree of dispersion which offered him an opportunity to defeat the enemy in detail, and he ordered the Australians to apply pressure at Derna while O'Moore Creagh concentrated the whole of the 7th Armoured Division for an attack on the Italian tanks at Mechili. This attack failed because bad patrolling by Creagh's infantry allowed the Italian armour to withdraw unnoticed into the Jebel during the night of 26th January, where his subsequent pursuit was halted two days later by mud, mechanical breakdowns, and a shortage of fuel. Thus the Italian armour was saved, and in some strength, Graziani then having 100 medium and 200 light tanks, of which half were still serviceable. The British on the other hand were almost on their last legs with only 50 cruisers still running. They had thoroughly frightened their opponents, however, and after the clash at Mechili Graziani changed his mind about fighting in the Jebel. He concluded that a delaying action in the Jebel could only result in the final destruction of his shattered army and decided to save what he could by withdrawing to Sirte where a strong defensive position was already being prepared.

After his failure to destroy the enemy armour at Mechili, O'Connor too made a new appreciation and took the third great decision of the campaign which at this point entered upon its final phase. Although he now held both Derna and Mechili the Italians were better concentrated for the defence of the Jebel, possessed a considerable force of armour even if it was not of very good quality, and showed every sign of fighting hard in the region's defence. As a result a direct advance from Mechili against Benghazi could expect to meet strong opposition in good defensive country and could not hope to turn an enemy flank.

On the other hand an advance across the desert to Msus would be entirely unexpected and might provide an opportunity to encircle and crush what was left of the 10th Army. Wavell agreed to this plan on 1st February, and O'Connor issued his orders.

The Australian Division, less one infantry brigade, was to advance along the coast from Derna while the 7th Armoured Division and the extra infantry brigade were to go to Msus and then, if the Italians showed signs of making a stand at Benghazi, to Solluch and an assault on Benghazi from the south. Alternatively, if the enemy continued to retreat, the armour was to go south-west to Antelat and cut off Graziani's escape from there.

The timing of these moves seemed to depend on two factors in particular, the condition of the 7th Armoured Division, and the perennial problems of supply. The supply situation was in fact improving. By 1st February Tobruk was handling 900 tons of stores daily and plans were made to establish FSD 14 south-west of Mechili and to stock it with supplies for 10 days. The stocking it was thought would take ten days to complete and O'Connor hoped to begin his advance between 10th and 12th of February, by which time his armour would have been reinforced by two fresh cruiser tank regiments from the 2nd Armoured Division which had recently arrived in Egypt. When he made these plans the 7th Armoured Division was reduced to 50 serviceable cruiser tanks, most of which were already long overdue for repair. Subsequently he reorganized his armour by transferring tanks from the 7th Armoured Brigade to the 4th in order to bring one brigade up to full fighting strength.

Suddenly, on 2nd February, O'Connor learnt that the enemy would probably shortly begin to retire along the coast. It was not long before this news was confirmed, and deciding that he could not wait for new tanks or supplies, O'Connor ordered O'Moore Creagh to advance south-west from Mechili and to keep going until he either cut off the enemy or his division collapsed. The Division was to advance on 4th February with full tanks, and would be followed by a convoy with supplies for two more days, but after that was to expect no further help.

The advance began on time and by dawn on 5th February the bulk of the division was near Msus while armoured cars of the 11th Hussars were approaching Antelat, having covered 124 miles in 24 hours across country that had not been reconnoitred because of the need for secrecy.

At this point, and in order to speed up the advance, O'Moore Creagh decided to send a motorised force under Colonel J. F. Combe to cut the coast road south-west of Antelat, and soon after, acting on information supplied by the RAF about the enemy retreat, to send his main strength in the same direction rather than towards Solluch. O'Connor subsequently gave this second decision the chief credit for the complete success of the Beda Fomm battle.

By the afternoon of 5th February, "Combe Force" (1 squadron each of the King's Dragoon Guards and the 11th Hussars, "C" Battery of the Royal Horse Artillery, the 2nd Battalion of the Rifle Brigade, and nine Bofors guns), had established itself across the coast road and was busily engaged with the retreating Italians. For the next two days the enemy tried unsuccessfully to break up this blocking force and the 4th Armoured Brigade, whose forward units had reached the coast road near Beda Fomm soon after "Combe Force" had cut it further south and were then attacking the Italian columns.

At this stage the Italians were in the process of being crushed between the hammer of the advancing 6th Australian Division, which was to take Benghazi on 6th February, and the rather small anvil of the 7th Armoured Division, or what was left of it. Nevertheless, south of Benghazi they were still greatly superior to the British in numbers of men and of tanks and a properly planned and supported attack against the tired and dispersed armoured division might have cleared the way for their escape. As it was they tried to break through in a number of piecemeal assaults only to be driven back with great bravery and skill by the tiny British force, and early on 7th February they began to surrender at Beda Fomm, with the leading Australians only two hours away. The 7th Armoured Division then had 24 serviceable cruiser tanks.

The battle of Beda Fomm marked the end of the Italian 10th Army, and XIII Corps counted 25,000 prisoners, 100 medium tanks, and 100 guns captured or destroyed.

This, O'Connor's latest victory, had been achieved despite a startling disparity in numbers of men, and an enemy superiority of 4:1 in cruiser tanks, of which most were little worn when compared with the British armour which had fought continuously for nearly ten weeks over hundreds of miles of difficult country.

The speed of the cross desert dash from Mechili had completely surprised the Italians, although they had foreseen the possibility of such a move, and should have realized their danger when the 11th Hussars arrived at Msus on 4th February.

On the other hand the British commanders having also recognized the fantastic risks involved in the chase across the desert, balanced them against the chance of destroying the enemy completely and were lucky enough to see events prove their judgment right. This short campaign of ten weeks was the first to be fought by modern armies with comparable air support over what was for the most part completely open country, and during its course a British force of one armoured division, an infantry division, and a few corps troops utterly destroyed an enemy army of 10 divisions, and, for the loss of 1,928 men killed, wounded, and missing, took 130,000 prisoners, 380 assorted tanks, and 845 guns.

The RAF, despite the loss of aircraft and equipment to the campaign in Greece gave invaluable direct support and information to the army, and achieved almost complete air superiority, so that after the early stages the Italian air force played no significant part in the campaign.

The Royal Navy opened the ports of Solium, Bardia, and Tobruk; carried supplies, and bombarded the enemy whenever weather and targets permitted, doing great damage to both Italian equipment and morale. Inter-service co-operation throughout the campaign was excellent.

There were three main reasons for the British victory. In the first place Wavell and O'Connor knew the sort of force that was required in the desert and managed to create one despite their other responsibilities. It was small and short of equipment, but was well trained and brilliantly led, and was always used in actions where the ends to be achieved were correctly balanced against the means available. Secondly, deception and surprise, especially by an unorthodox manoeuvre, were characteristic of O'Connor's command, and contributed greatly to his series of remarkable victories.

Finally, the supreme quality of the men and vehicles of XIII Corps enabled them repeatedly to meet outrageous demands upon their skill and endurance, and still to have enough drive at the end to complete the destruction of a numerically superior enemy.

All in all the winter campaign of 1940–41 in North Africa must rank among the very greatest feats of British arms.

Chapter 4

The Advent of Rommel

With the destruction of the Italian army at Beda Fomm the threat to Egypt seemed to have been removed and on 16th February the British Government decided to hold Cyrenaica with the smallest possible force while the rest of the army and air force concentrated in Egypt and prepared to move to Greece. Wavell and most of his colleagues then believed that although German troops were beginning to arrive in Tripoli the enemy would not be able to launch a strong attack before May, by which time the desert army's losses to the Greek campaign would have been made good by the arrival of two new divisions and aircraft from the United Kingdom. He therefore ordered the forces in Cyrenaica to adopt a defensive attitude and to be ready to stop any enemy thrust at El Agheila, which had been occupied by O'Connor on 8th February.

O'Connor himself was strongly opposed to the plan to halt his advance and argued powerfully that he should be allowed to invade Tripolitania and capture Tripoli itself. The advantages of holding Tripoli were very great as successive commanders-in-chief realized when they planned its capture as the culmination of their several campaigns. With the province in British hands the security of Egypt would be guaranteed as not until they had successfully landed a large army in North Africa would the enemy be able to consider another advance towards Cairo, and their chances of mounting a large scale amphibious operation of this nature were poor indeed. In addition the RAF would be able to use the North African airfields to attack Sicily and Italy, and help to Malta would be more easily forthcoming, although convoys passing through the Sicilian Narrows would still be beyond the range of fighter cover. There was also the chance that close contact with the French in Tunis and Algeria would be valuable in the future. Thus with Italian morale and fighting power shattered after the Beda Fomm debacle, and the possibility that Tripoli could be taken quickly, O'Connor put forward a plan to seize the whole of Tripolitania by advancing with a striking force of the 7th and 2nd Armoured Divisions while a seaborne brigade was landed near Tripoli itself.

He was probably right in thinking that he would meet little or no resistance en route to Tripoli, and Rommel himself supports this argument, but in other directions it would seem that O'Connor took too little account of the many different problems which existed in the Mediterranean at this time. The navy was already fully extended in covering and maintaining the extremely long lines of communication between Egypt and Benghazi, and with the Luftwaffe building up in Sicily the prospects of successfully increasing these responsibilities were remote, particularly in view of the RAF's numerical weakness. The defence of Tripoli was also bound to make heavy demands upon the resources required to oppose a German invasion of Greece or Turkey, and Wavell simply did not have the men to fulfil his various tasks without a dangerous dispersion of strength.

And even without the need to send help to the Greeks the logistical problems of an advance to Tripoli were so great that it is questionable if it was ever a practicable propostion at this stage in the war. O'Connor had very few serviceable tanks left after Beda Fomm; the 2nd Armoured Division was far from desert worthy; and his transport echelons were in a shocking state after their exertions of the two previous months. If the lack of shipping and the certainty of enemy air superiority are also considered it seems probable that the capture of Tripoli, however desirable, was, even in February, 1941, a hope for the future. Even so O'Connor might have continued his advance had not the British Government been convinced of the need to retain the ability to intervene in the Balkans, a power which could not be achieved if an army was to be maintained west of El Agheila, and he might well have reached Tripoli. Less certain would have been his ability in the circumstances to hold Tripolitania against growing German strength, it being reasonable to assume that an immediate threat to Tripoli would have been followed by a speeding up of the transfer of German troops to North Africa.

In the event, the British Government decided to act according to the long-term strategic needs, and so that help could be sent to Greece, gave orders for XIII Corps to be reduced to a weak holding force and for the Tripoli venture to be postponed.

The decision to send a force to Greece was taken after a Ministerial Mission which included Eden, the Foreign Secretary; Dill, the CIGS; and Wavell had reported on 22nd February that Britain had no alternative but to support the Greeks to the limit. Mussolini had attacked Greece in October 1941 in the hope of a cheap victory but had been defeated, and in early 1942 it was obvious that Hitler was preparing to take a hand in order to rescue his ally and prevent the establishment in Greece of a British force capable of threatening his southern flank.

The Greeks, like the Turks, had hitherto refused all offers of direct military assistance in the hope that Germany would not then be provoked into an attack, but as this possibility receded General Papagos, who had succeeded Metaxas as Prime Minister, agreed to accept a British force to help defend his country.

The British were concerned chiefly with the security of the northern flank of the Middle East but also with the need to ensure that a German attack would be resisted, and the Eden Mission were unanimous in recommending that troops should be sent from the desert to help the sternly fighting Greeks. The whole business was fraught with danger but it was considered that the alternative of allowing the Germans to occupy the whole of the Balkans unopposed was far worse and on 7th March the War Cabinet authorized the despatch of a British force equivalent to 4 divisions.

In the circumstances the decision was inevitable, although as many must have thought at the time, defeat was probable, the force that could be sent being far too weak to withstand a powerful German offensive. Not to send troops would have left the Middle East Strategic Reserve intact but of no use outside the desert, and it was sent to Greece in hope rather than expectation of military success but in the certain knowledge that its committal would have great political merit. The Eden Mission had in any case reported that there was a reasonable chance of stopping the Germans, and the short-term consequences were risked in order that the wider advantages would be guaranteed, chief among them the impressions that would be created in the USA, Turkey, and the USSR by Britain's action. The consequences of refusing to send help to an ally might, on the other hand, have been disastrous.

As it was the campaign in Greece proved to be one more in a long list of defeats but it did show quite plainly that Britain was prepared to help any nation that was attacked, a fact which did not go unnoticed in Turkey, the USA, and the world at large. It is possible that the decision to send help to the Greeks cost Wavell the cheap and easy conquest of Tripoli, and it is certain that the denuding of XIII Corps left the way wide open for Rommel's first advance, but the strategic needs of the time required the despatch of a British force to Greece and there is no indication that the advantages of securing the North African coast would have outweighed or even balanced the consequences of failing to go to the help of an ally.

The decision to reduce the British force in Cyrenaica was one of two which in due course led to a radical change in the military situation in North Africa. The other was taken by Hitler on 11th January when he ordered a German force to be sent to Tripoli as soon as possible. Mussolini had asked for such assistance in the summer of 1940, but in October, after receiving the report of General Von Thoma whom he had sent to investigate the situation and who had advised against the sending of German troops until Matruh was firmly held, Hitler seemed to lose interest in land operations in the theatre. He was confirmed in this attitude after listening to Admiral Raeder's arguments about the impossibility of clearing the Royal Navy from the Mediterranean and did not alter it until O'Connor's victories threatened to bring about the complete collapse of the Axis position in North Africa, and even of Italy itself. The Führer then decided that for strategic, political, and psychological reasons Tripolitania must be held and that German inter-vention was necessary.

On 5th February he informed Mussolini of the conditions under which he was prepared to send help and gave details of the forces which he proposed to make available. At this time Fliegerkorps X was already establishing itself in Sicily with orders to attack the British fleet and sea communications, and to give general support to Axis ground forces in the theatre, and the 5th Light Division was preparing to leave for Tripoli. This division would be followed in late March by the 15th Panzer Division but only if the Italians stood firm at Sirte and made no further withdrawals. The German divisions would then become the Deutsches Afrika Korps, and together with the two Italian mobile divisions which were to be sent out in the meantime, would be commanded by Lieutenant-General Erwin Rommel, an officer high in Hitler's favour who had demonstrated a flair for armoured warfare in France in 1940. For general tactical purposes the DAK would fall under the control of the Italian Commander-in-Chief, but in the field was always to be commanded directly by German officers and to be kept intact as a formation. Fliegerkorps X would remain directly responsible to Reichsmarshal Goering.

When Rommel landed in Africa on 12th February, two days before his first troops, the British command had also undergone a major recon-struction. O'Connor had returned to the Delta to become the GOC Egypt; Wilson became the Military Governor and Commander-in-Chief in Cyrenaica; and Major-General T. Blarney, with the Headquarters of the 1st Australian Corps, had replaced O'Connor and the XIII Corps Headquarters. Subsequently Wilson, Blarney, and the Australian Corps

HQ went to Greece and Lieutenant-General P. Neame, V.C., was brought from Palestine to be the Commander-in-Chief of Cyrenaica Command. This was primarily an organization for the civil administration of the region and in no sense a properly constituted Corps Headquarters, and Neame, without the staff or the signal equipment needed to maintain control of mobile forces in operations over a large area, found it increasingly difficult to carry out his dual task.

The RAF too had been reorganized, Longmore having withdrawn the Headquarters of 202 Group and 3 squadrons to refit and prepare to move to Greece, and replaced them with a Cyrenaica Headquarters having 2 fighter, 1 army co-operation, and 1 Blenheim squadron under command.

The British forces in the desert in mid-February were thus very weak. The 6th and 7th Australian Divisions; the New Zealand Division; a Polish Brigade Group; an Armoured Brigade Group (from the 2nd Armoured Division); and a large number of Corps troops had been sent to Greece; the 7th Armoured Division had been withdrawn to refit, and only the 9th Australian Division and half of the 2nd Armoured Division were available to hold Cyrenaica and protect Egypt.

The story did not end there, however, for the 9th Division had not only lost two of its best brigades to Greece in the general reorganization but the replacements were not so well equipped and trained as their predecessors and had no battle experience, while to their chronically bad vehicle state was added an acute shortage of anti-tank guns and signal equipment. For its part the 2nd Armoured Division consisted only of the very weak 3rd Armoured Brigade and an incomplete Support Group. Its commander, Major-General M. D. Gambier Parry, could call on only two cruiser and two light tank regiments, a total of some 200 tanks, and the mechanical state of the cruisers was frightening. This dismal picture was completed by the fact that the divisional staffs were also undertrained, understrength, and lacking in battle experience.

Inevitably it seemed, the supply situation too could only be bad. In early February Tobruk had begun to replace Solium as the main sea head but bad weather and attacks by the Luftwaffe, which had arrived in the Mediterranean in January, delayed progress, and contrary to expectations Benghazi proved to be of little value. Before the harbour there had been swept of mines the Germans had begun their air attacks and on 23rd February sank H.M. ships *Terror* and *Dainty*. Thereafter, without Anti-Aircraft protection, and faced with a shortage of small craft, Admiral Cunningham found it impossible to build up the port as a major advanced base, and the 450 mile coast road remained as the chief supply route between Tobruk and the army at El Agheila.

Besides reducing the value of the newly captured ports the Luftwaffe's appearance imposed severe restrictions on the freedom of movement of British shipping in the Mediterranean. The direct sea route to the Middle East now became too dangerous for convoys, and by mining the Suez Canal the enemy were able to delay the shipping turn round at Suez itself. At the same time the bombing of Malta made it impossible for the British to interfere seriously with the Axis supply routes across the Mediterranean, and in February and March the enemy forces in North Africa received 200,000 tons of supplies, only 20,000 tons being lost as a result of British attacks on their ships and aircraft.

Chapter 5

Rommel's First Offensive

S oon after his assumption of command Neame had reported to Wavell that Cyrenaica could not be defended with the forces at his disposal, suffering as they did from great tactical dispersion and administrative weaknesses. Wavell listened but could only repeat that no reinforcements should be expected before May and that an enemy offensive before then was highly improbable. At the same time, however, he gave Neame permission, if an enemy attack did develop, to fall back towards the Jebel where the probable Axis superiority in aircraft and armour would be less dangerous. In such a case the 9th Australian Division would withdraw along the coast road while Gambier Parry's armour waited in the Antelat region to discover the direction of the main enemy thrusts and to attack their flanks. It was known then that a German armoured force was forming in Tripolitania but Wavell believed, not without reason, that it could not be ready to mount a major attack before he was himself in a much better state to repel it. He had realized, however, that his original estimate of the numbers required to hold Cyrenaica had been far too low, and that it was now too late to repair the omission.

The difficulty of maintaining the army remained a major cause of anxiety. FSDs had been established in and around the Jebel in February and March but there was no coherent supply organization with which to implement an Administrative Plan had one existed, and the army was forced to rely for its supplies on isolated fixed depots at Msus, Tecnis, Martuba, Mechili, and Tmimi. Such a system would have been serious enough with ample transport available but the vehicle shortage now rendered its successful operation extremely unlikely. Group Captain L. O. Brown, the local RAF commander, was one of the few who recognized the danger and acted accordingly, and he warned his squadrons at Barce and Benina to be ready to move at an instant's notice as there was no hope of the army providing an effective defence against a strong enemy ground attack.

The vehicle shortage then obliged Neame, much against his will, to alter his tactical dispositions. Unable to occupy the good defensive positions west of El Agheila because of their distance from the army's supply points, and forced to deprive the armoured division of its mobility by tying it to a series of fixed dumps, he found it necessary in mid-March to withdraw an infantry brigade from the Mersa Brega position and to replace it with the Support Group. The one bright spot was the arrival of the 3rd Indian Motorized Brigade. This consisted of three motorized Indian cavalry regiments, rifle armed, without tanks or anti-tank guns, and with only half their wireless sets, but it was a mobile force of a sort and Neame placed it at Martuba, whence, in theory, it could move either north to Derna or south to Mechili.

In the third week in March, therefore, the Support Group was holding an 8-mile front at Mersa Brega with the 3rd Armoured Brigade on its left, while five infantry battalions of the Australian Division, without a recce regiment, divisional artillery, tracked carriers or adequate signals were trying to cover Benghazi and to prepare for the defence of the Jebel. The 9th Division's other brigade sat in Tobruk, unable to move forward because there were no vehicles available to lift it. In the meantime the two divisions had no direct contact with each other. At sea, however, the RN had consolidated its superiority in the Eastern Mediterranean by its victory at Cape Matapan.

Rommel had now been in Africa for five weeks during which his advanced units had moved forward to Nofilia, which they had reached on 19th February. Their build up was then delayed by bad Italian fuel and a shortage of transport, most of Germany's vehicle production at this time going into the preparations for the attack on Russia. Rommel himself seemed to care little about the details of military administration. He issued his orders and expected adequate supplies to be available when they were needed, his staff being left to resolve the problems of detail as best they might.

Units of Fliegerkorps X had also begun to arrive in Tripoli in the middle of February, their commander, Major-General Frohlich, then having 50 Stukas and 20 Me 110s under his immediate control, and the power to call on some long-range Ju 88s and He IIIs from Sicily. His orders were simple: to destroy the enemy air in Cyrenaica and to co-operate with General Rommel.

The Axis armies at this time consisted of the German 5th Light Motorized Division; the Italian Ariete Armoured Division, with half its tanks; and four Italian infantry divisions, a total of some 50,000 men. The Germans had formed the 5th Light Division without the benefit of desert experience, and though as a result its tanks at first had no suitable air or fuel filters, it was not long before it became a very powerful and effective weapon. It had 78 light and 80 medium tanks, these last armed with a 50 mm gun; a powerful reconnaissance unit; 12 pieces of field artillery; a small number of 88 mm dual purpose guns; an anti-aircraft unit, and 4 battalions of motorized infantry well supplied with anti-tank guns. The division thus created was a well-integrated, heavily armed, and very mobile fighting formation; well trained, and practised and experienced in mechanical warfare.

Rommel had gone to Africa under orders to conduct a policy of aggressive defence and to safeguard Tripoli, a task he had accomplished by the middle of March, when, with his troops holding a line from El Agheila to Marada, all danger of an immediate threat to Tripoli had been removed. Thereupon he proposed that an offensive should be launched in May which would lead first to the recapture of Cyrenaica, and secondly to the invasion of Egypt and the seizing of the Suez Canal. General Gariboldi, who had succeeded Graziani as C.-in-C, gave his approval, and Rommel sent the plan to OKH with demands for German troops over and above the promised 15th Panzer Division. A visit to Berlin saw him return without reinforcements but with instructions not to advance beyond Agedabia, which place he was authorized to attack in May.

Back in the desert Rommel was undeterred by the limitations imposed in Berlin, and on 23rd March advanced to and captured El Agheila and its excellent water supplies. There he paused for a week in order to prepare for a further advance, set to begin on 30th March with Mersa Brega as its objective.

On 31st March the Germans attacked the British right at Mersa Brega and induced a withdrawal which soon developed into a major retreat, the armour moving back to Msus. Four days later, while watching the continuing British retreat, Rommel decided to cross the desert to find out if Neame intended to fight for the Jebel, and in any case to threaten the southern flank of the British army. That night his forward units ran out of fuel and stopped, and he ordered all the available vehicles in the 5th Light Division to return to El Agheila, 40 miles in the rear, to fetch up fresh supplies. Rommel's staff estimated that this operation would take four days but he allowed them 24 hours, was obeyed, and on the night of 4th/5th April prepared to resume his advance. He formed his army into four columns, pressed the visiting General Kircheim into the command of one, and sent them severally up the coast and towards Tmimi, Mechili, and Tobruk with orders to keep moving at all costs. Gariboldi, who had protested strongly

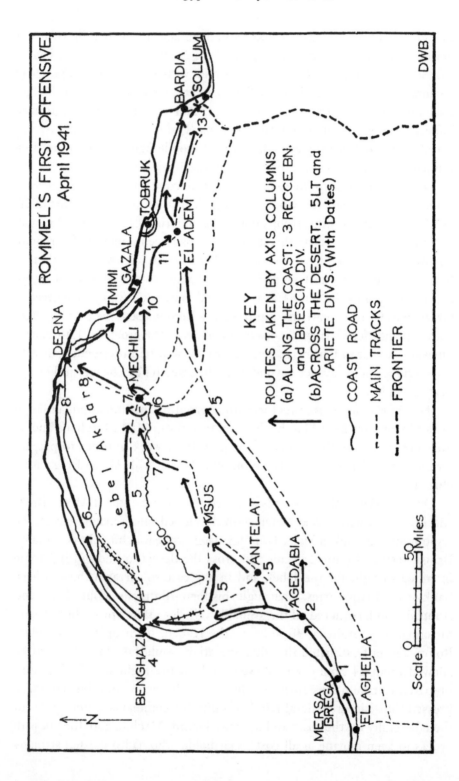

ROMMEL'S FIRST OFFENSIVE, April 1941.

KEY

ROUTES TAKEN BY AXIS COLUMNS
(a) ALONG THE COAST: 3 RECCE BN. and BRESCIA DIV.
(b) ACROSS THE DESERT: 5LT and ARIETE DIVS. (With Dates)

COAST ROAD
MAIN TRACKS
FRONTIER

Scale 0 [____] 50 Miles

DWB

at the passing of Agedabia, did so again but was overruled by the dominant German who insisted on having complete freedom of action.

The British during this period experienced little but trouble. On 2nd April Wavell flew up from Cairo, and then summoned O'Connor, whom he intended to place in command. Subsequently Wavell decided to leave Neame in command with O'Connor to advise him, a curious arrangement, which even more curiously seemed likely to work. Wavell still believed that the enemy were not ready to mount a large scale offensive and prepared to fight a defensive battle for Benghazi, which he thought must be the main German objective though both Neame and O'Connor considered a move across the desert to be more than likely. Fortunately perhaps, Wavell's orders for this defensive battle were not received until 4th April by which time Rommel's columns moving towards Msus and Mechili had penetrated the British southern flank and it was too late to act upon them.

Between 3rd and 6th April a state of rare confusion existed in XIII Corps, caused by an absence of information, hopelessly bad signal communications, and the speed of the German advance. O'Connor's and Neame's fears of a cross desert drive by the enemy had been fulfilled and on 6th they ordered a general withdrawal in an attempt to save what they could of the army. Twenty-four hours later, both these generals and Gambier Parry of the 2nd Armoured Division had been captured in a chance encounter with a German patrol; the 3rd Armoured and the Indian Motorized Brigades, caught near Mechili, had ceased to exist; and while one German column threatened the Derna airfield another was moving to cut off Tobruk.

The desert was then littered with German units waiting for fuel but there was no British armour to threaten them and when fuel arrived they hurried forward, driven on by their dynamic commander. On 11th April Tobruk was surrounded and the German and Italian mobile forces continued their pursuit of the British towards Bardia and Solium, Rommel having announced the previous day that Suez was his objective. In due course the coastal towns fell to the Germans but the British had begun by then to regain some coherence and Gott's Support Group held the frontier for some days until, after heavy skirmishing, he was forced back to the Buq Buq-Sofafi line on 26th April. There he stuck while the 7th Australian and 6th United Kingdom Divisions prepared a strong defensive position just forward of Matruh.

By this time Wavell had decided to hold Tobruk in strength, and if possible, to form in the frontier area a powerful mobile force which would operate against the flanks of enemy attacks on the fortress while a strong defensive position was established in the Matruh area as had been done the year before. He had foreseen early in April that a crisis might shortly arise, and hoping to be able to form a stable front west of Tobruk had obtained London's permission to use the 7th Australian Division from Greece, and the incomplete 6th British Division, originally intended for operations against the Dodecanese Islands, for this purpose. The Chiefs of Staff immediately gave the desert first call on supplies and equipment, and promised more aircraft to the Middle East, but then the speed of Rommel's advance and the disorganization of the armourless British army made this plan impracticable and Wavell was obliged to leave a garrison in Tobruk and to stabilize the front just inside the Egyptian frontier.

Wavell himself did not think Tobruk a good place to hold indefinitely. The position was not naturally strong, its water supply was vulnerable, and the garrison was too small to provide a secure defence. The airfields could only hope for very restricted use and the harbour could be closed by mines. On the other hand the garrison had ample supplies, its morale was good, and it could be a constant danger to Rommel's communications by threatening to break out in his rear. For this reason, and because he was anxious to deny the enemy the use of the port, and because Admiral Cunningham approved of the holding of the fortress and guaranteed to supply its troops, Wavell eventually decided to defend the position as strongly as possible.

In the meantime the destruction of the 2nd Armoured Division and the capture of the three generals had necessitated another reorganization of the command and the army, and in mid-April Beresford-Peirse was recalled from East Africa to take command of the reconstituted Western Desert Force. From his headquarters at Matruh he controlled the 7th Australian Division (Major-General J. D. Lavarack), newly recalled from Greece; the incomplete 6th Division (Major-General J. F. Evetts); and a reorganized Support Group, renamed the Mobile Force, under Brigadier W. H. E. Gott. Major-General L. J. Morshead with 24,000 fighting men and 12,000 others held Tobruk, for which he was responsible directly to the Commander-in-Chief. Also back in the desert at his old headquarters was Air Commodore Collishaw with the Headquarters of 204 Group, 3 squadrons each of Blenheims and Hurricanes, and parts of two more light bomber squadrons under command.

At Tobruk itself the repair work on the perimeter defences, begun by Neame's order in March, had been completed and on 9th April the garrison drew inside them. At the time Morshead had under command the 3rd

Armoured Brigade, in process of re-equipping from Egypt with 26 cruiser, 15 light, and 4 I tanks; the 9th Australian Division with the 18th Infantry Brigade in reserve; and a huge number of "tail" troops. In fact 12,000 of the 36,000 men in Tobruk were members of base units, Libyan refugees, and enemy prisoners, all of whom required feeding while adding little or nothing to the fighting strength of the garrison.

Characteristically Morshead was determined to fight as aggressive a defence as could be imagined. He convinced his men that although occasional break-ins could be expected on a front where one battalion held five miles of perimeter defences these would be crushed, and that further retreat was unthinkable. His men reacted appropriately and the morale of the garrison rapidly rose to a remarkably high level.

Between 11th and 17th April Rommel tried three times to capture Tobruk only to be beaten off with considerable losses. These reverses left the Germans surprised and bewildered, and badly scattered in difficult and unpleasant country. Morshead, unable to risk substantial losses of men or equipment, then subordinated his personal inclination to counter-attack to his duty to hold the port safely, and contented himself with vigorous patrol activity and sorties by small forces which inflicted both damage and casualties on the besiegers.

Thus the ground situation was somewhat improved but in the air it was another matter. The Luftwaffe attacked continually and by 14th April only 14 Hurricanes remained in the desert squadrons. These could only be used for occasional daylight patrols over Tobruk though Collishaw's bombers raided the enemy airfields at Gazala, Benina, and Derna whenever possible in attempts to reduce the weight of the bombing attacks on the fortress.

At the same time the sea flank was firmly held by the navy despite repeated air attack and mining. The maintenance of Tobruk was their chief task but destroyers, cruisers and gunboats also shelled enemy supply routes and airfields in Cyrenaica, and mounted a commando raid on Bardia on the 19th/20th April, while in the central Mediterranean the battle fleet bombarded Tripoli on 21st April and increased its attacks on the sea routes between Italy and North Africa.

On the enemy side the Italians had become fearful after Rommel's failure to capture Tobruk and Rome urged OKH to halt the advance for reorganization and refitting before Egypt was again invaded. Hitler agreed and insisted that Rommel capture Tobruk before renewing his offensive. Rommel's reaction was to demand reinforcements for his army, in particular more support units and guns, and a stronger air element with more transport aircraft to guarantee his supplies of fuel, ammunition, and water. At OKH, however, Halder, the Chief of the General Staff, had become very anxious about affairs in Africa, and fearing that it might become necessary to send more troops to extricate Rommel from a dangerous predicament at a time when Germany needed all the men she could muster for the attack on Russia, he sent General Paulus to Cyrenaica to examine and report on the situation.

At this point it is relevant to consider the factors which contributed most to the British defeat. As Wavell subsequently admitted when he accepted full responsibility for the defeat, he had underestimated the time the Germans would need to prepare for an offensive, and the strength he himself required to hold Cyrenaica. Even so his original appreciation was not unreasonable, the disaster arising largely from the fact that the armoured division existed in name only. Neame in fact could hardly have done more than he did even with an effective corps headquarters, for he did not possess a mobile force which he could use to strike at the enemy's lines of communication and to discourage a major advance until later in the year.

Equally important, however, was the fact that in their new adversary the British found a general who, more than most, had a genius for recognizing and exploiting casual opportunities, especially with armoured forces. The German pursuit was a great tactical and personal triumph for Rommel. Like O'Connor he knew his army's capabilities and used them to the full. In this he was greatly helped by the organization of the German army. The Germans had foreseen that in a mechanized war tactical changes would call for the rapid regrouping of units, and the army, and the panzer divisions in particular, were so organized as to permit this to take place easily. And by thorough training on a single doctrine they made it possible for small units to settle in with other groups and new commanders with the minimum of fuss. In the hands of a man like Rommel formations with such attributes were hard to beat and could achieve marvels. Rommel knew this and drove his men to incredible lengths and great successes.

His personal qualities too, seemed well suited to war in the desert. He had a Spartan attitude to personal comfort, and administrative problems had no more power to daunt his ambition than the protests of a local C.-in-C. whom he despised. He had a genius for improvization which showed in his tactics and administrative methods, and a great capacity for keeping his opponents guessing as to his intentions, Neame for one, failing to discover the direction of the German thrusts until it was too late. A firm belief in using speed of movement to secure the advantages of surprise, a ferocious and boundless energy, and great personal bravery were characteristic of the man. He also possessed moral courage of a high order, certainly enough to defy the orders of OKH when he saw an opportunity to inflict a heavy defeat on his enemy.

On two counts, perhaps, he can be criticized. He tended to take too little account of administrative problems, and was inclined to fight like a general of the 18th rather than of the 20th century. During the advance in April, 1941, for instance, he led in person numerous local attacks and was everywhere in the battle except at his own headquarters, where his staff were liable to be as surprised as his opponents by his movements. Nevertheless he was successful, and victory disarms criticism.

It is of particular interest to remember that Rommel at this time provided notable examples of the power a "fighting soldier" sometimes has to upset the careful calculations of the more formally learned of his colleagues, in this case the staffs in Cairo, Berlin, Rome, and London, and both his own immediate C.-in-C. and all the opposing British commanders.

When Von Paulus arrived at Rommel's headquarters on 27th April he found that a fourth assault against Tobruk had been planned for the 30th. He eventually gave his approval to this operation but made it clear that OKH were determined not to allow the desert theatre to become an embarrassment to the Führer's ambitions elsewhere.

For his attack Rommel had Kircheim with half the 5th Light Division and 70 tanks; some units of the newly arrived 15th Panzer Division; and the Italian Ariete and Brescia Divisions, a strong if somewhat unprepared force. Tobruk, however, had also gained in strength since Rommel's last attack, the minefields had been improved, and 12 I tanks had been added to Morshead's small force of armour.

On the evening of 30th April the Germans attacked and established a narrow lodgment at Ras Meduar in the south-western sector of the defences. Thereafter, however, the assault collapsed in a welter of indeterminate and scattered actions, the general confusion being made worse by sandstorms and the resilience and bitter fighting of the defenders. An attempt by Morshead to retake Ras Meduar failed and the battle died down on 4th June, the Germans having lost 1,150 men. Throughout this period the RAF provided excellent cover for the garrison and nullified the enemy's powerful attempts to bomb the fortress into submission.

Thus the second major battle for Tobruk ended with the Germans gaining a good observation point, and perhaps a possible place for starting a future attack, but failing completely to secure their main objectives.

Paulus then forbade further attacks unless the British withdrew of their own volition and defined the task of the DAK as the holding of Cyrenaica, irrespective of whoever held Bardia, Solium, or even Tobruk. In the meantime the Axis forces were to lie in depth round Tobruk and to prepare a defence line on the east of the Jebel with its left on Gazala and its right well back into the desert.

His report, sent to OKH on 12th May, stated that the tactical and administrative situation of the DAK gave cause for concern, and showed that the Germans in their turn were finding that problems of supply were probably the most difficult part of war in the desert. British naval and air attacks on the Cyrenaica harbours and convoys were forcing the Axis powers to rely increasingly on the 1,100 mile land route from Tripoli for the supply of their armies outside Tobruk and on the Egyptian frontier, and although this was a relatively safe route, the shortage of vehicles and the lack of a good administrative headquarters made the maintenance of the enemy forces exceptionally difficult. Paulus appreciated this and stated that the security of the harbours and coastal shipping routes east of Tripoli should be the first consideration of the Axis high command. After that ammunition, petrol, vehicles, and medium and anti-tank artillery, in that order, should be sent out, with troops to follow when a satisfactory stock of equipment had been built up. At OKH, Haider's reaction was that Rommel's exceeding of orders had created a situation for which the Axis supply organization was unprepared and inadequate, and that as a result the outlook was far from good.

Back in Egypt Wavell was also beset with many difficulties. For the time being at least Tobruk was firmly held, and thanks to the navy's determination to supply the garrison, even at high cost, was unlikely to be starved out, but in Egypt his armoured strength was dangerously low, and the chances of stopping an attack by the 15th Panzer Division were far from good. The British armour at this time consisted only of the small mixed unit in Tobruk and a cruiser squadron at Matruh, although between 30 and 40 tanks were expected to return from workshops by the beginning of June. Even with these, however, Beresford-Peirse could not hope to fight off a strong enemy attack, and the Tobruk garrison did not have the strength to break through the investing forces in order to attack the enemy's supply lines which ran well to the south of the fortress.

In London meanwhile, the Defence Committee had recognized the danger and on 21st April decided to send the Tiger convoy, with 53 Hurricanes and 295 tanks through the Mediterranean. When this convoy arrived at

Alexandria on 12th May, having lost only 10 aircraft and 57 tanks, Wavell believed that his armoured strength was again sufficient to permit him to return to the offensive himself.

He had seen that after the failure at Tobruk on 4th May Rommel had temporarily been fought to a standstill, and he planned to attack the Germans before they had time to recover from their difficulties of dispersion and supply. Wavell was in fact so eager to attack while Rommel was off balance that, without waiting for the Tiger convoy's reinforcements, he ordered Gott and the Support Group to take Solium and Gapuzzo and to exploit towards Tobruk. For this operation, code-named "Brevity", Gott was given all the available armour so that his Support Group would have a reasonable chance against the 30/50 enemy tanks known to be in the frontier area.

Gott now planned a three-pronged advance along the coast and above the escarpment, while the RAF concentrated on attacks against the enemy's supply lines west of the probable battlefield. Collishaw had decided on the basis of past experience that tanks were unprofitable targets for aircraft but believed that by cutting off an enemy column's supplies he could either halt it or force it to withdraw.

Unfortunately "Brevity" failed completely, Gott's armour having neither the strength nor the support required to enable him to take full advantage of his early successes. Chief credit should be given to Rommel, however, for gauging correctly the weight of the British attack and deciding that it could be stopped by determined resistance.

In the air Collishaw's men had successfully attacked enemy transport behind the battle but it is doubtful if at any time he possessed enough aircraft to achieve the ends he had in view. Thus Wavell's acceptance of high risks in the hope of making great gains had come to nothing, but he knew that Rommel was still facing great administrative difficulties and went on with the preparations for Operation "Battleaxe", of which "Brevity" had been no more than the premature offspring.

Chapter 6

The Second British Offensive. Operation "Battleaxe"

Wavell had begun to plan for "Battleaxe" as soon as Rommel's advance had been halted but there were other and much more weighty reasons than his own determination to defeat the Germans that made a new British offensive necessary. Towards the end of May the Chiefs of Staff reported to the Government that although Turkey was not in imminent danger of attack some political and military action was needed in order to ensure the security of the allies' northern flank in the Mediterranean. Furthermore the German occupation of Crete had enabled them to supply Cyrenaica via the western coast of Greece and it was essential to establish the RAF between Solium and Derna if this and the Tripoli supply routes were to be attacked, and if Malta was to be easily maintained.

At the same time the Prime Minister badly needed a victory to offset the succession of defeats in Greece and Crete, and to counter the enemy's distracting activities in Iraq and Syria; to justify the risks taken in passing the Tiger convoy through the Mediterranean, and to encourage the Australian people by the relief of their soldiers besieged in Tobruk. He also saw, as Wavell had done, that Rommel was in a very difficult situation with regard to his supplies and the German military directorate, and pressed very strongly for an offensive aimed at destroying the enemy in the western desert.

Always eager to attack the enemy Wavell had given his preliminary instructions for "Battleaxe" on 1st May, and on the 28th he issued his main orders. The Western Desert Force was to seize the Halfaya Passes and secure the Bardia–Sollum–Capuzzo–Sidi Azeiz area; to defeat the enemy between Tobruk and El Adem; and then to exploit these successes by further advances towards Derna and Mechili. The Tobruk garrison would operate against the enemy rear, its tasks being defined by Beresford-Peirse, the commander of the Western Desert Force.

The need to build up a strong force of armour by reconstituting the 7th Armoured Division now imposed some delay and "Battleaxe" was set to begin on 15th June. In February the 7th Armoured Division had been withdrawn and its men largely dispersed, and before it could join battle with any hope of success it needed to be reorganized and retrained. Meanwhile the 82 cruiser, 135 Matildas, and 21 light tanks delivered by the Tiger convoy were being overhauled and modified for desert conditions and crews were being trained to use the new models. Churchill raged and fumed at the inevitable delays but Wavell insisted that 15th June was the earliest day on which he could move and the Prime Minister had to be content with that.

The Germans were also building up their strength and with the 15th Panzer Division now complete Rommel placed it in the frontier area in support of the Italian infantry and withdrew the 5th Light Division into reserve, meanwhile continuing to work on the construction of a defensive position at Gazala.

To face the 100 medium tanks and 40,000 men Rommel had at the frontier and at Tobruk Beresford-Peirse had the rebuilt XIII Corps, consisting of the new 7th Armoured Division under Sir Michael Creagh; the 11th Infantry Brigade of the 4th Indian Division (Major-General F. W. Messervy), now in the process of returning from East Africa; and the 22nd Guards Brigade. His armoured force then consisted of some 200 gun-armed tanks.

The RAF in the desert had 105 serviceable bombers and 98 fighters to put against the 84 and 130 similar aircraft of the Axis air forces, Air Marshal Tedder, who was standing in for Longmore, having accepted serious risks elsewhere in order that local air superiority should be guaranteed for "Battleaxe". Unfortunately four of his squadrons had no experience of either the desert or the Germans, and many of his other crews had no battle experience whatever, having come directly from the United Kingdom to make up for the losses in Greece and Crete.

Three plans were prepared before Wavell decided on the precise nature of the action to be taken. A holding operation on the coast while the armour swept leftwards towards Tobruk was ruled out because not enough men and transport were available, and Wavell rejected a plan in which the armoured division was to seek an encounter battle because it involved dispersion of his army and was not certain to bring about the desired conflict. The plan which he finally accepted ensured that the largest force which could be maintained in the field, namely XIII Corps as it then existed, was certain to play a part in the battle.

In the first phase the two infantry brigades and the 4th Armoured Brigade were intended to advance and smash the enemy in the Halfaya-Sollum-Capuzzo-Bardia area while the rest of the armour guarded the left flank and gave what help it could to the operations further north. For this action Beresford-Peirse took the 4th Armoured Brigade from the 7th Armoured Division and placed it under Messervy's command on the understanding that if a major tank battle developed it would return to Creagh's control. This arrangement gave Messervy the use of two regiments of I tanks and left the armoured division with the Support Group and the two cruiser regiments of the 7th Armoured Brigade. This Brigade was then ordered to advance to the Hafid Ridge district while Messervy cleared the upper and lower Halfaya Passes with a two-pronged attack by his infantry and the 4th Armoured Brigade. No time was set for the beginning of the first of these attacks because Beresford-Peirse hoped that a general tank battle would develop as a result of the advance of 7th Armoured Brigade in which case the 4th Armoured Brigade would have to rejoin its original division. He proposed to make no call on the Tobruk garrison until XIII Corps had moved to within supporting distance of the fortress.

With the plan for his attack completed Beresford-Peirse set up his headquarters at Sidi Barrani which though 5 hours' driving time from the likely battlefield was the most advanced position from which sure communication with the RAF headquarters, 100 miles behind at Maaten Baggush, could be established. Sidi Barrani also possessed the most advanced airfield that tactical reconnaissance aircraft could use.

The Air Plan provided for the strategic bombing of enemy supply routes and dumps to continue until 12th June, when the weight of the attacks would be shifted to the area between Tobruk and the frontier, and every Axis airfield within reach. Tedder then promised that fighter cover would be available throughout the battle and placed his medium bombers on army call to attack enemy columns in the battle area should the need arise.

The navy's tasks were to continue to supply Tobruk and to be ready to open the port at Solium. The traditional bombardment was left out of the battle plan because fighter cover for the fleet could only be provided by reducing the army's tactical air support. Then, as preparations for the offensive went ahead, Wavell received news which led him to entertain certain misgivings about the probable success of the operation. His cruiser tanks were discovered to be subject to frequent mechanical breakdowns; the I tanks were too slow for armoured battle in the open desert and were vulnerable to the 88 mm German anti-tank guns; and because his armoured cars were inferior to those of the enemy his ability to obtain reliable information before and during the battle was likely to be sharply reduced. He reported these facts to the CIGS on 28th May, adding that while he believed his initial superiority would be such as to allow him to be successful in the first phase of the battle he doubted whether he would have sufficient strength to complete the second and third stages of the offensive.

When the battle began all seemed to go well for the British but when the day ended it was found that only in the centre, where Fort Capuzzo had been captured, had there been any real success. On the flanks the enemy still held the Halfaya Pass and the Hafid Ridge, and their anti-tank guns, including a dozen 88s, had inflicted heavy casualties on the British armour. Nevertheless the 15th Panzer Division's tank regiment had been driven north of Capuzzo and for the next day Beresford-Peirse planned another attack against the Halfaya positions while his armoured division, once more he hoped, reunited, destroyed the enemy tanks in the Hafid Ridge area.

Before these plans could be put into effect, however, Rommel had launched a counter-attack. The previous night he had called up the 96 tanks of the 5th Light Division and he now sent these across the desert towards Sidi Omar to attack the British left and rear while 15th Panzer tried to recapture Fort Capuzzo. Only the first of these moves met with any success, the 5th Light Division reaching Sidi Omar that evening after a continuous but inconclusive battle with the 7th Armoured Brigade. At Capuzzo meanwhile Messervy not only beat off the German attacks but succeeded in capturing the barracks at Solium, though the enemy pressure was such that he remained unable to release the 4th Armoured Brigade to rejoin Creagh's division.

The outcome of the battle was thus still in the balance when early on the 17th, Rommel struck towards Halfaya with both his armoured formations in an attempt to cut off the British in the Sollum-Halfaya-Capuzzo area, and to force Beresford-Peirse to withdraw into Egypt. By 8 a.m. the 5th Light Division had driven back the 7th Armoured Brigade and Support Group, now reduced to 39 runners, and reached Sidi Suleiman, and shortly afterwards Messervy ordered his forces in the Capuzzo area, the 22nd Guards Brigade, to withdraw before they were encircled and destroyed. On hearing of this latest development, Wavell, who had joined Beresford-Peirse earlier that morning, cancelled the instructions he had given for an armoured counter-attack at Sidi Suleiman, and ordered his army to break off the action and withdraw to refit, recovering as many

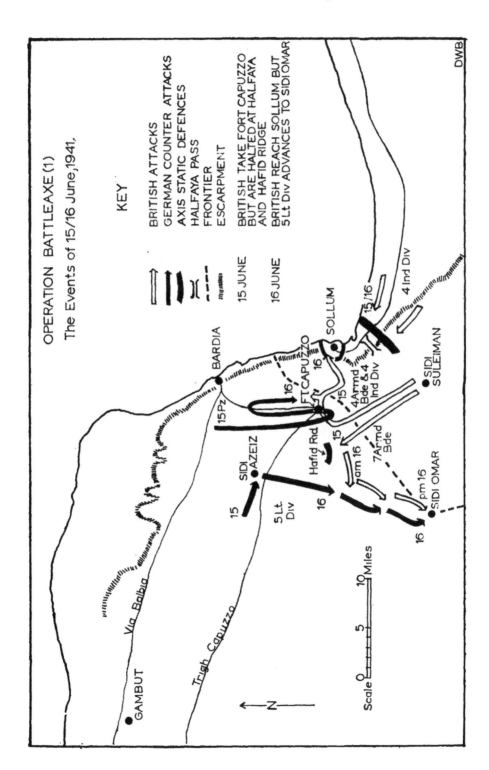

OPERATION BATTLEAXE (1)

The Events of 15/16 June,1941.

KEY

BRITISH ATTACKS
GERMAN COUNTER ATTACKS
AXIS STATIC DEFENCES
HALFAYA PASS
FRONTIER
ESCARPMENT

BRITISH TAKE FORT CAPUZZO
BUT ARE HALTED AT HALFAYA
AND HAFID RIDGE

BRITISH REACH SOLLUM BUT
5 Lt Div ADVANCES TO SIDI OMAR

15 JUNE

16 JUNE

DWB

BARDIA

GAMBUT

Via Balbia

Trigh Capuzzo

SIDI
AZEIZ

5 Lt.
Div

15

15 Pz

16

FT CAPUZZO

16

Hafid Rid.

SOLLUM

16

15

15

am 16

4 Armd
Bde & 4
Ind Div

7 Armd
Bde

16

pm 16

SIDI
OMAR

16

SIDI
SULEIMAN

15/16

4 Ind Div

N

Scale 0   5   10 Miles

damaged tanks as possible. By dark on 17th June the British army was back on the Sidi Barrani-Sofafi line having lost 969 men, 91 tanks, and 33 aircraft. The enemy had lost 678 men, 12 tanks, and 10 aircraft, and though 50 more of their tanks had been damaged most were recovered and after repair were able to rejoin the panzer division.

The RAF had played its part well, notably so on the last day when the fighters gave the retreating army excellent cover and protection, a debt fully acknowledged by Wavell, though their losses, particularly in fighters, were very heavy. Tedder attributed these casualties to a lack of training and experience among the pilots, and to the shortage of aircraft which meant that in order to give continuous cover to the army his patrols had to be weak in numbers and therefore increasingly vulnerable.

"Battleaxe" was thus the third successive defeat to be suffered at the hands of Rommel in the space of six months, and was the most salutary, coming as it did in the course of an intended British offensive. The reasons for the defeat are many and varied, some with immediate and local origins, and others with histories reaching back into the period before the outbreak of war.

The speed at which the operation was mounted, the result of Churchill's urging and Wavell's own wish to strike again at the enemy, had unhappy consequences, particularly for the 7th Armoured Division. The hasty re-equipment of that division, to a large extent with new crews and untried tanks, meant that training at all levels was below the desired standard. Neither of the armoured brigades nor the division as a whole had found it possible to train as complete formations, and the arming of the 7th Armoured Brigade with cruisers and the 4th with Matildas, slower and much shorter of range, made the fighting of the division as a cohesive formation difficult if not impossible. The close association of such ill-balanced formations without combined training and the practice of the tactics to be used in an encounter battle was a strong argument against using the 7th Armoured Division either as the instrument for seeking out and destroying the German armour, or for driving deeply into enemy held territory. And the absence of the transport required to maintain large scale armoured operations and the consequent need to secure the Halfaya and Solium positions for supply purposes reinforce the criticisms levelled at the organization of the British armoured force and the conception of its use in this offensive. On the other hand it should be remembered that in the battle itself the handling of our armour was sufficiently skilful to ensure that, after it had failed to achieve its aim, the division was able to concentrate and avoid defeat in detail, a fact commented on by Rommel himself.

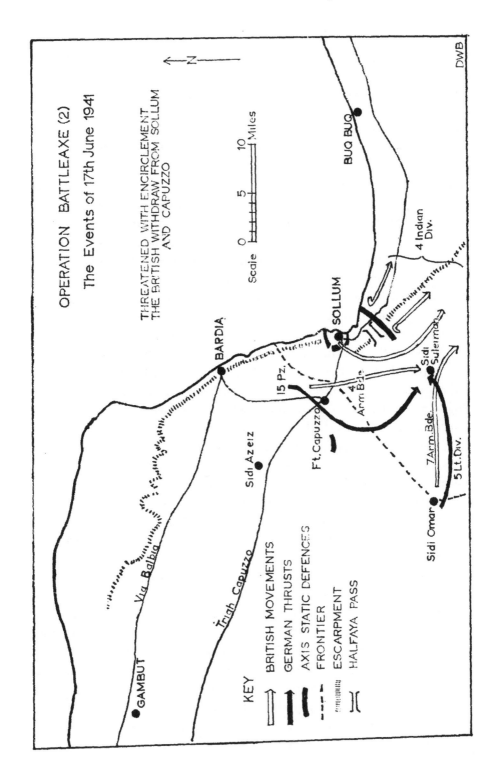

OPERATION BATTLEAXE (2)
The Events of 17th June 1941

The complicated command system, evolved in order to allow the I tanks to be used for infantry support as well as in the highly mobile operations planned for the 7th Armoured Division, greatly reduced the ability of the army and divisional commanders to fight flexible actions. It can only be a serious weakness of organization that requires the commander of an armoured division to consult with his infantry counterpart before being able to concentrate his whole tank strength for battle. As it happened Messervy's inability to release the 4th Armoured Brigade sharply curtailed Creagh's power to fight according to the opportunities and needs which arose in the course of the battle because he did not possess the required number of armoured vehicles. Fortunately the divisional commanders got on well with each other and with Beresford-Peirse and the potential for chaos was not realized, but the system invited trouble and meant that local setbacks could not be ignored in the interests of the larger battle. The splitting of the armoured division might have been less of a weakness, however, had the communication system permitted Beresford-Peirse to set up his headquarters nearer to the battlefield.

The poor state of training in the British army was another most serious handicap, and was not confined to the armoured division for the infantry had not practised with the I tanks, and neither realized nor understood the pattern and degree of co-operation between the two arms that was necessary if success was to be achieved.

It was also felt, despite the real successes that had been achieved, that army/air co-operation could be improved, and perhaps the most valuable lesson learnt by the British from "Battleaxe" was the need to study and resolve the problems of integrating the efforts of the two services before major actions were fought in the future. For once this lesson was recognized and acted upon promptly, although its full benefits were not to be forthcoming until 1942.

The British army thus compared badly with Rommel's in three ways. The enemy were well trained in the techniques of mobile armoured warfare, the Panzer divisions being organized for just such operations. Their tanks were reliable, and in their ability to fire high explosive as well as armour-piercing ammunition, had a distinct advantage over the British, to whom the appearance of the 88 mm gun in an anti-tank role came as an additional and most unwelcome surprise. And the German system for the recovery of damaged tanks was greatly superior to that of the British.

Most important of all, however, was the German philosophy of modern armoured tactics. In the main this gave the anti-tank guns the task of smashing an enemy's armour while their own tanks dealt with the opposing infantry and soft-skinned vehicles. The British on the other hand, envisaged tank battles as being like those of naval fleets and planned and trained accordingly. Unfortunately the German school of thought was the better, and with no lack of money and materials, their concentrated training in preparation for war, and their experiences in Poland and France, they were able to develop a superior battlefield technique.

During the battle it soon became apparent that the British tanks were suffering heavily at the hands of the German anti-tank gunners whose long-barrelled 50 mm guns were numerous and well handled, and appreciably out-ranged the British 2 pounders. There was little to choose between the tanks on either side although the high explosive shells of the 75 mm gun of the German Pzkw IV could sometimes disable the British cruisers at long range.

It is unreasonable to blame either Churchill or Wavell for the failure of "Battleaxe." The organization of the army was certainly badly suited to the needs of the campaign in the desert but the circumstances in which the offensive was mounted make it easy to understand how this came about. The conduct of the battle was orthodox and the Germans won largely because Rommel was better at this type of warfare and better equipped to fight it than were his opponents. The real blame, if blame is to be apportioned, lies with the politicians of the 1930's who failed to recognize the rising threat of Hitler's Germany and refused to rearm, and the British people, battered by the 1914–1918 war and the Great Slump, and unwilling to support a political party with rearmament among its policies.

Although the army was also seriously at fault in failing to find the correct answers to the questions posed by new weapons and theories of war it was the years of financial retrenchment and popular distaste for any form of rearmament that were in the main jointly responsible for reducing tank production in the United Kingdom almost to nothing. Meanwhile Hitler was rebuilding the German army and by 1939 the British, who had been the first exponents of armoured warfare, had fallen far behind the Germans in its theory and practice.

When in 1938 Britain did at last decide to rearm there was confusion in the minds of the planners as to the nature of the war which was daily becoming more likely, and demands were made for light and cruiser tanks for mobile operations as well as for heavier models, the I tanks, to support the infantry. In the early months of the war priority was given to the building of I tanks, and when after Dunkirk the need for medium or cruiser tanks was recognized it was too late to alter the pattern of manufacture because with invasion imminent the chief need was for tanks in large numbers and no delay in production could be accepted. As a result some of the new armoured divisions were equipped with I tanks which were not well suited to mobile operations, especially in the deserts of North Africa. In fact the Germans had great respect for the Matildas, which they thought a good tank, though they could not understand why it had no capacity to fire H.E. ammunition, but the British Cruisers, Crusaders and Valentines soon acquired a reputation for mechanical unreliability as well as sharing the chronic British weakness in armament. The 2-pounder was not a bad gun but fired only solid shot, whereas by 1940 the German 50 mm was in production and capable of firing armour-piercing and high explosive ammunition. In consequence a weapon gap arose which was not closed in the desert until the Grants and Shermans with their 75 mm guns appeared in 1942. In 1938 the General Staff had asked for a heavier gun than the 2-pounder but for many reasons production of such a weapon did not begin until early 1941, and its delivery to the Middle East until November of that year.

As late as May, 1942, only about 100 6-pounder anti-tank guns had reached the Middle East and it was another month before the first 6-pounder tank guns reached the theatre. The design of a 17-pounder tank and anti-tank gun had begun in April 1941, but it was January 1943, long after the time when mobile operations were the way of war in the desert, before any reached Egypt.

Chapter 7

The Replacement of Wavell and the Preparation for "Crusader"

After the failure of "Battleaxe" Wavell's days as Commander-in-Chief in the Middle East were numbered. In the political climate of the time no commander could survive two defeats and Churchill took the opportunity to make what he believed were long overdue changes in the Middle East command.

Ever since September 1940, the Prime Minister had been concerned over what seemed to him to be an unreasonable disparity between the number of troops in the theatre and the number of fighting formations and serviceable aircraft that could be put into the field at any one time, and in order to find the answer to this question he badgered Wavell with numerous telegrams.

Wavell's reply was to explain that no army could operate in the North African desert without a scale of administrative support that would be unthinkable in a more developed country. In January 1941, he considered that administrative weaknesses would be the chief reason for the current British advance coming to a halt, and gave point to this opinion in the following month, when, much to Churchill's bewilderment, he asked for drafts of non-divisional troops to be sent to the Middle East rather than the completely new division offered by the Chiefs of Staff. The Prime Minister was not convinced but turned his attention to the RAF and in May 1941, called Longmore to London to explain why a higher proportion of serviceable aircraft was not maintained in his command. On 19th May Longmore was replaced by Air Marshal Tedder and Wavell's dismissal soon followed.

By June that year Wavell was in fact showing signs of tiredness and strain. He had after all borne heavy responsibility for a long time, and his disputes with Churchill over supplies, the events in Syria and Iraq, when he had offered to resign, and the defeats in Greece, Crete, and Cyrenaica had affected him deeply. As the Prime Minister was later to admit an unfair burden had been placed on Wavell's shoulders, and though Churchill had sought since February to discover a means of easing it, it was 28th June before the means were found and Oliver Lyttelton appointed as Minister of State in the Middle East. This was an appointment of a sort that Wavell had recommended twelve months before but he was not to reap its benefits, for the Prime Minister, who had never had absolute confidence in him, decided that the time had come for a new hand in the theatre, and on 5th July appointed General Sir Claude Auchinleck to be the Commander-in-Chief in the Middle East, Wavell then going in Auchinleck's place to become Commander-in-Chief in India.

As soon as he arrived in Egypt Auchinleck was asked by Churchill to say when he proposed to resume the offensive and replied that until British power in Iraq and Syria had been consolidated no resumption of the attacks in the desert should be considered. There could be no gainsaying this view but it was not long before the Premier and the Defence Committee were again pressing hard for an early offensive.

The arguments in favour of such a step were very powerful. It was essential for political and military reasons that some direct help be given to the newly acquired Russian ally who was now in dire straits, and a desert offensive would force the enemy to fight on two fronts at an inopportune moment. At the same time a British success would encourage both the USA and Turkey, might induce the Spaniards to think twice before joining the Axis, and could conceivably draw the French in North Africa away from Vichy. Even more important, perhaps, the recapture of the Cyrenaica airfields would enable the RAF to give better cover to the fleet, to increase its attacks on the enemy, and to bring some relief to the beleaguered Maltese. Furthermore, with air superiority guaranteed and no enemy attack on the Middle East likely before the end of September, the British were in a relatively favourable position to take the offensive in the desert where the Tobruk garrison could help in an early attack and so justify the great strain its support was placing on the navy. In addition, after the early autumn Auchinleck could expect no reinforcements because of the invasion threat to the United Kingdom itself.

In Cairo the three Commanders-in-Chief accepted the need for an offensive but differed from London as to its purpose and timing. They saw the first task as the elimination of the enemy in North Africa but doubted whether they could muster the strength required to mount a successful offensive before the end of the year. With armour the key to success in the desert, Auchinleck calculated that to overcome the 15th and 21st Panzer and the Ariete Armoured Divisions with their 390 medium tanks, and four Italian infantry divisions, and to regain the whole of Cyrenaica, he would need at least two and preferably three armoured divisions of his own as well as suitable infantry strength. At the time he could assemble more than 500 tanks but more than half of these were I tanks, and for his mobile armoured force he could only count on the 7th Armoured Brigade of the 7th Armoured Division which was equipped mainly with Crusaders, and the 4th Armoured Brigade Group which was about to convert from Matildas to the American Stuarts. Late September was the earliest time at which these formations could be brought up to strength, and with the time needed for training and for adapting the Stuarts to desert conditions Auchinleck estimated that it would be mid-October before his mobile armoured force could be ready for battle. He reported these facts to London and added that the difficulty of maintaining a large armoured force in the desert made it essential to have a reserve equal to 50 per cent of his tank strength immediately available before he could embark on a major offensive.

The Defence Committee then promised to arrange for the 22nd Armoured Brigade of the 7th Armoured Division to arrive in Egypt in mid-September thus giving time for retraining and the modification of vehicles, and set in motion a reinforcement programme designed to give Auchinleck the armour he needed in order to begin his advance on 1st November. Thereafter the flow of tanks was well maintained but it was 4th October before the 22nd Armoured Brigade arrived, and very little time was left for its training.

Nevertheless the army was growing and by 25th October Auchinleck had in the desert the 7th Armoured Division (7th and 22nd Armoured Brigades and the 7th Support Group); the 4th Armoured Brigade Group; the 4th Indian, the New Zealand, and the 1st South African Divisions; and the 135 I tanks of the 1st Army Tank Brigade. At Tobruk were the 70th British Division, which had replaced the Australians, and the 32nd Army Tank Brigade; and in general reserve in Egypt the 2nd South African Division was bringing itself up to strength and completing its training. The armoured formations were still neither fully nor uniformly trained but the whole force of 532 cruiser and 204 I tanks, and some 150,000 men was the largest and best equipped army that Britain could put in the field, and to command it Auchinleck chose Alan Cunningham, the conqueror of Ethiopia.

At the same time he regrouped his command into two armies, the 8th in the western desert and the 9th in the region east and north of the Suez Canal. The 8th Army was next organized as two Corps, XIII Corps under Godwin Austen, and XXX Corps, containing the 7th Armoured Division and the 4th Armoured Brigade Group, under Willoughby Norrie. Wilson, whom Churchill with some justification had wished to see as the commander of the 8th Army, became the head of the new 9th Army.

Meanwhile Rommel had become the commander of Army Group Afrika though to save the faces of the Italians he was made nominally subordinate to Bastico who had succeeded Gariboldi. This was a paper transaction which the Germans had no intention of honouring. At the same time their failure to achieve decisive success in Russia obliged them to postpone their plans for the conquest of Malta and Gibraltar and to concentrate on the capture of Tobruk, which Rommel hoped to achieve in October. During the summer he too received valuable reinforcements in the shape of the specially trained and equipped German 90th Light Division, the Italian Motorized Trieste Division, some Italian artillery, and 100 Italian medium tanks for the Ariete Division. His German armoured strength also increased, as vehicles returned from repair, from 180 to 250 tanks.

In September when Auchinleck began the tactical preparation for "Crusader" he was well informed as to the enemy's dispositions and estimated that the balance of strength was such that the enemy had enough supplies for three months' fighting and would enjoy a 3 : 2 superiority in the air, but that the 8th Army would benefit from a numerical advantage of 6 : 4 in tanks.

At first he ordered Cunningham to study two possible courses of action, one for an advance from Jarabub to Jalo to cut the Axis lines of communication south of Benghazi; the other for a major thrust towards Tobruk accompanied by diversionary attacks further south. Cunningham disliked the precarious supply situation and the dispersal of armour inherent in the first of Auchinleck's suggestions and proposed instead an advance by his tanks against Tobruk so that Rommel would be forced to choose between allowing the siege to be raised or committing his armour to battle against superior forces, and perhaps being destroyed, which was the British hope. This plan was accepted by Auchinleck on 3rd October with the naval and air commanders-in-chief in full agreement.

Cunningham's intention was for XXX Corps to cross the frontier between Sidi Omar and Fort Maddalena and move north-west hoping to meet and defeat the enemy armour near Tobruk, after which the siege could be raised with the help of a sortie by the garrison. In the meantime XIII Corps would hold and then envelop the enemy on the frontier, and then go on to clear the country between Bardia and Tobruk.

His orders for the first day provided for XXX Corps to advance to Gabr Saleh whence it could move either to Bardia or Tobruk according to the direction of Rommel's expected counter-thrust. This advance, Cunningham thought, would be certain to draw the DAK, then waiting near Gambut, into action, after which, with Rommel's intentions known, he could issue his orders for the further development of the battle. He intended to keep the direction of the battle firmly in his own hands and in order to be able to give his new instructions promptly arranged to travel with Norrie and the headquarters of XXX Corps as the armour advanced.

The defeat of the enemy armour would be followed by a sortie from Tobruk with the object of seizing the ridges at El Duda and Sidi Resegh between which ran the Trigh Capuzzo, the main supply route for the Axis forces east of Tobruk. The timing of the Tobruk sortie was to be left to Norrie who would then add the garrison to his own command. Meanwhile XXX Corps was strengthened by the addition of the 1st South African Division which was first to protect the southern and western flanks of the armoured advance, and later to help with the capture of the vital ridges.

XIII Corps' share of the operation was to begin with the 4th Indian Division covering the gap through which XXX Corps would advance and the forward bases and railheads of the army. Subsequently, when the DAK had been fully committed, it was expected that Cunningham would order the New Zealand Division to drive northwards from Sidi Omar against the rear of the enemy along the frontier, who would thus be forced to choose between being cut off, or withdrawal, and pursuit by the whole of Godwin Austen's corps.

The diversionary attacks in Cunningham's plan were assigned to the 29th Independent Infantry Brigade Group and the 6th South African Armoured Car Regiment, now named the Oasis Force. This force would advance to Jalo, protect an airstrip 100 miles west of Jarabub from which the RAF would bomb the coastal areas south of Benghazi, and endeavour to create the impression that a major attack was about to develop from the south. To support this deception plan bogus dumps were prepared in the southern desert and a heavy concentration of false signals traffic was maintained. At the same time the Long Range Desert Group continued to watch the coast road as far west as El Agheila, to carry out general reconnaissance, reporting on the going and enemy movements, and to harass the Germans whenever a suitable opportunity occurred.

At this point Auchinleck introduced a modification into the plan which reduced its probable effectiveness. In order to destroy the enemy armour which he thought would come in against the flank of Nome's advance Auchinleck had placed all his cruiser tanks in XXX Corps with the intention of leaving Norrie a free hand and a good chance of success in the general tank battle which he and Cunningham were trying to bring about. Cunningham and Godwin Austen, however, were fearful of the results should Rommel decide to ignore the advance of XXX Corps and instead turn his armour against the British infantry whose only anti-tank weapon was the ineffective 2-pounder, and Godwin Austen asked for the 4th Armoured Brigade to be placed under his own command. Auchinleck would not agree to this but he did make Norrie responsible for the protection of the left and centre of XIII Corps.

Norrie objected to this arrangement on two counts. He argued that the advance to Gabr Saleh was by no means certain to draw the DAK into battle and sought permission, if circumstances allowed, to move on immediately into the Sidi Resegh-El Adem area where the Germans would be forced to fight in defence of their supply routes. He also much disliked the responsibility for protecting the left of XIII Corps as it would mean that he might be unable to concentrate all his armour against the enemy panzers.

About this time the Ariete Division moved to Bir Hacheim and Cunningham, impressed by the possibility of a new threat from the south-west and Godwin Austen's fears, held to his decision to concentrate in the central position at Gabr Saleh whence the armour could be sent in any direction. Thus Norrie's well-reasoned criticisms were overruled, and although he retained control of all the armour he was saddled with the potentially embarrassing role of protecting XIII Corps, and no guarantee of being able to fight the armoured battle in his greatest strength.

"Crusader" was a nightmare for the administrative staff of the 8th Army, who were faced with the task of arranging for the supply of the army as it advanced 210 miles beyond its railhead and fought a battle of manoeuvre in a roadless and waterless region.

Huge stocks of fuel, ammunition, and water had to be established within easy reach of the fighting and this alone required an extension of the railhead. Wavell had ordered this to be begun in May but "Battleaxe", in particular, had delayed progress and it was September before serious work was resumed. Thereafter two companies of New Zealand railway troops laid two miles of track each day and on 15th November a new railhead was opened at Misheifa. Three forward bases were then set up, one near Sidi Barrani for the coastal sector; one at Thalata for XXX Corps; and the third near Jarabub for the Oasis Force. Beyond these, and fed from them, six Field Maintenance Centres were established. These were bigger versions of the FSDs and, proving highly successful, became permanent features of the army's administrative system. 32,000 tons of stores were then placed in the depots for the first week's fighting after which it was hoped that Tobruk would come into use as an advanced sea head for supplies.

Inevitably water supply presented a major difficulty. The absence of sources west of the Matruh-Siwa road and the lack of transport meant that the water pipeline also had to be extended beyond Matruh. This task was completed on 13th November when the water pipe reached Misheifa but even then water was in short supply and the daily ration of 6 pints per man was strictly accounted for.

Also included in the Administrative Plan were the preparations for opening the ports at Tobruk, Derna, and Benghazi; for a water build up of 600 gallons per day at Matruh, intended to last until the wells in the Jebel were reached; and arrangements for the evacuation by sea of casualties and prisoners of war.

The RAF was growing in strength at the same time as the army and by the time "Crusader" opened 204 Group had become the Desert Air Force (DAF) under the command of Air Vice-Marshal Arthur Coningham. Under his immediate control were 16 fighter, 8 bomber, and 3 tactical reconnaissance squadrons, and he could also call on occasional help from the Wellingtons of 205 Group, further back in Egypt, some transport squadrons, and the Fleet Air Arm. The flow of aircraft reinforcements was now sufficient to allow substantial reserves to be built up although it was still very difficult to make good losses in aircrews.

Of particular value at this time and later was the development of a system of command and maintenance that allowed the DAF to retain a high degree of flexibility in its operations and movements with the result that the effectiveness of its support for the army was greatly increased. Coningham himself retained the control of all operations and set up his headquarters alongside those of the army so that the two commanders were able to co-operate to the full and ensure that no local crisis was allowed to jeopardize the first duty of the DAF, the maintenance of air superiority over the army's field of operations.

This arrangement involved a change in the practice established after "Battleaxe" whereby an Air Support Control Section had been included in each Corps and Divisional Headquarters but Cunningham supported the changes made by his RAF colleague and the new scheme more than proved its worth. Perhaps its greatest merit lay in the fact that it became much easier to keep the essential needs of the land battle always in the air commander's mind.

At the beginning of "Crusader" the RAF had 550 serviceable aircraft to range against the 342 of the Axis in Cyrenaica, and could rely on help from 66 more based in Malta. This constituted a valuable local superiority in numbers, and although the enemy had a potential reserve of 750 more aircraft in the Mediterranean these were prevented from taking any part in the campaign until late December by the acute shortage of aviation fuel in North Africa, a direct result of allied attacks on enemy shipping.

By the middle of November, therefore, while Rommel was preparing to make his fifth attempt to capture Tobruk, all unknown to him a numerically stronger British army was about to launch a powerful attack against his positions in Cyrenaica. Rommel fully expected that some attempt would be made to divert his attention from Tobruk but was so oblivious of the real danger that he went to Rome for a conference only four days before "Crusader" was due to start.

Chance alone then decided that, its administrative preparations being completed before those of the Germans, the 8th Army rather than the DAK was the first to move, after which Rommel's refusal to react quickly to the advance of XXX Corps created an unforeseen problem for Cunningham. In the event Cunningham's decision to delay the development of his plans until some German reaction became apparent had the result of temporarily hamstringing his army. This was a curious and unhappy state of affairs and an abdication of the initiative difficult to understand in a clever, thrustful, and hitherto successful commander.

Chapter 8

The Third British Offensive Operation "Crusader" (1). The Opening Phase, 18th-23rd November, 1941

The "Crusader" fighting lasted for the better part of two months, beginning with the advance of XXX Corps on 18th November, 1941, and ending on 13th January 1942, when elements of the 8th Army, unable to make further progress, faced the Germans on a line from Mersa Brega to Alam al Mgaad.

In the air, however, the battle had begun five weeks before the tanks rolled westwards. Coningham had been given three tasks: to establish air superiority in Cyrenaica; to obtain information about the enemy's movements; and so to disrupt his supply system that he would be seriously handicapped in the coming battle. And all was to be done without arousing Rommel's suspicions.

The air operations subsequently fell into two phases. In the first, workshops, dumps, transport concentrations, enemy ports on both sides of the Mediterranean, and forward airfields were attacked, and in the second, beginning on 13th November, the DAF directed its efforts against the enemy air in Cyrenaica and to the task of covering the assembly and concentration of Cunningham's army. In this it was wholly successful although a Special Air Service raid on the Gazala and Tmimi airfields came to nothing. The bad weather which was largely to blame for this minor failure then proved to be an unexpected ally because the enemy air forces became bogged down on their own airfields just before the offensive was due to start, when its discovery might have had unfortunate results. Thus in the days before the battle the RAF not only prevented any interference with the British preparations but ensured that the attack would come as a complete surprise to the enemy.

The navy too had been busy during this period. In November 40 per cent of the tonnage despatched from Italy was sunk, Rommel's supply build-up thus receiving a very serious setback, and with air cover once more available for the fleet it was planned to resume the usual tasks of bombardment and supply in support of the army as soon as the offensive started. Elaborate arrangements were also made for the fleet to share in the deception plan, and in order to distract enemy attention and aircraft from the land battle plans were made for the simulation of a convoy passage from Gibraltar to Malta between the 16th and 19th November, and for a convoy from Malta to pretend to land a seaborne force near Tripoli on the 22nd.

The land battle itself fell into four phases, the most critical action taking place in the area Sollum-Maddalena-Bir Gubi-Tobruk, a region which merits precise description. Except near the coast and after heavy rain desert-worthy vehicles could move freely over most of this area, but between Bardia and El Adem there are two East-West ridges whose northern faces form scarps passable by vehicles in a few places only. These ridges lie parallel, one north of the Trigh Capuzzo, and the other crossing it between Belhamed and Sidi Resegh. Near this point the by-pass road built by the Axis to replace that part of the Via Balbia made useless by the British occupation of Tobruk passed between and could be commanded by two minor hill features at El Duda and Belhamed. Thus whoever held the Sidi Resegh-El Duda-Belhamed triangle could control the lines of communication of all the enemy forces east of Tobruk, and it was here that the most bitter fighting of the whole offensive took place.

The first phase, which was to last from 18th November until the 23rd began with a virtually unopposed advance to Gabr Saleh by XXX Corps. The same day Rommel had returned to the desert from Rome and though warned by Cruewell, the commander of the DAK, and the Italians, that a strong British attack was likely refused to make any change in the dispositions of his armour in the belief that the British advance was no more than an attempt to divert his attention from Tobruk, whose capture now had an almost obsessive quality for him. At the time 15th Panzer was at Gambut, 21st Panzer 20 miles west of Sidi Azeiz, and the Ariete at Bir Gubi, watching the desert flank. Four Italian divisions and one German surrounded Tobruk, another Italian division was spread along the frontier, and a sixth lay in reserve at Bir Hacheim.

Placed on the horns of a dilemma by Rommel's refusal to react to his advance Cunningham compromised, and on the 19th ordered 7th Armoured Brigade to move to Sidi Resegh while the 4th and 22nd remained at Gabr Saleh. At this point mechanical breakdowns had reduced 7th Armoured Brigade to 119 runners, and the 22nd Armoured Brigade to 136. Gott then attacked the Ariete Division with the 22nd Armoured Brigade, only to be beaten off with the loss of 25 cruisers, and nightfall came with the British armour split into three parts. The 7th Armoured Brigade was in an exposed

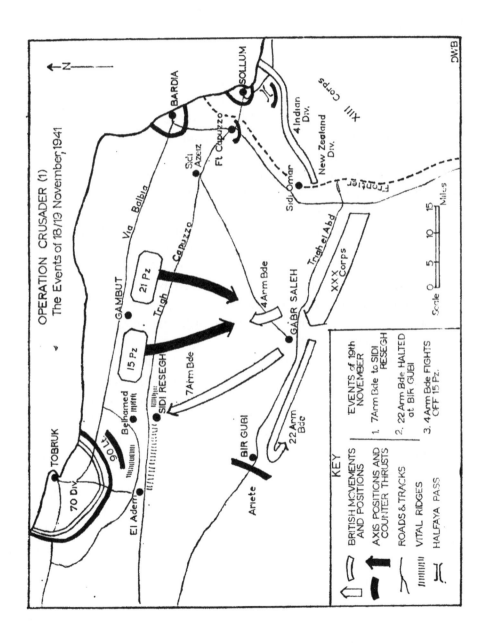

OPERATION CRUSADER (1)
The Events of 18/19 November, 1941

KEY

EVENTS of 19th NOVEMBER
1. 7Arm Bde to SIDI RESEGH
2. 22Arm Bde HALTED at BIR GUBI
3. 4Arm Bde FIGHTS OFF 15 Pz.

BRITISH MOVEMENTS AND POSITIONS
AXIS POSITIONS AND COUNTER THRUSTS
ROADS & TRACKS
VITAL RIDGES
HALFAYA PASS

Scale   0   5   10   15   Miles

position at Sidi Resegh; the 22nd was licking its wounds south of Bir Gubi; and only Gatehouse's 4th Armoured Brigade Group remained in the chosen battle area at Gabr Saleh, where it had been attacked during the day by a battle group from 21st Panzer sent to protect the German reconnaissance units near Sidi Azeiz.

Rommel had still failed to react as Cunningham had hoped, and for the next day the British commander decided to exploit his initial successes by sending the 7th Support Group to join the 7th Armoured Brigade at Sidi Resegh while the 22nd Armoured Brigade and the South African Division cleared Bir Gubi. That done they would be ready to move to Sidi Resegh in their turn.

On the 20th the Support Group duly joined Gott at Sidi Resegh but before Bir Gubi could be taken the initiative passed to the enemy. Rommel had at last accepted the fact of the British offensive and ordered Cruewell to destroy the British armour before it could interfere with his assault on Tobruk. That afternoon Cruewell began the defeat of the British in detail by again attacking the 4th Armoured Brigade and driving it south of the Trigh el Abd where it was eventually rejoined by the 22nd Armoured Brigade, recalled from Bir Gubi by Norrie. Thus by nightfall on the 20th Cunningham found himself with two of his armoured brigades once more concentrated near Gabr Saleh.

This apparent advantage was soon to be dispelled, however, for Rommel, thinking that Gatehouse's brigade had been smashed, ordered Cruewell and the DAK back to Sidi Resegh to deal with the 7th Armoured Brigade and the Support Group, and at dawn on the 21st the panzers began to move westwards, followed by the 4th and 22nd Armoured Brigades.

At this point Cunningham and Norrie, misled by bad information, appear to have thought that the vital armoured battle had been fought and won and they ordered their tanks to pursue the retreating enemy while the Tobruk garrison broke out to meet the 7th Armoured Brigade at Sidi Resegh, where they would be joined by the 5th South African Brigade from Bir Gubi. The Tobruk sortie involved a change in plan, the German armour not having been destroyed, that was to have a favourable influence on the later progress of the battle.

Unfortunately events did not turn out as Cunningham had hoped. The 4th and 22nd Armoured Brigades, delayed by the need to refuel, bad going, and the German anti-tank screen did not reach Sidi Resegh until the afternoon of the 22nd by which time the 21st Panzer Division had reduced the 7th Armoured Brigade to 10 tanks, and Gott with the remnants of the

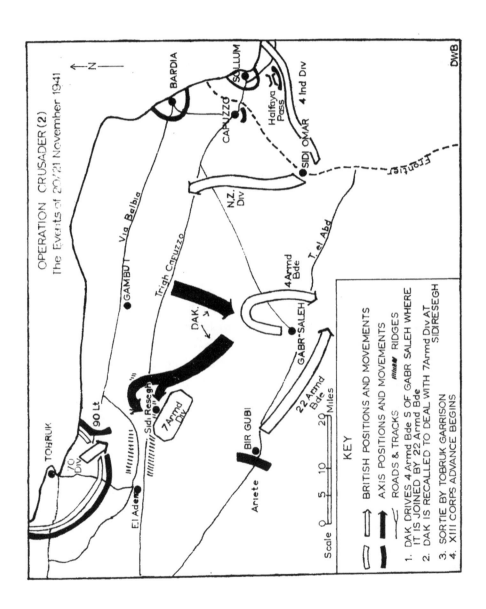

OPERATION CRUSADER (2)
The Events of 20/21 November 1941

TOBRUK
70 Div
El Adem
90 Lt
Sidi Resegh
7 Armd Div
BIR GUBI
Ariete
22 Armd Bde
GABR'SALEH
4 Armd Bde
Tel Abd
N.Z. Div
DAK.
GAMBUT
Trigh Capuzzo
Via Balbia
BARDIA
CAPUZZO
SOLLUM
Halfaya Pass
SIDI OMAR
4 Ind Div
Frontier

DWB

KEY

⟹ BRITISH POSITIONS AND MOVEMENTS
◀ AXIS POSITIONS AND MOVEMENTS
ROADS & TRACKS
⁄⁄⁄⁄ RIDGES

1. DAK DRIVES 4 Armd Bde S OF GABR SALEH WHERE
   IT IS JOINED BY 22 Armd Bde
2. DAK IS RECALLED TO DEAL WITH 7 Armd Div AT
   SIDI RESEGH
3. SORTIE BY TOBRUK GARRISON
4. XIII CORPS ADVANCE BEGINS

Scale 0   5   10   20
               Miles

Support Group had decided to fall back southwards on to the 5th South African Brigade north of Bir Gubi. The other armoured brigades suffered nearly as heavily as the 7th. Both were badly battered by the German anti-tank guns as they tried to check the German attacks and break through to Sidi Resegh, and then 15th Panzer Division, coming from Gambut to join the battle, overran Gatehouse's headquarters with the result that his brigade was put out of action until 24th November.

In the meantime, Norrie having reported that the enemy were in full retreat, Cunningham ordered XIII Corps to join in the pursuit, and Godwin Austen sent the New Zealand Division and 200 I tanks out along the Trigh Capuzzo towards Sidi Resegh and Tobruk while the 4th Indian Division dealt with the enemy's frontier garrisons. Cunningham, encouraged by reports of the destruction of 230 enemy tanks, and ignorant of the fact that XXX Corps had been reduced to 44 cruisers, was chiefly concerned at this moment for the success of the Tobruk sortie. That in fact had gone well, a sizable salient having been driven between the 90th Light and Bolzano Divisions on the south-east of the perimeter, before Major-General Scobie, realizing that two panzer divisions were about to place themselves between him and the 7th Armoured Brigade, called a halt.

22nd November ended with each commander thinking that final victory lay within his grasp. Rommel believed with some reason that on the 23rd he could complete the destruction of XXX Corps and go to the help of the frontier garrisons whose fate had replaced Tobruk as his main cause of concern, and he planned a concerted attack by all his armour on the British south of Sidi Resegh. Cunningham, on the other hand, knowing nothing of the disasters at Sidi Resegh was reorganizing his command. He thought that the battle would henceforth develop as an infantry action and early on 23rd transferred to Godwin Austen the responsibility for continuing the advance and relieving Tobruk, while XXX Corps finished its task of breaking up the enemy armour. It was only on his return to Maddalena after telling Godwin Austen of the new arrangement that the army commander received accurate reports of the fighting at Sidi Resegh, learning that nothing was known of the 7th Armoured Brigade and that the 4th and 22nd had only 54 tanks between them.

For this latest blow Cruewell was responsible. He had first sent the 15th Panzer to join the Ariete and on its way south it had smashed the Support Group, and then in the afternoon he had struck north from Bir Gubi with the 21st Panzer and the Ariete and routed the 5th South African Infantry and the 22nd Armoured Brigades. His own losses had also been

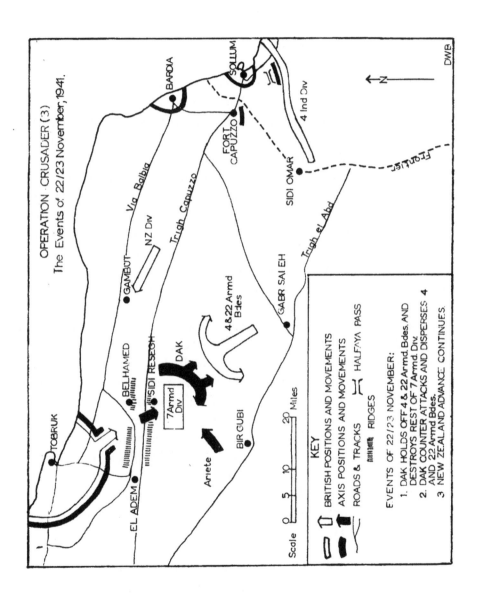

OPERATION CRUSADER (3)
The Events of 22/23 November, 1941.

TOBRUK
EL ADEM
BELHAMED
SIDI RESEGH
7 Armd Div
DAK
Ariete
BIR GUBI
GAMBUT
NZ Div
Via Balbia
Trigh Capuzzo
4 & 22 Armd Bdes
GABR SAI EH
Trigh el Abd
BARDIA
SOLLUM
FORT CAPUZZO
4 Ind Div
SIDI OMAR
Frontier
N
DWB

KEY

BRITISH POSITIONS AND MOVEMENTS
AXIS POSITIONS AND MOVEMENTS
ROADS & TRACKS   HALFAYA PASS
RIDGES

EVENTS OF 22/23 NOVEMBER:

1. DAK HOLDS OFF 4 & 22 Armd Bdes. AND DESTROYS REST OF 7 Armd Div
2. DAK COUNTER ATTACKS AND DISPERSES 4 AND 22 Armd Bdes.
3. NEW ZEALAND ADVANCE CONTINUES.

Scale   0   5   10   20 Miles

heavy but whereas the British had now suffered almost catastrophic casualties Rommel's armoured strength remained considerable.

It then seemed to Cunningham that he had lost the crucial battle, and with only 44 tanks to pit against the enemy's 120, the superiority in armour on which the whole offensive depended. He therefore decided that the only course left open to him was to break off the battle and to withdraw his forces to their starting positions. The preliminary orders for the move of the headquarters had actually been issued when Brigadier Galloway, Cunningham's chief staff officer, believing that the battle could still be won and that only disaster could follow a disengagement, spoke to Headquarters Middle East and asked that General Auchinleck should come forward to the headquarters of the 8th Army.

The situation which confronted Auchinleck when he arrived at the army headquarters on the evening of 23rd November was fraught with danger. By virtue of his greater strength in cruiser tanks Rommel was in a position from which he might cut off the remains of XXX Corps; attack Godwin Austen's unprotected infantry and the supply base at Thalata; and if successful against XIII Corps, find no substantial British force between him and the Delta. Should he, Auchinleck, therefore continue the offensive or break off the battle and adopt a defensive attitude ?

As has been seen Cunningham favoured the latter course but Auchinleck, supported by Norrie, Godwin Austen, Freyberg, and Galloway, decided to fight it out. In his view Rommel could hardly be less disorganized than the 8th Army; Tobruk was still a threat to his rear; and, perhaps equally important, a British disengagement could only end in the surrender of the initiative and any chance of final victory that still remained. The danger inherent in committing his last reserves to an unfinished battle which had gone well for the enemy were great, but relying on his men's fighting ability, his power to bring up fresh troops from Egypt, and the enemy's disorganization Auchinleck ordered the offensive to continue. The German armour was to be destroyed as a preliminary to the reconquest of Cyrenaica and an advance on Tripoli, and the 8th Army was to continue to attack down to its last tank.

Cunningham then passed on these orders and completed the reorganization of the army. From midnight on 24th November Godwin Austen was to be responsible for all operations north of an east-west line through Sidi Azeiz, including those of the Tobruk garrison; was to capture the El Duda and Sidi Resegh ridges whatever the cost, and be ready to exploit westwards. Norrie was to reorganize XXX Corps, and to protect the flanks of the 1st South African Brigade and the New Zealand Division from attacks by enemy tanks, as well as the FMCs south of the Trigh el Abd.

Galloway's action in calling up Auchinleck was entirely correct as in the circumstances only the Commander-in-Chief could decide what should be done, and as it turned out Auchinleck's decision to fight on saved not only the battle but much else. It was one of the great strategic decisions not only of the desert campaigns but of the war as a whole.

Chapter 9

The Second Phase, 24th-30th November, 1941 Operation "Crusader" (2)

The second phase of the "Crusader" battle covered the seven days 24th to 30th November, 1941. During this period Auchinleck, who returned to Cairo on the 25th, remained in effective control of the 8th Army although Cunningham and then Ritchie nominally held the command, and Rommel embarked on a spectacular but ineffectual armoured drive to the Egyptian frontier before being forced to return to the Tobruk front by Godwin Austen's continuing advance.

On 23rd November Rommel's position was much as Auchinleck had foreseen, and it was not until 6 a.m. on the 24th, with his army in great confusion, that he learnt from Cruewell of the defeat of the British armour at Sidi Resegh. The problem now was how best to use his 100 remaining tanks to exploit the previous day's success. Cruewell wanted to continue the Sidi Resegh action and complete the destruction of XXX Corps, but Rommel, who had hitherto been unwilling to move east at the cost of raising the Tobruk siege, decided to strike towards the frontier in a bold attempt to finish the battle once and for all.

He believed that the British armour could be disregarded and with the threat to his forces outside Tobruk thus removed, and the 8th Army demonstrably off-balance, there had arisen an opportunity to cut off Cunningham and at the same time bring relief to his frontier garrisons. It is almost certain that Rommel remembered the effects on the British of earlier sudden appearances of large enemy armoured forces in their rear *e.g.,* Mechili and "Battleaxe") and saw no reason why a similar move should not have comparable results. At the worst Cunningham would be seriously embarrassed, and at best the British army would be cut off or forced to withdraw. Therefore, leaving a small force under General Böttcher to keep the New Zealanders out of Tobruk, he ignored Cruewell's objections, called the Ariete and Trieste Divisions to follow him, and at 10 a.m. set off at speed in the direction of Sidi Omar with the DAK under his personal control. The risks involved in taking his main strength away from the epicentre of the battle were great but the psychological advantages to be gained outweighed them, for Cunningham feared above all an armoured thrust against his unprotected left and rear. Fortunately for the British it was Auchinleck and not Cunningham who had to decide how the 8th Army should react to this new and startling development.

Startling it certainly was for by 5 p.m. Rommel and the DAK had reached the frontier at Gasr el Arid having driven through and scattered the headquarters of XXX Corps, 7th Armoured Division, 7th Armoured Brigade, the Support Group and the 1st South African Division in the process. Neither the 4th nor 22nd Armoured Brigade had made a serious attempt to interfere with the German advance and they remained in position on the left flank of Freyberg's New Zealanders who continued to march westwards along the Trigh Capuzzo.

Back on the frontier Rommel was making plans to destroy the British by sending the 21st Panzer Division round their rear to link up with his forces at Halfaya while 15th Panzer drove north along the frontier itself. Cruewell, in his role as the keeper of Rommel's orthodox military conscience, demurred once more. He had disliked the plan from the outset and his apprehension grew as the scheme unfolded. He feared an administrative breakdown that would leave the DAK stranded and was anxious lest disaster should follow upon the confusion and dispersal created by the piecemeal arrival of the two German divisions. As it happened he was right to be apprehensive because for the next two days the DAK was to fight in a state of uncertainty and muddle rarely equalled.

Meanwhile Auchinleck and Cunningham were at Maddalena discussing what they thought were the latest happenings. Their information at this time was particularly vague. Neither the armoured cars nor the RAF, who were much handicapped by the need to use rear airfields and the difficulty of distinguishing between friend and foe in the confusion of the battlefield, had been able to discover anything of value, and recurrent signal failures simply made a bad situation worse.

Cunningham, fearing for the safety of his main base at Thalata and his water supplies, had already given orders for a general defensive action but Auchinleck refused to be made more anxious than was absolutely necessary. He believed that Rommel's latest thrusts, apparently aimed at Misheifa, could be stopped and turned back, and ordered the New Zealanders to continue their advance towards Tobruk while the 4th Indian Division stood firm on the frontier, meanwhile detaching a brigade to cover Misheifa. An initial weakness in armour was remedied by drawing tanks out of the

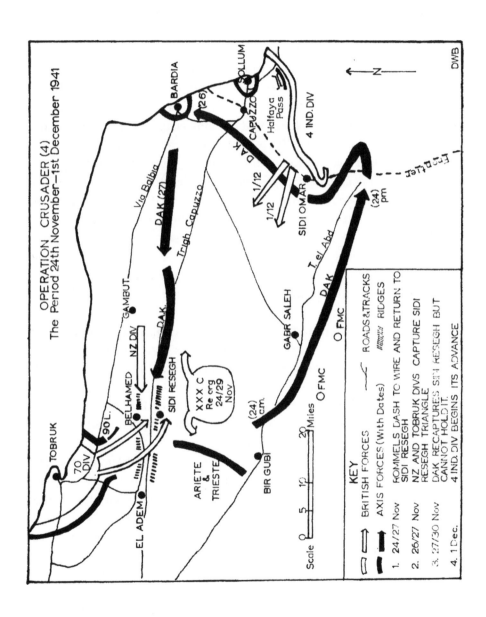

OPERATION CRUSADER (4)
The Period 24th November–1st December 1941

TOBRUK

EL ADEM

70 DIV

90 L.

BELHAMED

NZ DIV

GAMBUT

SIDI RESEGH

Via Balbia

DAK (27)

Trigh Capuzzo

DAK.

BARDIA

SOLLUM

(26)

CAPUZZO

Halfaya Pass

DAK

1/12

1/12

SIDI OMAR

4 IND. DIV

(24) pm

Frontier

T. el Abd

DAK

O FMC

GABR SALEH

XXX C
Re org
24/29 Nov

ARIETE & TRIESTE

BIR GUBI

(24) c.m.

O FMC

O FMC

N

DWB

Scale 0   5   10   20
                  Miles

KEY

⟹ BRITISH FORCES   ROADS & TRACKS
                                     RIDGES
⟹ AXIS FORCES (With Dates)

1. 24/27 Nov   ROMMELS DASH TO WIRE AND RETURN TO
                 SIDI RESEGH
2. 26/27 Nov   NZ AND TOBRUK DIVS CAPTURE SIDI
                 RESEGH TRIANGLE
3. 27/30 Nov   DAK RECAPTURES SIDI RESEGH BUT
                 CANNOT HOLD IT.
4. 1 Dec.   4 IND. DIV BEGINS ITS ADVANCE

army reserve, and by Norrie's recall of the remnants of XXX Corps. These concentrated south of Gabr Saleh during the night of 24th/25th November, together with the 22nd Guards Brigade from Bir Gubi which Norrie had previously recalled to protect FMC 62 in the same area.

The frontier fighting on 25th and 26th November was as confused and unconnected as any yet seen in the desert. Neither side knew what was happening, the Germans because the Luftwaffe was outfought by the DAF and was operating from very distant landing grounds, and the British because there was not enough reliable information on which to construct a satisfactory situation report. In the end Auchinleck had the advantage, thanks to the progress made by the New Zealanders, the determined resistance of the Indian Division, and Rommel's neglect of certain basic principles.

The German commander began by making impromptu changes of plan which reduced his power to control the battle and then committed his armour a little at a time only to see it outfought, notably by the gunners at Sidi Omar, and later run out of fuel. The result was that both panzer divisions were obliged to break off the battle and go to Bardia where they joined forces on 26th November. The Italian armour did not even reach the frontier, the 1st South African Brigade having held up the Ariete Division at Gabr Saleh.

The DAF's operations in this period had been unusually successful. For once it had been possible to use all the day bombers against enemy columns, and they had made the most of their opportunities, smashing one major attack almost before it had begun. In contrast the Luftwaffe was unable to intervene in the fighting largely because by capturing the Gambut airfields the New Zealand Division had forced the enemy fighters back to landing grounds out of range of the battlefield.

In the meantime Freyberg had advanced steadily and late on the 26th Rommel decided that he would have to return to Tobruk if he was to save Böttcher, who was then in danger of being crushed between the 70th Division and the 4th New Zealand Brigade, and he ordered 21st Panzer to move west at dawn next morning. The 15th Panzer Division was to clear up in the Solium area and follow in due course.

His attempt to outflank the whole 8th Army thus ended in failure. His attack had created confusion and some dismay but failed either to relieve his frontier forces or to force Auchinleck to alter his general plans. Moreover, while the DAK was losing 30 of its tanks in a fruitless battle XXX Corps had been able to reorganize and refit. Rommel's greatest disappointment, however, perhaps lay in the fact that the British outside Tobruk had completely ignored his outflanking move and were going on to achieve precisely what he had previously spent so much time and effort in preventing. Had he stuck to his original objective, or even listened to Cruewell, things might have gone much worse for the British.

26th November was also important because it saw a major change in the British High Command with Major-General Neil Ritchie replacing Cunningham as Army Commander. Cunningham, who had not been fully fit since September, was now showing signs of strain and overwork and Auchinleck, doubting his ability to press the offensive to the bitter end, felt obliged to relieve him of his command. It was a painful decision, especially for Auchinleck who had appointed Cunningham in the first place, to remove a good general who had fought hard and bravely, but this was the least of his difficulties.

The removal of the opposing commander was certain to encourage the Germans and reduce British prestige everywhere, Cunningham's replacement being seen as a confession of defeat, and Auchinleck had no way of measuring the effects that the change in command might have on the morale of the army. Most important of all, however, was the need to find a suitable successor. As the new commander had to be an officer who was fully acquainted with the progress of the battle and with future plans, and who was "in the mind" of the Commander-in-Chief, the choice lay between one or other of the Corps Commanders and Ritchie, Auchinleck's Deputy Chief of Staff. And as the promotion of either Norrie or Godwin Austen would have removed an essential commander in the middle of the battle and probably involved other consequential changes, Ritchie, though junior to both, was the only alternative.

By the time these changes and decisions had been made the New Zealand and 70th Divisions had made contact and between them had captured Belhamed, Sidi Resegh and El Duda thus confirming Cruewell's worst fears for the safety of his lines of supply. Help was at hand for the Germans, however, as the DAK drove west on the 27th, and Ritchie was faced with a singularly nasty situation for it seemed that his three infantry brigades outside Tobruk, now seriously weakened and short of supplies, with only artillery and a few tanks to protect them and the DAF unable to help because of bad weather, were about to be attacked from the rear by the DAK.

That night Rommel lay within easy striking distance of the Sidi Resegh-El Duda-Belhamed triangle, planning to prevent the relief of Tobruk. He had already beaten off an attempt by the reorganized and strengthened XXX Corps to halt his move west and now intended to pinch out the New Zealand

and South African brigades by attacking them from the east and south-west with the 21st and 15th Panzer Divisions. These attacks were successful in that after two more days of most bitter fighting the British were pushed oíĩ the Sidi Resegh and Belhamed ridges and Tobruk was isolated once more, but it was a short-lived victory. On the frontier Rommel's forces were still pinned in their defensive positions, and Ritchie was preparing to bring up the 2nd South African Division so that the 4th Indian Division could be released for renewed attacks outside Tobruk.

Rommel's cares had thus become uncomfortably heavy and he emphasized the gravity of the situation when he conferred with Bastico on 30th November. Not only was the 8th Army still in being, but an attrition battle had developed in which the advantage was bound to lie with the British who could bring up fresh troops and re-establish a general superiority whereas no Axis reinforcements could be quickly forthcoming because of the naval situation in the Mediterranean.

Therefore, by 1st December, with "Crusader" about to enter upon its third and decisive phase, the beginning of the end was in sight for Rommel. With Auchinleck able to bring in fresh troops against the diminishing resources of the Germans the result could only be a matter of time, and British determination and doggedness had brought its reward. Auchinleck had recognized the Sidi Resegh area as ground which Rommel dared not give up and although he still held it after two weeks' costly fighting, and Tobruk was still sealed off, the future lay with the 8th Army, and Auchinleck's decision on the 24th to continue the offensive and his refusal to be put off by Rommel's dash to the frontier had been justified. For this he had in large part to thank the fighting qualities of his troops, his armoured force as such having failed to perform the task it had been set.

He also owed a great deal to the DAF for its performance during this very dangerous period. Despite the difficulty of maintaining air operations in very bad weather they managed to cover the army on two fronts 50 miles apart, and so outfought the enemy air forces that these took little or no part in the battles. The long-range bombers continued their attacks on supply routes, ports and airfields, and the fighter squadrons, while helping in the land battles, were always ready to move forward as soon as a new landing ground was safely in British hands.

Chapter 10

Operation "Crusader" (3). Phases III & IV, 1st December, 1941–17th January, 1942

Ritchie, appointed by Auchinleck for the express purpose of continuing the offensive, announced his plans on 1st December. While XIII Corps held its ground outside Tobruk and the 2nd South African Division tidied up on the frontier, XXX Corps was to capture El Adem and send columns on towards Tmimi and Acroma. The same day Auchinleck returned to the army's headquarters where he was to remain for the next ten days, ready to advise Ritchie, but chiefly to arrange for the arrival of the infantry reinforcements which he had summoned from Syria and Cyprus, and of units of the 1st Armoured Division which had begun to land in Egypt in the previous month.

Godwin Austen soon reported that XIII Corps was ready to attack at any time and Ritchie then left it to Norrie to decide when the armoured advance should be resumed. Norrie had hoped to start on 3rd December but was held up by delays in supplies and two more attempts by Rommel to relieve his frontier garrisons. These counterattacks, made despite Cruewell's objections, failed miserably as did an attempt to recapture El Duda, and on 4th December Rommel, now thoroughly frightened of being outflanked from the south, began to withdraw from the eastern perimeter of Tobruk.

Three days later, on 7th December, faced with growing British superiority on the ground and in the air he decided to disengage and fall back to Gazala where defensive positions had been prepared in the previous May. That morning Ritchie had ordered both Norrie and Godwin Austen to advance but possibly because the 8th Army had temporarily fought itself out they were unable to break through the enemy rearguards and Rommel withdrew without much difficulty.

Then, on 10th December, after a siege of eight months, Tobruk was at last relieved. This event not only had a tremendous tonic effect on the British nation, but of more immediate importance opened the airfields at Tobruk itself, El Adem, Sidi Resegh, and Bu Amud to the DAF whose fighters were thereafter able to give cover to the army well beyond El Adem and Bir Gubi as well as to the supply ships entering Tobruk. Unfortunately they failed to prevent the enemy from reinforcing the DAK by an airlift of infantry from Crete.

By coincidence both sides had chosen 9th December to reorganize their command systems and policies. That day Rommel became the field commander of all the Axis forces in the theatre, and he warned Bastico that an outflanking move round his right by the 8th Army would necessitate a withdrawal, certainly to Agedabia and perhaps to El Agheila. The Italians, however, anxious to save what they could of their dwindling empire wished to fight at Gazala, and Bastico gave orders to this effect on the 12th. Rommel perforce had to agree but repeated his warning that without the air power to prevent a cross desert move by Ritchie's armour he could not defend the Gazala positions for any considerable period.

Changes had also taken place in the 8th Army where XIII Corps was made responsible for all future operations in Cyrenaica, and XXX Corps, less 7th Armoured Division, was charged with the reduction of the enemy still on the frontier. As the largest force that could be maintained west of Tobruk was of a size that one Corps Commander could control, Ritchie argued that there would be less delay in continuing the advance if the task were given to Godwin Austen whose headquarters were now well established in Tobruk. He was anxious that the enemy should be allowed no respite, and ignoring Norrie's suggestion that XXX Corps was the formation best suited to conduct mobile operations, transferred the one armoured brigade left in 7th Armoured Division to Godwin Austen's command. It is open to doubt whether XXX Corps was at this stage in any condition to carry out a long pursuit and in any case Auchinleck was considering its transfer to army reserve as an insurance against a possible defeat on his northern front.

On 11th December, therefore, the 4th Armoured Brigade and the 4th Indian Division joined XIII Corps at Tobruk and next day the rest of XXX Corps departed for Egypt. Ritchie himself took the 22nd Guards Brigade under his personal command and announced his intention of sending it across the desert to capture Benghazi and cut the enemy's escape route into Tripolitania. This in fact was never done, and it is difficult to understand why the third phase of the battle ended without this formation having been committed.

This reorganization marked the end of Phase III of "Crusader" and the beginning of Phase IV, which was to last until 13th January 1942.

Phase IV began with an attempt by Godwin Austen to cut off the enemy in the Gazala positions, but this failed, largely because the Stuart tanks of the 4th Armoured Brigade had too short a range to enable them to force action upon the enemy, and on 16th December Rommel ordered a withdrawal out of Cyrenaica to avoid being cut off by a cross desert move by the British through Mechili to the coast. His intention was now to reach a position where he could regroup and concentrate his army in safety, meanwhile forcing Ritchie to operate at the end of ever lengthening supply lines.

Ritchie did try to cut off the retreating enemy but was handicapped by shortages of tanks, fuel, and MT, and failed to discover Rommel's intention to retreat to Agedabia until it was too late. Then, on 28th and 30th December, Cruewell counter-attacked the 22nd Armoured Brigade, which had replaced the 4th, south of Agedabia and did so much damage that Ritchie was forced to withdraw it to refit.

The British commander was still seeking to gather a force strong enough to turn the enemy out of Agedabia when on 1st January Rommel began to fall back to El Agheila. Four days passed before Ritchie was convinced that a further retreat had begun, but lacking armour and supplies he could have done little to prevent or hinder it, and it was not until 13th January that contact with the enemy was regained, by which time the Germans were well established in a position between Mersa Brega and Alam el Mgaad that was far too strong for any force that Ritchie could muster to break through.

Ritchie's supply problems were now immense and by late December it had become clear that pursuit by anything more than a weak British force was out of the question. He was 300 miles from his main base at Tobruk, and this, together with petrol wastage and a shortage of vehicles, increasing attacks by enemy aircraft and U-boats on British shipping, and the impossibility of using captured ports made his whole administrative position extremely precarious.

Throughout the later stages of the campaign the DAF had been able to do little to help the army. At Gazala an opportunity to hammer the enemy ground forces had been lost because of poor army/air co-operation and thereafter, with bad weather imposing severe restrictions on air operations, the earlier hopes of inflicting wholesale destruction on the retreating enemy columns came to nothing.

The frontier battles ended on 17th January when the enemy at Solium and Halfaya, hungry, short of water, bombed by the RAF, and shelled by the navy, finally surrendered. Bardia had surrendered two weeks earlier to the South Africans after three days of heavy fighting. As early as 19th December the Italian High Command had ordered their forces at Halfaya and Bardia

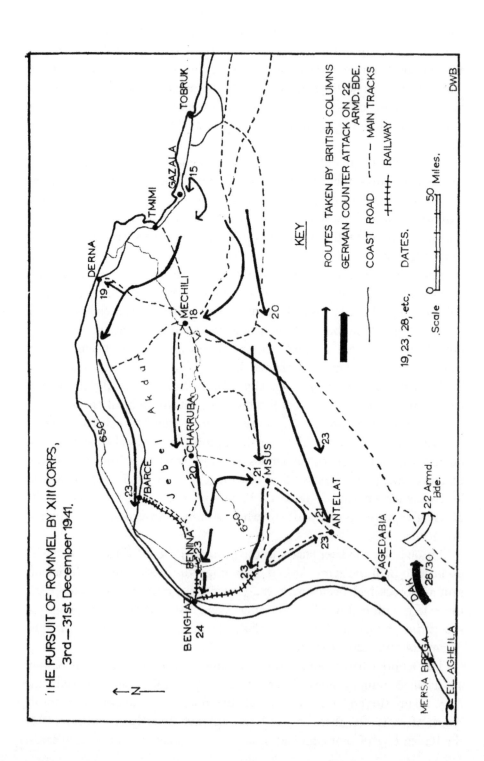

General Sir Archibald Wavell (right) and Major-General R. N. O'Connor are here in conference before the final assault on Bardia on 5 January 1941.

Major-General F. W. Messervy giving orders to a staff officer, south-west of Gazala, Libya. (*Wikipedia – public domain*)

(*Above*) Two British tank officers are pictured reading an Italian newspaper on 28 January 1941. According to the original caption, the mascot held by one of the men is a puppy found during the capture of Sidi Barrani, one of the first Italian bases to fall in the fighting in North Africa. (*NARA/Martin Mace*)

(*Below*) General Erwin Rommel with the 15th Panzer Division between Tobruk and Sidi Omar, 1941. (*NARA*)

Heinrich von Vietinghoff.
(*Bundesarchiv*)

Hans-Jürgen von Arnim,
seen here in the centre of the
photograph. (*Public domain*)

(*Above*) Two soldiers pictured at work producing a military newspaper or information sheet during the Siege of Tobruk. (*US Library of Congress/ Martin Mace*)

(*Left*) Standing amongst the rubble, a soldier looks through holes made by Axis bombs into a church in Tobruk, 1941. (*US Library of Congress/ Martin Mace*)

(*Above*) A Junkers Ju 87 Stuka dive bomber attacking a British supply depot near Tobruk, Libya, during October 1941. (*NARA/Martin Mace*)

(*Below*) A British patrol is on the lookout for enemy movements over a valley in the Western Desert, on the Egyptian side of the Egypt-Libya border, in February of 1942. (*NARA/Martin Mace*)

(*Left*) A 25-pdr field gun of 11th Field Regiment, Royal Artillery in action during the First Battle of El Alamein, July 1942. (*9th HAA Regiment Archive*)

(*Below*) A captured German 88mm surrounded by ammunition, west of El Alamein, 7 November 1942. (*Estate of Philip Warner*)

(*Right*) The Victor of Alamein – Field Marshal Bernard Montgomery. The tank behind is a Grant. (*Estate of Philip Warner*)

(*Below*) Field Marshal Archibald Wavell (centre) is pictured with Field Marshal Sir Claude Auchinleck (right) and Field Marshal Bernard Montgomery. This photograph was taken on 17 June 1946, in the Viceregal Gardens, New Delhi. (*Martin Mace*)

11 - 4 - 64

Dear Essame.

Thank you exceedingly for arranging that I got a copy of Braddock's book on the North African Campaign 1940 – 1942. It is high time that somebody wrote a concise treatise for serving officers on the whole conduct of operations in the desert war, and I shall read the book with great interest.

Yrs. sincerely

Montgomery of Alamein.

A letter from Montgomery written in April 1964, and forwarded to the author by Major General H. Essame, who upon its publication had sent a copy of the book to Montgomery for his consideration.

to fight to the end as by doing so they were holding down a British division, and by blocking the coast road and preventing the extension of the railhead to Capuzzo, were severely restricting the supplies reaching XIII Corps, which as it advanced badly needed the use of the Trigh Capuzzo and the Via Balbia. The enemy garrisons resisted bravely and it took three weeks of combined attacks by all three British services before the roads to the west were finally cleared.

Away in the southern desert the Oasis Force had reached its objectives but then shortages of fuel and supplies limited its activities and it neither took part in the offensive nor influenced the tactics of either side.

"Crusader" ended in January, 1942, with Cyrenaica once more cleared of Axis troops but with the 8th Army worn out after two months hard fighting and with its supply lines so stretched that when it reached Agedabia its striking power had gone. Auchinleck had won the battle but had not destroyed Rommel's army, and now as he waited at El Agheila, the German commander was in a much improved administrative position.

The DAF's contribution to the offensive was invaluable. Before the advance began it established its superiority in the desert and guaranteed that the attack would at least start with the advantage of surprise, and though in the later stages of the campaign its ability to deal crushing blows against the enemy declined somewhat, and there were several disappointments, Army/Air co-operation in "Crusader" was much the best seen by the British since the desert war began. In particular, high praise is due to the fighter squadrons which were always prepared to move forward in support of the army as soon as suitable airfields were cleared of the enemy. Altogether some 12,000 sorties were flown during "Crusader" and the enemy's losses in aircraft comfortably exceeded the 300 lost by the RAF. Much of the credit for these successes is owed to the commander of the DAF, Air Vice-Marshal Coningham. He it was who, with the full support and encouragement of the army commander, before "Crusader" began, evolved and applied the system by which the two commanders lived and worked together and were thus able to ensure that the most important needs of the army in terms of air support were promptly met.

Typically, the navy's role in "Crusader" was rarely spectacular but it was always of the highest importance. Tobruk was kept open in difficult circumstances, and later thousands of tons of supplies were moved up under the navy's protection. Naval bombardment played its part in the reduction of Bardia, and there were also the constant attacks on the enemy's trans-Mediterranean convoy routes. Here Force K wreaked havoc among enemy shipping, and ensured that the supplies reaching Rommel fell far below his needs.

Then in early December the naval situation underwent a radical change. The British fleet was first reduced by the need to send ships to the Far East, where war with Japan broke out on 7th December, and then, in the five weeks between 14th November and 20th December, and consequent upon the appearance of German U-boats, H.M. ships *Ark Royal, Barham, Neptune, Galatea,* and *Kandahar* were sunk. At the same time Italian "human torpedoes" attacked Alexandria and put the battleships *Queen Elizabeth* and *Valiant* out of action for several months.

This meant that Admiral Cunningham had lost the hard core of his fleet just at the time when the army's capture of the Cyrenaican airfields had made it possible for the RAF to give it air cover in the central Mediterranean where there were still four Italian battleships, and by the end of the year the Royal Navy was no longer in command of the situation at sea.

On the land, however, a comparison of casualty figures shows "Crusader" to have been a great British victory. Between November 1941, and January 1942, the 8th Army lost 17,700 men, 15 per cent of the number engaged, whereas the enemy suffered 38,300 casualties or 32 per cent of their total strength.

Losses of equipment were very high on both sides, especially among the Italian infantry divisions, but the British lost many more tanks in combat and through mechanical breakdown than did the Germans despite the improvement that had been made in their recovery and repair systems. Up to 1st January the British lost 600 light and cruiser tanks, of which 231 were subsequently repaired, and 200 I tanks, while the Germans lost 220 and the Italians 120 tanks of all marks.

The relative weakness of the British anti-tank guns was a particularly disquieting feature of the campaign, and without the 25-pounder field gun, which they used in an anti-tank role to the detriment of its other functions, the British would have suffered even more than they did in the armoured clashes at Sidi Resegh and elsewhere. The latest British cruisers were also very prone to mechanical failure in which respect they compared very badly with the German Pzkw III and IV. The Stuarts, which were reliable, were under-armoured and had only a very short range, characteristics which drastically limited their value as fighting vehicles.

The weakness of the 8th Army's communication system was yet another factor contributing to the British failure to gain a decisive victory. Signals security was extremely bad and as a result Rommel was able to acquire a great deal of valuable information; while the acute shortage of wireless sets in the

British army meant that much of the information that reached Cunningham and Ritchie was imprecise and unreliable. Moreover their staffs were much less skilled than those of the enemy at reading intercepted messages, and at interpreting the information that they did receive.

In the administrative sphere the problems facing the opposing commanders were very different. The 8th Army had at all times to operate at the end of very long lines of communication across the open desert with the result that wear and tear on the supply vehicles was unusually high and the consumption of petrol was enormous, difficulties which increased with each battlefield success.

The Germans who had also begun the winter battles with extremely long supply lines had, however, been able to establish major depots in their forward areas between June and November, and most of the fighting took place within easy reach of these bases. Nevertheless, when they operated at a distance from these dumps the enemy frequently ran out of fuel, and in some cases survived only by making use of captured supplies, and then, as the fighting continued and their forward dumps were worn down, their supply position became precarious in the extreme.

Paradoxically Auchinleck's victory did nothing to reduce his administrative problems or to increase Rommel's, and although the attacks by the Royal Navy and RAF against his supply lines were a serious embarrassment they were never sufficient to paralyse his supply system to the extent which made battlefield defeat certain. And by his retreat to El Agheila the German commander restored his administrative security at the same time as he saved much of his army. Maintenance difficulties certainly restricted the part played by the Luftwaffe in "Crusader" but its main task at this time was the reduction of Malta and in this it suffered little interference, especially as the DAF's power to retain control of the air declined with the army's advance beyond Benghazi.

The navy's work in helping to supply the army was invaluable but by the end of the year the losses of ships to the Far East, the decline of British air superiority, the appearance of the U-boats, and the growing strength of the Luftwaffe made this task increasingly difficult and dangerous, and greatly reduced its effectiveness.

In the final analysis, however, it was bad tactics and a weakness in command that contributed most to the British failure to gain a thoroughly decisive victory, the underlying factor being the inability of their senior officers to handle large forces of armour on the battlefield. The British had been correct in their appreciation of the action that Rommel was likely to take in response to an advance by XXX Corps towards Tobruk, but Cunningham, first by deciding to halt his armour at Gabr Saleh, and then by allowing it to be dispersed before Rommel had reacted, failed to develop thoroughly the plan made on the basis of the appreciation with the result that the British armour was defeated in detail.

The second great tactical weakness of the British was their failure to co-ordinate, as did the Germans, the action of tanks, anti-tank guns, artillery, and infantry on the battlefield, with the result that the armoured commanders were restricted in their power to manoeuvre by the need to protect the infantry of XIII Corps.

Had XXX Corps advanced to Sidi Resegh as a concentrated force there is little doubt that Rommel would have been drawn into battle, and XIII Corps would have been in no danger, their ability to look after themselves being proved by their successful advance during Rommel's dash to the frontier.

Even so Auchinleck and Cunningham were not entirely to blame. The handling of large forces of armour was an art never practised in the pre-war British army, there being neither the men nor the weapons available, and now in the desert it was being learnt in a process of trial and error by an inexperienced and unfit army commander, and an inexperienced Corps Commander, Nome, who nevertheless stuck better to sound principles than did his superiors. It should be remembered, however, that this was not only the first time since 1918 that a British army of such a size had been employed in mobile operations, but that largely for political reasons it was the first time in peace or war that a British armoured corps had ever been assembled. And it found itself in the unfortunate position of having to fight an enemy with the experience of armoured operations in five campaigns behind him. No British armoured division existed before 1939, and then a series of defeats meant that no time was available for proper training, and all too often unprepared formations were pushed into battle to learn by experience, a dangerous and costly practice for men and commanders alike.

At the command level "Crusader" must be considered chiefly in the light of the personalities of the two British officers most closely concerned.

Auchinleck was a brave and capable general, always popular with his commands and, like Wavell, ready to try an unorthodox approach, but in his appointment as Commander-in-Chief he suffered from certain major disadvantages. Most unfortunately he had crossed Churchill soon after he had assumed command in the Middle East, and thereafter found it very difficult to convince the Prime Minister of the truth about the situation in that theatre. Churchill also pressed him unceasingly to renew the offensive though in view of Auchinleck's own wish to attack it is open to question how far "Crusader" was brought forward as a result.

He was, moreover, while almost totally ignorant of the conduct of large scale mobile operations, hampered as a commander by one serious personal weakness, the inability to choose suitable subordinates. The first of these characteristics though potentially dangerous, was in fact, balanced by his outstanding ability in battle, and in any case his knowledge of the subject was no worse than that of most other senior British officers. In battle Auchinleck could be superb and his decision to fight on at Sidi Resegh was in the dogged tradition of the British army's most famous leaders. Marlborough at Malplaquet, Haig at First Ypres, and Montgomery at El Alamein and Caen were cast in the same mould, and it was Auchinleck's ability to dominate the situation in a crisis, allied to the British soldier's habit of fighting to the end in the belief that determination must eventually triumph, that enabled him in "Crusader" to put the 8th Army on the road to victory.

The ability to impose his will in a crisis is one of the hallmarks of a commander and probably his greatest test, and though in this Auchinleck was outstanding, as the later battles show his claims to a place among the very greatest generals must be questioned.

His choice of Cunningham to be the 8th Army's first commander also invites comment. Auchinleck himself chose Cunningham despite the Prime Minister's preference for Wilson, because of his successes in East Africa and his known liking for rapid action, but the new commander had no experience of armour and by mid-September 1941 was not as fit as a man in his position needed to be.

In East Africa Cunningham had commanded an army of four brigade groups in a campaign where his skill as a fighting soldier had a special value, and had won a brilliant victory, but in the desert he was called upon to face a very different situation. The 8th Army consisted of two corps and was expected to fight a great armoured battle, a form of war in which Cunningham had had little or no experience or training. Moreover, the corps and divisional commanders on whom he had to impose his will and leadership were robust characters who knew much more than he did about both armour and the desert. Altogether it was an uncommonly difficult situation made worse by the fact that he had had to give up smoking because of an eye infection; the knowledge that the Prime Minister had preferred Wilson; and the realization that he alone carried the hopes of the British nation for a badly needed victory. The final blows were probably the very short time that was available for him to become accustomed to the scale of operations in the desert; the speed at which the offensive had to be prepared; and the length of time, since February, for which he had been working under extreme pressure.

In the end Cunningham paid the bill for the vacillations of pre-war British Governments and military planners, and wore himself out mentally and physically in preparing and fighting a battle for which he had not had the time to train himself. He fought magnificently as far as he was able and was replaced only because ill-health and overstrain had so affected him that he was no longer his natural self. Fully fit he was never the man to give up a battle before the last hope of victory had been tried and lost.

On the enemy side Rommel's performance was a strange mixture of the brilliant and the bizarre. His decision to withdraw from Gazala despite the efforts of Kesselring and Bastico, OKH and Rome, to persuade him to stay and fight probably saved the DAK from a disaster as complete as that which had befallen the Italians ten months before. He saw the issue clearly, and having made the right decision stuck to it under intense pressure, and conducted a withdrawal worthy to rank with his spring advance as a piece of military virtuosity. On the other hand his first raid towards the frontier failed and the later attempts seem to have had a quality of despair about them as if he could think of no other way of breaking Auchinleck's grip on Tobruk and Sidi Resegh.

It may be asked if the first raid was ever likely to succeed in view of the difficulty of maintaining the DAK, the battering it had already received, and the British strength on the frontier. It was a bold and imaginative venture and perhaps well calculated to succeed against Cunningham but by the time it began Auchinleck was in effective command of the 8th Army and determined to stay where he was outside Tobruk.

Had the raid achieved its objects it would have been hailed as a strategic and tactical masterpiece; having failed it is criticized, with some justice, as being foolhardy. Great victories have often been won with unorthodox manoeuvres but in every case these followed accurate appreciations, and Rommel neglected to take this elementary precaution. Cruewell, the very able commander of the DAK, objected to many of Rommel's schemes, the dash to the frontier among them, usually because the German commander seemed to disregard first principles, and one may wonder if a more orthodox and carefully prepared use of the panzer divisions would have been more successful. In leaving Tobruk and Sidi Resegh to thrust eastwards Rommel lost sight of his chief aim and took what turned out to be an unjustifiable administrative risk by failing to ensure that his forces would be properly supplied. He also cut himself off from the battle outside Tobruk and thereby greatly reduced his chances of victory. Had it been possible to fight the eastern and western battles in concert the result might have been quite different. As it was Rommel's armoured thrust failed to induce a British withdrawal and instead embarrassed his own side by removing its main striking arm from the vital area at a crucial stage.

"Crusader" can be summed up as a hardly fought and costly victory won more by the bravery and tenacity of the British soldiers than by the tactical skill of their commanders. At the same time it should be remembered that it was only Auchinleck's strong nerve and ability to read a battle that made the victory possible.

Chapter 11

Rommel's Second Offensive and the Retreat to Gazala

In September 1941, with the preparations for "Crusader" well in hand, Auchinleck had turned his attention to plans for Operation "Acrobat", the invasion of Tripolitania, which he hoped would follow the successful completion of his winter offensive. By the end of the year, however, he realized that until a strong British force with suitable administrative support could be established somewhere west of Benghazi, "Acrobat" would remain a hope for the unspecified future. Nevertheless he was anxious that no time should be lost and ordered Godwin Austen as XIII Corps Commander to build up a force capable of advancing to Tripoli and to arrange for its maintenance and supply.

Godwin Austen soon found that this was an impossible undertaking in the short term, for the 8th Army had overreached itself in the pursuit to Mersa Brega and was in no condition, physically or administratively, to go any further for the time being. The supply situation was particularly bad. With enemy air attacks making it impossible to develop Benghazi as an advanced base, supplies for the army and the DAF still had to be brought 300 miles overland from Tobruk, and deliveries of stores were falling short of the amounts needed by more than 250 tons per day. As it was, the troops were still living on short rations and there was no hope of being able to accumulate the supplies needed to support a further advance before the end of February at the earliest. Moreover the transport shortage meant that only a weak force could be maintained in contact with the enemy and the tactical situation soon approximated to that of February 1941, with Cyrenaica once more guarded by half an armoured division and two-thirds of an infantry division.

In December the 7th Armoured Division had been replaced by the 1st, which at the time was already below strength, the 22nd Armoured Brigade having been taken for "Crusader" and then so badly mauled by Cruewell at Agedabia that Ritchie had been obliged to withdraw it. All the armoured cars had also been withdrawn to refit, and the 2nd Armoured Brigade, which then took over had neither desert experience, nor the petrol with which to continue its training. And with the Support Group in little better shape the division was in no state to fight a major action.

Godwin Austen's infantry at this time consisted of the well-tried 4th Indian Division, but this too was widely dispersed because it was not possible to maintain more than one brigade in a forward position, and in January had one brigade at Benghazi, another at Barce, and the third refitting at Tobruk. Perhaps the most important deficiency was the lack of armoured cars, since the success of a defensive operation under the conditions which then existed depended on the early receipt of information about enemy movements in order that enough time should be available for the British forces to concentrate for battle.

Nevertheless, Auchinleck and his senior officers felt reasonably confident. They had already begun to prepare for a further advance and were agreed that Rommel would be incapable of mounting a strong counter-offensive for a long time to come. With the information available at the time this was a fair conclusion but we now know that Auchinleck and Ritchie took too little account in January 1942 of Rommel's power of recovery, the improvement in his situation resulting from his rapid retreat to El Agheila, and his practice of attacking whenever an opportunity arose.

They did not entirely ignore the possibility of an enemy counterattack, however, and plans were made for XIII Corps to fight a defensive battle on a line from Agedabia to El Haseiat. The 1st Armoured Division, in effect the 2nd Armoured Brigade and the Support Group, was now ordered to hold a line south from Mersa Brega and to harass the enemy while the new offensive was being prepared, but at the same time to be ready to join with the 4th Indian Division should a major defensive action become necessary. Major-General Messervy accepted these tasks but asked for the Indian Division to be moved up to Agedabia in support of his armour, a request which was refused because Ritchie could not guarantee to supply any more units so far forward. Thus the 30 miles between Mersa Brega and the Wadi Faregh were left in the care of the 24 Stuarts of the Support Group, and a Guards battalion with some guns, while another Guards battalion remained at Agedabia, and the 2nd Armoured Brigade, with 130 tanks, assembled at Antelat, 90 miles behind the front, to carry out some long overdue desert training.

Also at Antelat were 9 fighter squadrons of the DAF under the command of 211 Group, set up by A. V. M. Coningham to relieve his own headquarters of the responsibility for Cyrenaica while he prepared for "Acrobat".

With further squadrons at Benina, Tobruk, Gambut and Bu Amud the DAF at this time had 280 serviceable aircraft, but spare parts and fuel were in short supply and it was becoming increasingly difficult to maintain a satisfactory percentage of machines at operational readiness.

Meanwhile the outbreak of war with Japan had created further problems for both army and air force in the Middle East. The policy was to do everything possible to build up allied strength in the Far East without withdrawing units from the Mediterranean theatre though several formations en route to Egypt were diverted to Indian ports. Auchinleck and Tedder were later asked to send tanks and aircraft to India but neither these transfers nor the diversion of the 18th British Division were regarded by those concerned as likely to affect the success of either "Crusader" or "Acrobat", although they did ask for the losses to be made good one month before the latter operation was due to start.

Rommel's position at the end of "Crusader" was much as Auchinleck had guessed. Having reached El Agheila with much of his army intact he was chiefly concerned to make the best use of the pause to prepare to meet a renewed British attack. In this he was greatly helped by a reinforcement of 54 tanks and their crews and a consignment of fuel which reached Tripoli on 5th January and the front ten days later.

The crucial day was 12th January when, as a means of delaying the expected offensive, Rommel decided to mount a spoiling attack against the British forward positions. At the time the Germans enjoyed a numerical superiority in the Cyrenaica border area and the dispersion of the British formations seemed to offer a chance of local success, though a shortage of German troops and supplies prevented Rommel from looking for any chance of far-reaching exploitation. By 17th January, however, his prospects had improved for he could count 84 German tanks well forward in his army; he had regained some of his strength in the air; and he knew from intercepted signals that XIII Corps was in administrative difficulties and not ready for battle.

To a certain extent this was also true of Rommel's forces, as although the 300 serviceable aircraft of the Axis air forces could be sure of a valuable local superiority, not one of the three German and seven Italian divisions in the army was up to strength or fully equipped. However, Rommel with 12,500 German and 25,000 Italian troops could still muster an army that was far larger than any force that Ritchie could bring quickly into battle, and he laid his plans for a simple and unambitious attack.

His intention was to advance in three columns between the coast and the Wadi Faregh and to disrupt the British preparations before retiring again to the safety of El Agheila. The attack was prepared under conditions of the greatest secrecy, and with the weather suddenly becoming very bad the DAF was unable to discover or interrupt the German build up so that when the enemy army began its advance on the morning of 21st January the British were taken by surprise.

Well supported from the air the Germans advanced some 25 miles that day and broke up the Support Group in the process. A speedy withdrawal saved the British advanced forces from complete destruction, however, and Messervy next ordered them to hold a front from Agedabia to El Haseiat while the 2nd Armoured Brigade moved up to Giof al Matar ready to strike at the flank of an enemy breakthrough in the centre.

This was not part of Rommel's plan, however, and on the 22nd he ordered his left hand column, the Marcks Group, to continue towards Agedabia which it reached at 11 a.m. Messervy's command was now in danger of being cut off completely as Rommel was making plans to send columns round his rear through Antelat and Saunnu, and inside the ring thus established to use the DAK and the Italian 20th Mobile Corps to drive the British south-east away from their supply lines.

By the evening of 22nd January the German ring was in position, Messervy having been too weak to prevent his right being outflanked although he did recall the 2nd Armoured Brigade from Giof al Matar. Godwin Austen, suspecting Rommel's intentions but uncertain how far the latter's plans had progressed, was now extremely anxious about the supplies for his armoured division and ordered Messervy to block the tracks between Msus and Agedabia and Saunnu while the 4th Indian Division closed the coast road and made ready to evacuate Benghazi.

At this point Ritchie returned to the desert from Cairo and examined the situation, only to misread it completely, first by underestimating Rommel's power to advance further, and secondly by exaggerating the ability of XIII Corps to deliver a strong counter-attack. He refused to believe that Rommel could maintain a strong force east of Agedabia and decided to delay his own counterstroke until the German commander had so overreached himself that an attack by the 1st Armoured and 4th Indian Divisions could not fail to succeed.

This attitude was characteristic of Ritchie who was normally optimistic even in unpropitious circumstances, but he was also doing his best to meet Auchinleck's wishes. Before Christmas Auchinleck had had to decide whether to maintain contact with the enemy about El Agheila, and accept the risk that his light forces might be driven back, or to withdraw to Benghazi

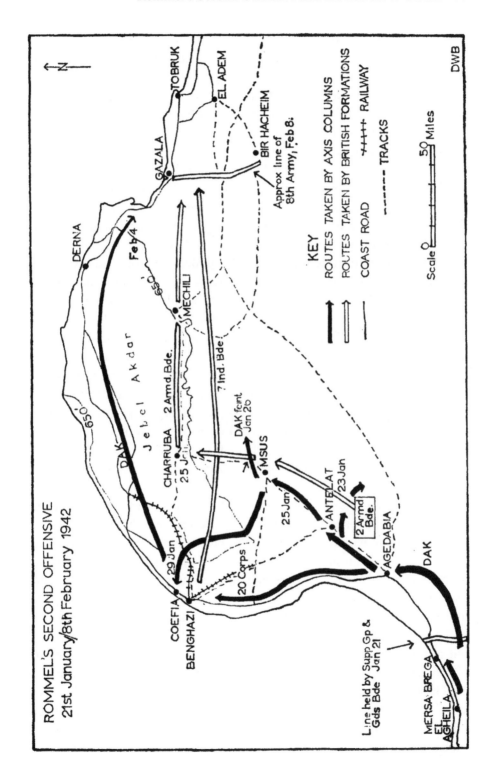

and Msus where the build up for the advance into Tripolitania could be carried out more easily and in relative safety. Believing that Rommel was too weak to mount a major attack, and wishing to keep up the pressure begun in "Crusader" Auchinleck chose the first course. It was a calculated risk and a bluff that failed, chiefly because of excellent German staff work and the dynamic leadership of Rommel himself.

Thus on 23rd January the situation was that Godwin Austen wanted to pull back Messervy's division before Rommel succeeded in encircling it. This attempt by the Germans failed because the 21st Panzer Division allowed a gap to be opened at Saunnu through which the 2nd Armoured Brigade fought its way to safety, and by nightfall the British armour was established across the Msus track north-east of Antelat.

Ritchie had meanwhile reported to Auchinleck that the battle was well in hand and that he proposed shortly to attack the isolated columns which he was convinced were all that Rommel could supply so far forward.

Elsewhere, the German commander, now promoted to the command of the Panzerarmee Afrika, was arguing fiercely with his C.-in-C. Bastico, thoroughly alarmed at the way in which a spoiling attack was developing into a full scale offensive, had complained to Rome, where Mussolini's reaction was a directive expressly forbidding a major advance. Rommel's reply was to the effect that as Germans were doing most of the fighting only Hitler could stop him, and he went on with the battle, only to spend a fruitless day in searching for the British troops which he thought were still south of Agedabia, before making plans to continue his northward advance on the 25th.

A command crisis had also arisen in the 8th Army where Godwin Austen, now fully alive to the dangers of the situation, had asked Ritchie for permission to withdraw from Benghazi towards Mechili as little damage seemed to have been inflicted on the enemy, and as he did not have the strength both to protect the desert flank and stop an advance along the coast road. Ritchie at first refused this request and ordered XIII Corps to concentrate at Msus for a counter-attack, but then changed his mind and gave Godwin Austen permission to withdraw if he thought it necessary, and to put in hand schemes for the demolition of stores and installations at Benghazi. He also warned Norrie to reconnoitre defensive positions in the Gazala-Tobruk area. By this time Godwin Austen had told Messervy to retire to Mechili if it was the only way to save his remaining tanks from a destructive running fight, and Coningham had ordered his squadrons to fall back in stages to the landing grounds at Gazaia, Gambut, and El Adem.

The DAF commander, disturbed by the progress of events and the conflict in the army command, had already withdrawn his radar and maintenance units and the air cover available to the army was much reduced. Fortunately, however, the enemy's air activity had also declined and the day passed without major incident.

On the 25th this all changed as the battle flared up once more, and by mid-afternoon the DAK, having driven Messervy's armour back to Charruba, reached Msus and Godwin Austen ordered the 4th Indian Division to evacuate Benghazi. Rommel then called a halt as he was running short of fuel and needed a pause in which to consider his next moves, and he spent the next 36 hours in replenishing his tanks, sorting out captured equipment, and thinking how best to exploit his gains. The success of the spoiling attack had ended Auchinleck's hopes for an early offensive, and with withdrawal out of the question, Rommel had to make up his mind whether to strike for Benghazi or to repeat his cross desert advance of the previous year. He discarded the latter alternative as it would have exposed his supply lines to a counter-attack from Benghazi, and then learning from intercepted British signals of the disagreements in the British camp, and that Benghazi might be given up, decided to attack the port from an unexpected direction. He proposed to deceive Ritchie by feinting with the DAK towards Mechili and then, while the 90th Light Division and the 20th Italian Corps moved up from the south, to send a reinforced Marcks Group straight across the terrible country between Msus and Benghazi to cut the coast road north of that city at Coefia. The attack was timed to begin on the 28th and unwittingly forestalled a British counter-attack by 24 hours.

Soon after Rommel had halted at Msus Auchinleck, and Tedder joined Ritchie at his headquarters where they too allowed themselves to be persuaded that the enemy could be driven back without undue difficulty. Believing that the capture of Msus had been the exploitation of an unexpected success by the DAK Auchinleck first allowed Ritchie to cancel Godwin Austen's orders for the evacuation of Benghazi and the withdrawal of the 1st Armoured Division to Mechili, and then to issue instructions for an attack to be made against the enemy communications north-east of Agedabia.

Godwin Austen, who considered that his 40 remaining tanks were too few to protect or support the Indian infantry in their counterattacks, protested strongly but Ritchie was adamant, and to give point to his orders took personal command of the 4th Indian Division. Godwin Austen then protested again, both against the plan and at Ritchie's lack of confidence in him as a Corps Commander, but gave the necessary instructions, only to find his own complaints followed by others from Messervy and Major-General Tuker of the Indian Division. These officers pointed out that they did not have the strength to do more than hold at Charruba, let alone attack southwards without armoured support, but Ritchie was not to be convinced and ordered the preparations for the attack, set for the 29th, to be continued.

Bad weather on the 26th and 27th once more restricted the activity of the DAF but late on the 27th Coningham's airmen reported the move of the DAK towards Mechili, and Ritchie, who had already learnt that enemy forces were pushing towards Benghazi from the east, ordered Messervy to attack its rear. Twelve hours later he had realized his mistake and agreed to Tuker's request to withdraw the 7th Infantry Brigade from Benghazi that evening, but when that time came Rommel was across the road at Coefia, and Brigadier H. R. Briggs was only able to escape by leading his men across the enemy rear areas to Mechili.

Benghazi fell to Rommel on the 29th and he was soon joined there by the Ariete Division, but short of fuel he was unable to pursue Godwin Austen in strength, and a week later the 8th Army had begun to establish itself in the comparative safety of the Gazala-Bir Hacheim line.

The decision to retire to Gazala had been forced on Ritchie by the reports made by Godwin Austen and the divisional commanders. Ritchie had believed as late as 30th January that the fall of Benghazi would see the end of Rommel's advance, and thinking of the resumption of his own offensive he was loth to give up ground without reason, but when Messervy reported that he could not withstand more than 25 enemy tanks the army commander accepted Godwin Austen's proposal to organize a defensive position at Gazala and ordered a general withdrawal.

Rommel at this time had problems of his own. Italian policy was still concerned with the defence of Tripolitania, and a directive from Mussolini to this effect, together with the news that no further supplies were to be expected for some time, reached Rommel on 4th February, just when he was considering the possibility of another attack on the weak and apparently demoralized British. As a result he decided to wait in the Jebel where he could reorganize and build up his command secure in the knowledge that the 8th Army would be in no condition to attack him for at least six weeks.

The war in the air during this period had taken a course almost opposite from that of the land fighting. At first the Luftwaffe had enjoyed a pronounced superiority and had subjected XIII Corps to a series of severe attacks, but it was not long before they were left behind by the speed and unexpected development of Rommel's advance, and air support for the

Axis army dwindled almost to nothing. The field was thus left open for the DAF, and although bad weather still curtailed air operations, more and more sorties were flown in support of the retreating 8th Army, the day bombers in particular finding good targets along the enemy's supply routes, although the fighters were restricted to watching for signs of new German thrusts.

The strain of fighting while conducting a gradual withdrawal was very high however, and it is greatly to the credit of the DAF that by the time the army reached Gazala the desert squadrons were firmly established at El Adem, Gambut, Sidi Barrani and Maaten Baggush, and ready to join battle once more in real strength.

Nevertheless Rommel had won another great tactical victory, having in two weeks driven the 8th Army back some 350 miles from the Tripolitania border, and at small cost to himself taken or destroyed 70 tanks and 40 guns. Meanwhile the DAF had lost 45 aircraft, and Ritchie's army 1,390 men.

This latest reverse to British arms caused understandable consternation in those circles concerned with the higher direction of the war, and was followed by a rapid increase in the telegraphic traffic between London and Cairo as reasons for the defeat were sought. Fundamentally the issue was simple. The British, apparently paying little attention to the lessons of Wavell's campaign, had not only badly overreached their administrative resources, but had deployed their forces in a fashion likely to invite attack at a time when the 8th Army lacked the strength to meet it with a fair chance of success. And Auchinleck, though in a different strategic situation, had repeated Wavell's mistake of badly underestimating the enemy's powers of recovery. It is relevant to ask whether he might have been better advised to have taken a leaf from Rommel's book and fallen back to Benghazi where his supplies would have been more certain and where he could have placed a stronger force in the field while preparing to resume the offensive. The chief fault, however, would seem to lie in the fact that with the territorial objectives of "Crusader" achieved the 8th Army was neither tactically nor administratively ready to consolidate its gains while preparations for a further advance were made. All the efforts of the 8th Army in the planning stage, and of Middle East headquarters while "Crusader" was going on, should have been directed towards ensuring that the resources for such operations were available when needed. The heavy losses suffered during "Crusader" were hardly enough in themselves to explain this shortcoming, and at this stage in the war there should have been time enough for the 1st Armoured Division to have completed its training and for armoured cars or other mobile forces to have been present in adequate numbers.

The old weaknesses in equipment and organization and of inexperience at all levels also contributed to the British defeat, and in communications to the Prime Minister Auchinleck repeatedly stressed the inadequacy of the 2-pounder guns and the mechanical unreliability of the British cruiser tanks. These were disadvantages which the fighting qualities of the army itself could not overcome and it was noticeable that morale was sinking as the troops lost confidence in their weapons.

The retreat to Gazala also brought into sharp relief the inferior quality of the training and organization of the British compared with that of the Germans. Whereas new British units and formations were frequently thrown into battle as soon as they arrived, the Germans, as a matter of policy, ensured that all their armoured formations at least received a very thorough basic training. The 1st Armoured Division was a case in point for when it first met the panzers it had only half its strength, and was badly undertrained, and it is greatly to the credit of the men who served in it that it did not suffer an even more shattering defeat.

The British also had much to learn from the German system of reinforcement. Whereas the British reinforced with raw troops and allowed those with desert experience to be withdrawn the Germans brought their formations up to strength by drafting new troops into established units so that a hard core of skill and experience was always present.

Finally, at the command level the British were not nearly so well served as the soldiers had a right to expect. Ritchie, largely through inexperience, was for some time unable to temper his desire to attack with the acceptance of unpleasant facts and the need to disengage, and by his inept handling of the situation he made it impossible for Godwin Austen to remain in command of XIII Corps. By disregarding his corps commander's advice and by taking personal command of the 4th Indian Division Ritchie had caused Godwin Austen to lose the confidence of his subordinates and on 2nd February he asked to be relieved of his command. Auchinleck had no choice but to agree to this request and it can have been no consolation to any of those involved to see Godwin Austen proved right. This command crisis is of particular interest in that, like "Crusader", it illustrates one of the most searching of all tests of generalship, the choice of the moment when a commander should order a subordinate to do what he, the subordinate, believes to be unwise. Ritchie, like Auchinleck was not afraid to override his subordinates in the interests of wider strategy, but whereas Auchinleck, with long experience of command behind him, based his decision of 24th November on an accurate appreciation and the advice of men like Freyberg, Norrie, and Galloway,

Ritchie's decision to countermand Godwin Austen's orders was founded on what is now seen to be wishful thinking, and in contradiction of the advice of an officer of wide experience.

The chief credit for the victory must, however, go to Rommel himself. Once again he attacked long before his opponents thought it possible, and when he did so his plans were sufficiently flexible for him to be able to exploit to the full any opportunities that arose. He completely dominated his allies and subordinates, turned every British weakness, including the weather, to his own advantage, and by doing the unexpected, as in his attack on Benghazi, utterly deceived and then defeated both Auchinleck and Ritchie. He was always prepared to do what he considered to be militarily correct whatever the opinions of his nominal superiors, and by his habit of taking personal command at the most important points ensured that his orders were carried out. This could be a dangerous practice and created certain strains within his army but it did mean that no attack would fail for lack of drive and determination. A less obvious benefit to his command lay in the fact that by sheer strength of personality he overcame many of the internal weaknesses of the Axis High Command in North Africa.

Chapter 12

The Lull, February to May 1942

As soon as the front was stabilized at Gazala Auchinleck and Ritchie resumed their preparations for the new offensive as a matter of the highest urgency. Tripoli still remained as the most important long-term objective but a more immediate need was to regain the airfields in Western Cyrenaica. Without these landing grounds it was impossible to supply or reinforce Malta except at prohibitive cost, and in the absence of offensive air and naval strikes from Malta the enemy in Africa could build up his strength with ease. It is not surprising, therefore, that as the months passed Churchill pressed Auchinleck to attack at the earliest possible moment.

The Prime Minister also had other equally important reasons for desiring a renewal of the offensive, for the war situation as a whole was unusually gloomy. On 12th February, the *Scharnhorst*, *Gneisenau*, and *Prince Eugen* had escaped from Brest, and three days later Singapore had fallen to the Japanese; the Russians were being hard pressed by the German spring offensives, and in April Malta was nearly bombed to destruction. At home the British people were depressed and anxious, the House of Commons was becoming restive, and finally the USA was beginning to show signs of losing interest in the African theatre. If Churchill had needed a victory in the autumn of 1941 he needed one twice as much in May the following year, and his pressure on Auchinleck increased directly with his anxieties about other theatres. The desert it seemed was the one place where victory was possible in the near future, and the sooner it was achieved the better.

Meantime outside Gazala Ritchie was busy consolidating his defences, preparing the build up for his offensive, and considering the prospects of recapturing the Derna-Mechili-Martuba complex of airfields while Auchinleck argued with London. The C.-in-C, calculating that by April he would have an army of 3 Armoured Divisions, 2 Armoured Brigade Groups, an Army Tank Brigade and 3 Infantry Divisions, had reported to London on 7th February that he intended to attack but gave no date for the beginning of the offensive, and found as a result that he had started a four-month telegraphic argument.

The chief bone of contention was the armoured strength necessary for the attack to begin. Auchinleck, fully supported by Cunningham, Tedder, and Casey, the new Minister of State in the Middle East, stated baldly that he would need a superiority of 3 : 2 in tanks before he could hope to defeat Rommel on ground of the latter's choosing and to invade Tripolitania.

He based his claim for this number of tanks on the existing arguments of the inferior quality and performance of the British armoured vehicles; the better training and greater experience of the enemy; and the difficulties involved in maintaining a large and effective force of armour in the field. These were, without exception, perfectly valid and cogent arguments, but the Defence Committee elected to ignore their force, and continued to insist that total numbers of tanks rather than the number which could be maintained in the field should be the criterion on which relative strengths were to be assessed. The Chiefs of Staff also thought that the High Command in the Middle East underestimated the enemy's difficulties and exaggerated his fighting strength, and on the 26th and 27th February Auchinleck received two telegrams. One came from the Prime Minister who referred to the numerical superiority of the British armour in North Africa and demanded to know what Auchinleck's intentions were, and the other was from the Chiefs of Staff who said simply that an advance into western Cyrenaica was essential if Malta was to survive.

Auchinleck replied that with the best will in the world an offensive before 1st June would incur the risk of defeat in detail and might well leave Egypt wide open to the enemy. Such an answer was guaranteed not to produce any satisfaction in London, and on 8th March Churchill asked Auchinleck to fly to the UK to discuss the situation. This the C.-in-C. refused to do, saying that his opinions were well known and that in any case he could not leave the Middle East for ten days at a time. The Prime Minister, thus snubbed, became more and more angry and on the 10th telegraphed to Auchinleck that the British Government had no intention of allowing Malta to fall without an attempt by the 8th Army to relieve the pressure on the island, and that Auchinleck was to attack in time to allow a convoy to reach Malta in June.

This telegram gave Auchinleck the chance of resigning or of obeying orders against his better judgment. In the end he signalled that he would comply with the Government's wishes but that success was by no means certain and would be neither rapid nor spectacular. At the same time he asked the Prime Minister to confirm that the 8th Army's main task was to destroy the enemy in Cyrenaica and not to create a diversion in order to help Malta.

The somewhat mollified Churchill confirmed this belief and accepted Auchinleck's reservations, and then invited the C.-in-C. to take charge of the coming battle in person. Auchinleck answered that in view of his widespread responsibilities throughout the Middle East he did not feel justified in taking over the 8th Army with the risk of becoming so deeply involved in one battle that his judgment of the needs of the theatre as a whole might be impaired.

This decision was a sound one though a good case could be made out for the other side. After all Auchinleck had already once taken over the army in all but name, and was to do so later without any ill effects on the rest of his command, although it is difficult to justify his retention of Ritchie as the army commander. His refusal to go to London, however, was ill-advised. Had he gone he could have made the local situation, including the undesirability of holding Tobruk in the event of a battlefield reverse, absolutely clear to the Prime Minister and could have resigned then if it seemed necessary. As it was, by remaining in Egypt he gave Churchill the impression that he was trying to avoid unwelcome pressures, and displayed a lack of political sensibility that was disconcerting in a Commander-in-Chief. The upshot of the whole unhappy affair was that neither fully understood the other's point of view and that decisions were taken which may not have been in best accordance with the facts.

Chapter 13

The Battles at Gazala (1)
The Period of Planning and Preparation

While he was arguing with the Defence Committee in London Auchinleck decided to reorganize the army so that in future armour, artillery, and infantry would work in close and permanent association rather than as semi-independent elements of the military whole. He began by giving the armoured divisions, which had hitherto been overloaded with tanks and weak in support units, an Armoured Brigade Group and a Motor Brigade Group only. The first was to have 3 tank regiments, a motorized infantry battalion and a mixed RA regiment; and the latter 3 motorized battalions and a similar Royal Artillery component. Both were to have their own anti-aircraft, sapper, and administrative units, and it was intended that they should fight as largely self-contained formations. He then gave similar orders for the infantry divisions to be reorganized into 3 Infantry Brigade Groups, each with its own artillery, and technical and administrative support units.

New weapons were also beginning to arrive at this time and it was hoped to replace the 2-pounder anti-tank guns with the 6-pounder, and to give each armoured regiment at least one squadron of the American Grant tanks. This tank was heavily armoured and very reliable and carried as its main armament a 75 mm gun capable of firing H.E. or Armour-Piercing shot and of outshooting any enemy tank or anti-tank gun except the 88 mm. It also mounted a 37 mm high velocity gun, and though limited in manoeuvre by having its heavy gun in a fixed sponson it was a very welcome reinforcement.

The new Crusaders had been given heavier frontal armour but were still very liable to mechanical failure and were no match for the Pzkw III Specials with a long-barrelled 50 mm gun and face-hardened frontal armour which were beginning to be delivered to the DAK. Even at this late stage the Stuarts were the only British tanks capable of firing capped ammunition and it was fortunate that only 19 of the German "Specials" arrived in time to take part in the early battles at Gazala.

Less fortunate for the 8th Army was the fact that the fighting flared up before Auchinleck's reorganization and reinforcement was complete. When Rommel advanced on 26th May only 112 6-pounders had arrived, and though some progress had been made in changing the composition of the infantry divisions neither of the armoured divisions had adopted the two brigade group organization, and most of the artillery regiments were still not integrated with the armoured or infantry formations. The 3 armoured brigades were not short of tanks, but almost inevitably it seemed, were not fully trained, especially with the Grants.

Nevertheless a powerful force was once more being gathered together and in its positions at Gazala the 8th Army was beginning to regain its confidence.

Throughout the spring the administrative build up went forward and by 25th May the advanced bases were up to 80 per cent of their capacity except at Belhamed where only two-thirds of the necessary petrol had arrived. Three such bases had been established, one at Tobruk with 10,000 tons of stores; another at Belhamed with 26,000 tons; and a small one at Jarabub with 1,000 tons. Belhamed was also the railhead, work on pushing the line forward having begun as soon as the enemy's frontier garrisons had surrendered in January. All the work of the build-up had to be carried out in the face of heavy air and U-boat attacks, and despite heavy shipping losses, but by the end of May Auchinleck and Ritchie had no reason to fear a collapse of their supply system, though they were later to discover that the Belhamed base was embarrassingly close to the battlefield when Rommel and not they who attacked first.

The DAF was kept particularly busy during the spring of 1942 in preparing for the coming offensive at the same time as they continued their defensive operations against the enemy. The DAF had lost heavily during "Crusader" and the retreat, when the fighter force had been worn down and then outclassed by the German Me 109s, but a steady recovery was made, and despite diversions to the Far East there was a good prospect in March that the August target of 80 squadrons would be reached. This total was to include 35 short-range fighter squadrons, among them 15 squadrons of Spitfires, and three heavy bomber squadrons, one of Liberators and two of Halifaxes. The aircrew shortage remained however, and the Air Ministry did not look kindly upon Tedder's requests for reinforcements.

Coningham meanwhile had found time to remedy some organizational weaknesses of his own that had been discovered during "Crusader", and among other changes created a Fighter Group in the DAF. Hitherto the fighters had operated in two wings directly under the control of Air Headquarters, and the new group was set up to take charge of all the operations, flying, early warning, and ground defence, of a much larger fighter force. Three fighter wings, each with between 4 and 6 squadrons, were formed and a Group Operations centre was established to control them while the DAF retained the responsibility for their administration and maintenance. The purpose of this reorganization was to improve the operational performance of the fighter force while relieving its senior officers of the burdens of administration. The Group Operations Centre itself was formed in duplicate to enable the fighters to carry out a leap-frogging advance as the army moved forward, and thus guarantee air cover for the men on the ground.

Gambut now became the main fighter base and the new Boston day bombers established themselves at nearby Bir el Baheira. The intention was to give the day bombers fighter escorts and this arrangement of bases was of great value in enabling combined training to be carried out.

The aircraft of four fighter squadrons were then modified to allow them to carry bombs. This had the advantage of increasing the DAF's bomb load, saving fuel, and speeding up the turnround of aircraft engaged in attacking enemy columns, and once they had dropped their bombs the fighters' performance was as good as ever.

In general the system developed for army/air co-operation in "Crusader" had worked well and it remained unchanged although no answer had been found to the problem of identification on the battlefield. It was hoped, however, that by two-hourly forecasts of troop positions the army would make it easier for the DAF to define a safe and effective bomb line.

Airfield defence was another thorny problem. The fears of the DAF about the degree of protection that the army could give to landing grounds during a battle had resulted in the acceptance of a policy of unified air defence, including AA guns, for rear areas, but in May 1942 it had not been adopted in the forward areas and many of the new airfields built after the retreat to Gazala were in very exposed positions.

Meanwhile, as Malta's ability to mount bomber strikes declined Coningham's bomber squadrons had to shoulder an additional burden, and with the recurring demands for reconnaissance, and strategical and tactical bombing of ports, supply routes, airfields and troop concentrations an average of 130 sorties a day were flown between 7th February and 25th May. Losses in these operations were high, nearly 300 aircraft, but this was the price that had to be paid for conducting an aggressive air policy with a largely obsolescent fighter force. In the same period 150 enemy aircraft were destroyed and much damage was done to enemy airfields and supplies, but at no time did Rommel's recovery programme suffer a severe setback as a result.

The virtue of the position where the 8th Army had halted on 8th February lay in the fact that it covered the tracks east to Acroma, and the Trigh el Abd and Trigh Capuzzo further inland, and on 4th February Auchinleck had ordered it to be held in strength while Tobruk was built up as the base for his next offensive. On the same day a defensive policy was discussed and Ritchie was told that although Tobruk was to be held if at all possible it was not Auchinleck's intention to allow a British force to be besieged there. If, by some misfortune, the enemy secured a position from which to encircle the port the garrison was to be evacuated and to withdraw with the rest of the army to the Egyptian frontier.

This immensely important decision was taken jointly by the three commanders-in-chief in the Mediterranean and was communicated to London on 7th February. They based their conclusion on the points that Wavell had listed in 1941 when assessing the value of keeping a strong garrison behind the enemy's front, namely, the heavy cost of supplying the garrison between April and December that year, and the negligible effect that it had had on Rommel's operations against Egypt.

Of the correctness of this decision there can be little doubt and the failure to hold to it had tragic results.

Even before Auchinleck had agreed to take the offensive in May it was known in the 8th Army that Rommel was himself preparing for an advance, and now, with the British not fully ready to attack, the prospect of fighting in prepared positions was not unwelcome. Even so Auchinleck's policy was still to take the offensive and on 16th May Ritchie issued an order in which he stated that his intention was to destroy the enemy's armour in the Tobruk-Gazala-Bir Hacheim triangle as the first step towards the recapture of the whole of Cyrenaica.

At the time he had XIII and XXX Corps in forward positions and the 5th Indian Division in army reserve at Tobruk, while the 1st Armoured Brigade and the 11th Indian Infantry Brigade in Egypt, and the 10th Indian Division in Iraq were also under orders to join the army in the desert. Gott, now a Lieutenant-General, had succeeded Godwin Austen at XIII Corps, in which he had the 1st and 32nd Army Tank Brigades, the 50th United Kingdom Division, and the 1st and 2nd South African Divisions. Norrie in XXX Corps had the 1st and 7th Armoured Divisions.

The main bulk of Ritchie's army was now disposed in a series of strong points protected by minefields between Gazala and the fortress of Bir Hacheim. Each strong point or "box" was well wired and dug, and contained a week's supply of food and ammunition, but though the intervening spaces were covered by minefields the boxes were too widely spaced to allow for mutual support or even for the minefields to be covered by gunfire. In the rear of the main front were other defended positions at Acroma and Knightsbridge. These were intended to guard the better tracks and communication centres and to be bases of manoeuvre for the army's mobile forces.

This deployment of the 8th Army was the result of a compromise. Ritchie and Auchinleck had had to decide whether to concentrate their forces, in which case Rommel would have little trouble in bypassing them, or to extend the front to its practicable limits thereby forcing an attacker to make a wide sweep to the south and increase his problems of supply and maintenance. They chose the latter course, believing that the weakening of the British front would be outweighed by the extra difficulties facing Rommel, but the German commander still drove right round the British position, and although the minefields affected the early pattern of the battle they were eventually breached and a way through them was opened for the Axis supply vehicles. Had Ritchie possessed the artillery to cover all the minefields the story might have ended differently although it was his failure to use XXX Corps as a concentrated striking force that was the real cause of his defeat.

Inside the Gazala position XIII Corps lay north of a line drawn just to the south of the track junction at Knightsbridge while XXX Corps guarded the region between there and Bir Hacheim and provided an armoured "mass of manoeuvre". This arrangement had two great weaknesses and suggests that the British commanders had learnt little or nothing from their recent unhappy experiences. Ritchie (cf. Graziani) had not only put most of his infantry and guns in a fixed line of isolated "boxes" which were open to outflanking movements if the minefields could be breached, but had also left a 20-mile gap between Sidi Muftah and Bir Hacheim to be covered by minefields alone. And his armour was spread out over the country between Knightsbridge, Bir Hacheim and Bir Gubi in direct contradiction of the well-established principle of concentration.

Auchinleck saw the dangers inherent in these dispositions and on 20th May wrote to Ritchie stating his belief that Rommel's most likely course would be a feint to the south to draw off XXX Corps followed by a break-in at the centre and a thrust northwards towards Tobruk. 8th Army, he thought, had two tasks, to hold the Tobruk-Gazala-Bir Gubi area and to destroy Rommel wherever he broke into the British positions. He therefore suggested to Ritchie that XXX Corps should be concentrated and placed astride the Trigh Capuzzo west of El Adem whence it could move against a break-in on the centre or against a sweep round the army's southern flank. Above all he insisted that the armoured divisions should fight as such under Norrie's control as the corps commander, and should in no case be committed to battle in bits and pieces.

Unfortunately the views held at army headquarters did not coincide with those of the C.-in-C. and Auchinleck was not prepared to insist on his plan being carried out. Ritchie for his part was certain that Rommel would attempt a flanking move round or through Bir Hacheim, while Nome foresaw a heavy blow against Gott's corps supported by a simultaneous southern thrust. This difference of opinion led to yet another compromise and a plan being made to counter either of these possible attacks, with the result that 7th Armoured Division was ordered to take up a position considerably further south than Auchinleck thought either necessary or desirable.

The rest of Ritchie's plan was unexceptionable. XIII Corps was to defend strongly and to counter-attack from the boxes whenever an opportunity occurred, meanwhile earmarking two brigade groups for a powerful counter-offensive. Gott was also ordered to form two mixed columns, one, "Stopcol", to hold the passage of the escarpment near Acroma, and the other, "Seacol", to work with the Navy to prevent any seaborne landings between Gazala and Tobruk. Meanwhile both corps fronts were to be covered by armoured cars, and these did their work so well that Rommel found it quite impossible to reconnoitre either the minefields or the defended localities, and had to begin his attack lacking valuable information.

By this time he had been given permission to attack at the end of May, to seize Tobruk, and to advance to the Egyptian frontier where he was ordered to remain until Malta had been captured. With that island in Italian hands the safety of the Axis supply lines would be guaranteed and Rommel could then invade Egypt. With the authority to attack in his hands Rommel made his plans. He proposed to hold down the 50th and 1st South African Divisions with a subsidiary attack between the Trigh Capuzzo and the coast while he led the whole of his armour and mobile forces, the DAK, 90 Light, and the 20th Corps round Bir Hacheim under cover of darkness, and the following day drove north behind XIII Corps towards Acroma. Cruewell was given two Italian infantry corps, most of Rommel's artillery, and a German infantry brigade, and told to use noise and movement to convince the British that a heavy attack was imminent while Rommel got into position for a crushing attack on the XIII Corps rear, and the Hecker Group landed from the sea and cut Gott's communications with Tobruk. That place would fall as soon as XIII Corps had been smashed, but to embarrass Ritchie even more Rommel proposed to push the 90th Light Division on towards El Adem with the object of creating havoc in the British rear and if possible to seize the Belhamed dumps. The supplies needed by his own forces were to be brought up in specially formed columns which would follow the DAK at a safe distance. Four days, he thought, should see the battle fought and won.

Rommel at this time had no high opinion of the 8th Army's ability to fight a fluid armoured battle, and though his knowledge of the British strength and dispositions was poor he decided to rely on surprise, boldness, and speed of movement to gain him the victory. On 25th May, however, he made a slight change in his plans and ordered the Ariete Division to capture Bir Hacheim while the main body of his armour swung further south to avoid a premature clash with British tanks.

To carry out his attack Rommel had 560 German and Italian tanks, of which 282 were Pzkw IIIs or IVs (including 19 Pzkw III Specials armed with the "long" 50 mm gun), and could rely on the support of 497 serviceable aircraft, including a considerable number of Me 109s, the best fighter in the desert. In reserve he had 77 more tanks including 28 Specials though not all of these were immediately available.

The 8th Army had 167 Grants, 257 Crusaders, and 149 Stuarts in XXX Corps, and 276 Matildas and Valentines in the Army Tank Brigades; with 75 more Grants and 70 more Stuarts in the 1st Armoured Brigade, now moving up from Egypt: but only 190 of the DAF's 320 aircraft were serviceable, and in the air the enemy had a decided superiority.

Chapter 14

The Battles at Gazala (2). The Fighting south of Gazala and the Fall of Tobruk

The actual fighting at Gazala took place in four phases, Rommel's attempt to crack open the British positions from the rear; his pause in the Cauldron to regroup and re-establish his communications; his counter-attack against the British armour; and the capture of Tobruk.

Phase 1 began on the afternoon of 26th May when the Cruewell Group closed up on the British between Sidi Muftah and Gazala, and Rommel started to move south-east. A little later British armoured cars reported that a heavy concentration of enemy vehicles was moving in the direction of Bir Hacheim but neither Ritchie nor Norrie made any use of this immensely valuable information.

Early next day the DAK overran the 3rd Indian Motor Brigade at Bir Hacheim and when the 90th Light Division shortly after forced the 7th Motor Brigade away from the half finished Retma Box to Bir Gubi the 8th Army's southern flank lay wide open. Messervy now asked Norrie for permission to take up the battle positions decided upon in the case of a major attack against the British left, but Norrie, who still thought the main attack would come in the centre, chose to wait for further information and refused the request.

In the meantime Messervy had ordered the 4th Armoured Brigade to go to the help of the Indians at Bir Hacheim but it clashed with 15th Panzer and was driven back beyond El Adem, finally coming to a halt in front of the Belhamed base. Shortly afterwards the headquarters of the 7th Armoured Division were surprised near Bir Beuid and Messervy was made prisoner. Two days later he escaped but in the interim his division had been without effective command, 8th Army having refused to believe the reports describing the scattering of its various units.

While these events were taking place Norrie warned the 1st Armoured Division to be ready to join the battle in the south and the 22nd Armoured Brigade started to move off in that direction. It had not gone far, however, before it was caught by the DAK and driven back towards Knightsbridge

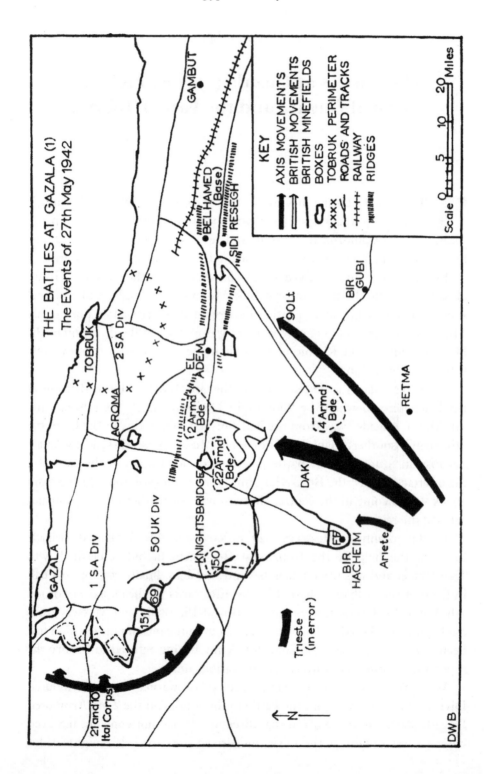

THE BATTLES AT GAZALA (1)
The Events of. 27th May 1942

KEY

AXIS MOVEMENTS
BRITISH MOVEMENTS
BRITISH MINEFIELDS
BOXES
xxxx TOBRUK PERIMETER
ROADS AND TRACKS
++++ RAILWAY
RIDGES

Scale 0 5 10 20 Miles

GAMBUT

BEL HAMED
(Base)

SIDI RESEGH

BIR
GUBI

90Lt

RETMA

TOBRUK

2 SA Div

ACROMA

EL
ADEM

(2 Armd)
Bde

(4 Armd
Bde

(22 Armd)
Bde

DAK

KNIGHTSBRIDGE

150

GAZALA

1 SA Div

50 UK Div

151 69

BIR
HACHEIM

Ariete

Trieste
(in error)

21 and
Ital Corps

N

DWB

with the loss of 30 tanks. Later in the day the brigade attacked again, and with the 2nd Armoured Brigade coming in against the German right from Bir Lefa, halted the enemy thrust.

That night the British were more satisfied than the Germans with the day's work, for although some of Rommel's columns had reached the Trigh Capuzzo he had lost a third of his tanks, 15th Panzer was running short of fuel and ammunition, and all contact with the 90th Light Division had gone. The Ariete had been beaten off at Bir Hacheim; the Trieste Division was gravelled on the minefields away to the west; and the striking force of the Axis army was not only dispersed among battered but still powerful British armoured formations but cut off from its supply columns, which were themselves in serious trouble between Bir Hacheim and Bir Harmat.

Rommel was not discouraged, however, and on the 28th he ordered his troops northwards again. This time the 21st Panzer captured Commonwealth Keep, 7 miles west of Acroma but 15th Panzer ran out of fuel and stopped; the Ariete was plundered by the 2nd Armoured and 1st Army Tank Brigades; and the 4th Armoured Brigade chased the 90th Light Division away from El Adem.

In the air meanwhile the Luftwaffe had been having the better of the battle and had given Rommel's troops excellent cover and support, although the DAF had attacked 15th Panzer and 90th Light Division with some success. In general, however, the speed of the German advance, their excellent fighters, and bad visibility prevented the DAF from giving much help to the British ground forces.

The day ended with Ritchie, who had captured Rommel's battle plans, believing that he had a good chance of winning a decisive victory. With 240 cruisers and 90 I tanks left, not counting the 1st Army Tank Brigade, and with 40 cruisers and 30 I tanks due to arrive next day, he reckoned on having a definite advantage in armour over the enemy who were thought to have some 250 tanks still serviceable. Auchinleck was also optimistic and he urged Ritchie to counter-attack before Rommel could recover his balance. Neither general knew at this time that the Pavia and Trieste Divisions had begun to clear the minefields in the undefended areas near the Trigh el Abd and Trigh Capuzzo.

Rommel himself was far from happy. Not only was his armour still scattered and short of ammunition but his headquarters had been dispersed, and he had at last discovered that his supply routes from the west were blocked by minefields, and near Sidi Muftah, by the 150th Infantry Brigade. By nightfall on the 29th, however, he had managed to concentrate his armour once more, having left the DAK and Ariete to fight a bloody and exhausting battle south-west of Knightsbridge while he went off in person to lead up his supply columns. From the British point of view the day's fighting had been inconclusive, the 4th Armoured Brigade being prevented from joining in the tank battle by a sandstorm, though they had deprived Rommel of one of his best officers by capturing General Cruewell. This loss was not badly felt, however, because Kesselring was visiting the front and agreed to take temporary command of the 20th Corps on the enemy left.

When he had regrouped Rommel changed his plan. He cancelled the proposed landing by the Hecker Group and gave orders for the British on his right to be held by an anti-tank screen while a gap was cut through the minefields on his left to open a supply route and give a way of escape should it prove necessary. His first attack had failed, and his position was extremely dangerous, but he was determined not to accept defeat while he possessed the means of fighting.

Ritchie, on the other hand, found himself unable to take advantage of Rommel's predicament. His armour had been committed piecemeal, had suffered periods of complete disruption, and even with the Grants had been unable to smash the Germans in the tank battles of the 28th and 29th May. As usual his information had been bad (he was often 24 hours late with news of the battle) and with the DAF unable to help, their lack of success was again beginning to take its toll of his men's confidence. Even so, on the 29th Ritchie had the best grounds yet for optimism. With Rommel's tanks pinned against the minefields west of Sidi Muftah they could perhaps be shelled to bits while his own armour sought out and destroyed the enemy supply columns, and cleared the way for a major counter-offensive.

The second phase of the Gazala battles, the fighting in the Cauldron, which began on 30th May and lasted until 10th June, was chiefly remarkable for a failure by Ritchie to take advantage of a golden opportunity to destroy Rommel completely.

The German commander had begun to clear the minefields on his left on 30th May, but found the way blocked by the 150th Brigade, and it was not until the afternoon of 1st June, with the Sidi Muftah box destroyed, that his rear was secured and a supply route opened from the west. Neither Norrie nor Ritchie had fully appreciated the desperate plight of 150th Brigade and attempts by XXX Corps to help the infantry were uncoordinated and on too small a scale to be of any use. Ritchie himself knew nothing of the ordeal of the 150th Brigade until 2nd June by which time the brigade had been smashed and an attempt to crush Rommel in the Cauldron by a

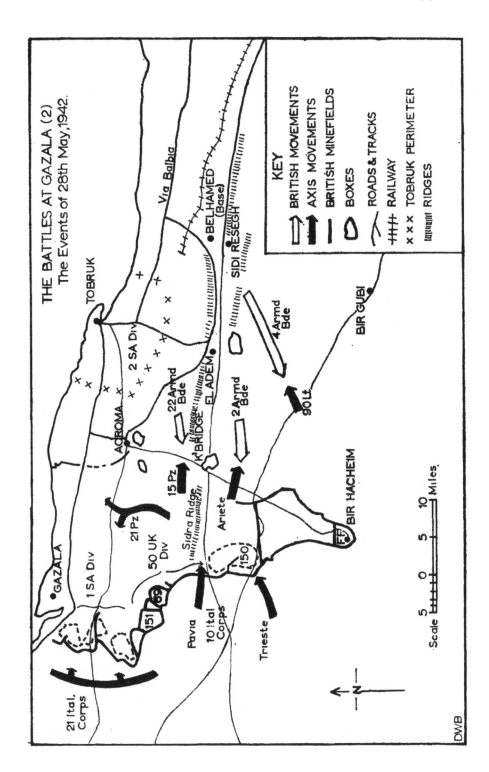

THE BATTLES AT GAZALA (2)
The Events of 28th May, 1942.

KEY

BRITISH MOVEMENTS
AXIS MOVEMENTS
BRITISH MINEFIELDS
BOXES
ROADS & TRACKS
RAILWAY
TOBRUK PERIMETER
RIDGES

TOBRUK

Via Balbia

BELHAMED (Base)

SIDI RESEGH

2 SA Div

ACROMA

22 Armd Bde

EL ADEM

K' BRIDGE

2 Armd Bde

4 Armd Bde

90 Lt.

BIR GUBI

15 Pz.

21 Pz.

Sidra Ridge

Ariete

GAZALA

1 SA Div

50 UK Div

69

151

Pavia

10 Ital Corps

'150'

Trieste

BIR HACHEIM

F.F.

21 Ital. Corps

N

Scale   5   0   5   10   Miles.

DWB

force totally inadequate for the purpose had ended in a fiasco. Undeterred Ritchie sat down to prepare for another attack two or three days later and apparently disregarded two warnings by Auchinleck that Rommel might renew the offensive before the 8th Army was ready to move against him.

Not for the first time Auchinleck had read Rommel's mind correctly, for with his administrative position much improved and the centre of the Gazala position firmly in his hands, the German general sent the 90th Light and Trieste Divisions south against Bir Hacheim on 2nd June, while 21st Panzer was ordered to demonstrate towards Eluet et Tamar to distract Ritchie's attention from Bir Hacheim, and to disrupt the preparations for the British attack. There now began the ten-day battle for Bir Hacheim, but elsewhere the front was relatively quiet as both sides gathered their strength for the next phase.

Meanwhile the DAF was passing through an uncomfortable period. It had maintained its attacks on enemy supply routes and troop concentrations but in the face of strong resistance had suffered heavily, and by 1st June, having lost 50 fighters, Coningham found it necessary to reduce the scale of his close support operations in order to conserve his remaining Kittyhawks.

About the same time Auchinleck was toying with the idea of a drive by XIII Corps towards Bir el Temrad but he failed to convince Ritchie and the Corps Commanders who thought that such a thrust would be vulnerable to attack by the DAK and planning went ahead for another attempt to crush Rommel in the Cauldron. On this occasion XXX Corps was to drive in behind the enemy south of Knightsbridge while XIII Corps seized the Sidra Ridge and closed the northern rim of the basin. This done, 1st Armoured Division would guard the northern and eastern exits from the Cauldron while the 10th Indian Brigade opened a path through the enemy anti-tank screen along which the 7th Armoured Division would drive to destroy the enemy armour. Command of this Operation "Aberdeen" was to lie with Briggs (5th Indian Division) and Messervy in turn, as the battle developed, and though it was intended that infantry and armour should fight together it should also be noted that their functions remained separate. Altogether it was a complicated plan and fraught with danger, but Ritchie and his colleagues were confident and looked forward to a resounding victory.

The attack began on 5th June with a heavy artillery bombardment after which the 10th Indian Brigade advanced and soon captured its appointed objectives, chiefly because Rommel's main defences lay further to the west.

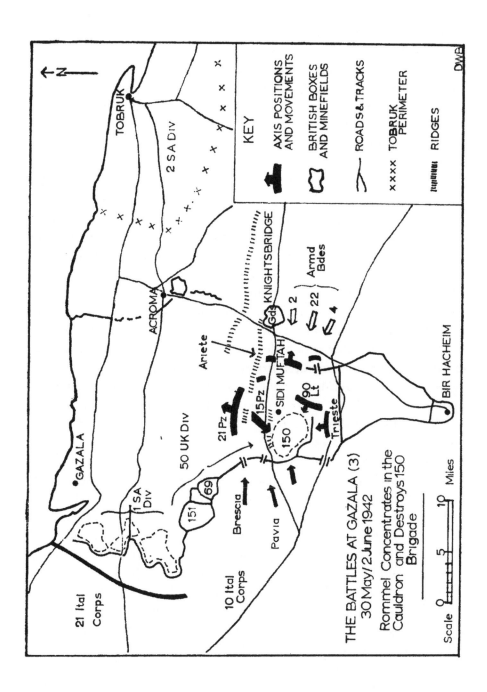

THE BATTLES AT GAZALA (3)
30 May/2 June 1942

Rommel Concentrates in the
Cauldron and Destroys 150
Brigade

Scale 0 [____] 5 [____] 10 Miles

KEY

AXIS POSITIONS
AND MOVEMENTS

BRITISH BOXES
AND MINEFIELDS

ROADS & TRACKS

xxxx TOBRUK
PERIMETER

RIDGES

There they had escaped the full effects of the artillery barrage, as was to be discovered when the 156 Stuarts of the 22nd Armoured Brigade, pushing on through the Indians, ran into the mass of the German guns and were driven off in the direction of Bir et Tamar. The infantry thus left unprotected were then counter-attacked by the DAK and driven back in their turn, while on the northern flank XIII Corps' attack on the Sidra Ridge was called off after 50 I tanks had been destroyed, many of them in an unsuspected minefield. By this time the command system had collapsed and with no one present to take full control each division was once again left to fight its own private battle.

Such a situation was hand-made for Rommel and he now counterattacked with great ferocity. With his northern flank safe after the repulse of XIII Corps he struck east towards Knightsbridge and sowed death and destruction in XXX Corps and the 5th Indian Division. The British by this time had lost all control of the battle and were unable to reorganize until their scattered forces had reached the security of the Knightsbridge and El Adem boxes. In the meantime the 22nd Armoured Brigade was pushed back beyond the Trigh Bir Hacheim, losing 60 tanks in the process, and four infantry battalions and four regiments of artillery were left in the Cauldron where they were systematically destroyed, Messervy being unable to bring either the 4th or 2nd Armoured Brigade to their rescue.

Nor had help been forthcoming from the DAF who, having rejected numerous requests for assistance on 5th June, found next day that bad weather and the absence of a recognizable bombline precluded the use of bombers in the battle area.

Thus for the second time Ritchie had failed to smash the Germans in the Cauldron but despite the heavy losses, which included 168 cruisers and 50 I tanks, the curious feeling persisted in the army that Operation "Aberdeen" had not been unprofitable. In fact, however, the enemy had had much the best of the battle. Rommel had prepared his defences well, had taken full advantage of the collapse of Ritchie's plans, and the men of the 8th Army had once more suffered heavily because of their commander's inexperience. It is difficult to understand how, at this late stage, Ritchie was prepared to allow a vital battle to be fought by junior commanders with a command system that could never be expected to equal the efficiency of the strong personal control habitually exercised by Rommel. He was also seriously at fault in using only one armoured brigade, an army tank brigade, and two infantry brigades in Operation "Aberdeen" when he should have left his bases to look after themselves and concentrated every possible British formation and

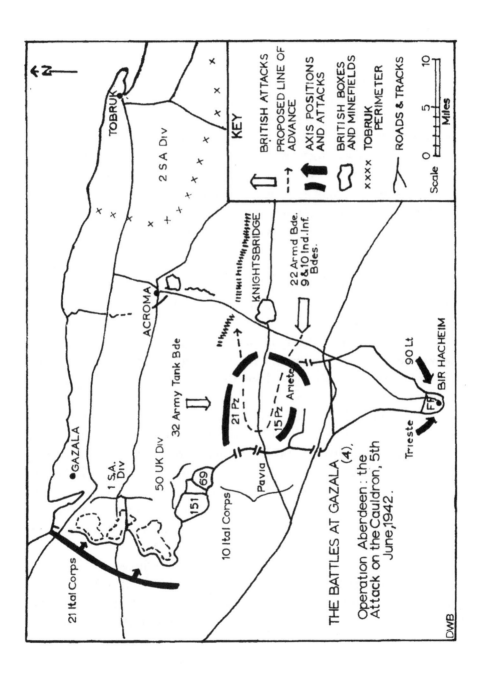

KEY

BRITISH ATTACKS

PROPOSED LINE OF ADVANCE

AXIS POSITIONS AND ATTACKS

BRITISH BOXES AND MINEFIELDS

xxxx TOBRUK PERIMETER

ROADS & TRACKS

Scale   0   5   10
                    Miles

TOBRUK

2 SA Div

KNIGHTSBRIDGE

22 Armd Bde. 9 & 10 Ind. Inf. Bdes.

ACROMA

32 Army Tank Bde

21 Pz

Ariete

15 Pz

90 Lt

BIR HACHEIM

GAZALA

1 S.A. Div

50 UK Div

151   69

Pavia

10 Ital Corps

Trieste

FF

21 Ital Corps

THE BATTLES AT GAZALA (4).

Operation Aberdeen : the Attack on the Cauldron, 5th June, 1942.

DWB

all the guns that could be made available to ensure the destruction of the enemy.

Meanwhile the battle at Bir Hacheim was continuing and it was to be 11th June before Ritchie ordered General Koenig to evacuate the position. Auchinleck had advised Ritchie to hold at Bir Hacheim on 6th June, when the army commander had been undecided whether to withdraw or not, and in the end its continued resistance served two important purposes. Originally it had made Rommel's supply routes long and costly, and then, after 6th June, it gave Ritchie a chance to recover from the Cauldron fighting. The conduct of the French troops was admirable and it is pleasant to record that two-thirds of the 3,600 garrison made good their escape, having withstood an unbelievable onslaught and obliged Rommel himself to take command of the attackers. It was here too that the DAF did its best work yet at Gazala, in giving great and much appreciated support to the beleaguered Free Frenchmen.

Phase 3 of the Gazala Battles began on 11th June, with Auchinleck and Ritchie deciding that their best course was to induce Rommel to attack their bent but once more continuous defences. At this point the positions of the 1st South African and 50th British Divisions south of Gazala were still intact, and five new strong points had been established between Alam Hamza and Acroma. A minefield ran from there to the coast; a Guards Brigade Group was at Knightsbridge; the 2nd South African Division was waiting in Tobruk; El Adem was covered by the 29th Indian Brigade; and Sidi Resegh and Belhamed by other units, the whole forming a framework for a strong defensive position. Less happy was Ritchie's situation in terms of tanks and artillery for he had lost 7 regiments of field artillery since 27th May and though he still had 185 cruisers, including 77 Grants, and 63 I tanks the condition of the replacements was the cause of many complaints and much uneasiness. Moreover the army's left flank was now parallel with and dangerously close to the Trigh Capuzzo, its main supply route.

Rommel too had suffered heavy losses, but reinforced with 33 tanks mounting long barrelled 50 mm or 75 mm guns he could still muster 124 good German cruisers and on 11th June he ordered 15 th Panzer, 90th Light and the Trieste to advance on El Adem while 21st Panzer attacked northwards from the Sidra Ridge.

By nightfall Norrie had seen enough of these moves to realize that Rommel had spread his force over a wide front and thought he saw an opportunity to smash him. He wanted to send the 140 cruisers of the 4th and

2nd Armoured Brigades to attack 15th Panzer but Messervy considered this division of the British armour to be undesirable and set off to confer with his corps commander. In the event he did not reach Norrie's headquarters for some hours during which the armoured brigades waited near Point 169 where they beat off a weak attack by 15th Panzer.

The British having failed to blunt themselves in a further assault on his anti-tank guns Rommel now decided to attack himself and gave orders for the DAK to crush the two armoured brigades in a converging assault, the 15th Panzer coming in against their front and the 21st from their rear.

At this point Norrie placed Lumsden in command of all three of his armoured brigades and he in his turn ordered the 22nd to move south from Knightsbridge. In the process it met and halted the 21st Panzer, but the delay did not last long, and during an afternoon's confused fighting the 2nd and 4th Armoured Brigades were driven back in the direction of Knightsbridge. The 4th was in fact pushed out of the battle but Lumsden managed to concentrate the 2nd and 22nd between Knightsbridge and Bir Bellefaa where he had decided to consolidate. He had now lost all contact with Norrie, and in the absence of higher direction decided to try and hold the Knightsbridge position for one more day.

Ritchie was at this time faced with an unenviable choice. With Rommel's advance threatening to cut off the 1st South African and the 50th Divisions he had to make up his mind whether to fight or to run. If he stood firm his armour might well be destroyed and his infantry cut off, but even if he withdrew to Egypt there was no guarantee that he would escape a severe mauling, and Tobruk would inevitably be left to the enemy. Characteristically he decided to stand and fight it out, a decision endorsed by Auchinleck and applauded by the Prime Minister.

For the coming defensive battle he transferred the 1st Armoured Division to XIII Corps and ordered Lumsden to hold the Acroma–Eluet–Knightsbridge area while fighting generally under the protection of Gott's guns and infantry. Further to the east the 10th Indian Division was directed to attack at El Adem and the 7th Motor Brigade to strike at the enemy rear between there and Knightsbridge.

By the time these instructions reached Lumsden on the morning of 13th June he was fully occupied with an enveloping attack on Knightsbridge by the DAK, an action which was to become the decisive armoured battle of the Gazala series. It was from this battle that Rommel emerged for the first time at Gazala definitely superior in armoured strength to the British, and at the end of the day, with XXX Corps reduced to 50 cruisers

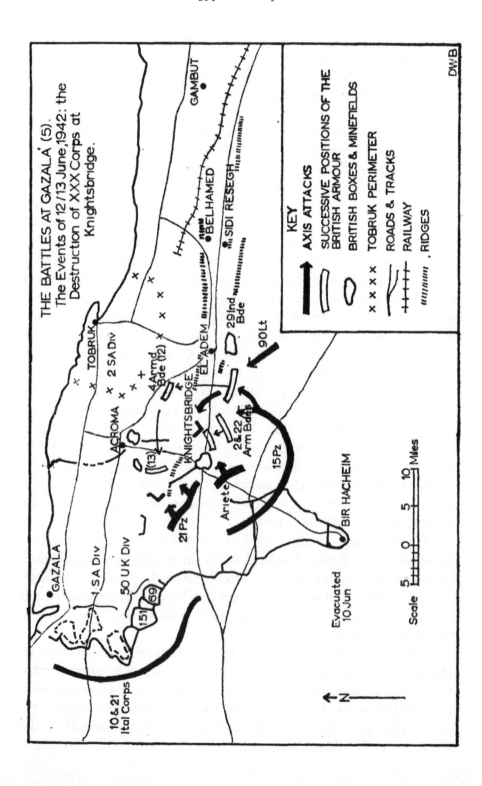

THE BATTLES AT GAZALÁ (5).
The Events of 12/13 June, 1942: the
Destruction of XXX Corps at
Knightsbridge.

KEY

AXIS ATTACKS

SUCCESSIVE POSITIONS OF THE
BRITISH ARMOUR

BRITISH BOXES & MINEFIELDS

x x x   TOBRUK PERIMETER

ROADS & TRACKS

RAILWAY

. RIDGES

GAMBUT

BELHAMED

SIDI RESEGH

29 Ind
Bde

90 Lt

TOBRUK

2 SA Div

4 Armd
Bde (12)

EL ADEM

KNIGHTSBRIDGE

2 & 22
Arm Bde

ACROMA

(13)

15 Pz

21 Pz

Ariete

BIR HACHEIM

GAZALA

1 SA Div

50 UK Div

151 69

Evacuated
10 Jun

10 & 21
Ital Corps

Scale 5 0 5 10 Miles

N

DWB

and unable to recover its damaged vehicles, Ritchie ordered Lumsden to withdraw. Up to this time the recovery and repair units had done sterling work but at Knightsbridge they were given no chance and the DAK won a great victory.

With Knightsbridge in enemy hands the 8th Army was in danger of being surrounded and on 14th June Ritchie decided to clear the Belhamed base. Two days later 1.5 million gallons of fuel had been leaked away, and except for 1 million rations the dumps were empty. This was a great disappointment to Rommel but Tobruk remained, filled with stores and badly defended, and he hoped for more success there. Ritchie's position, however, was worse than it had ever been, and with no armour to protect his southern flank it was imperative to withdraw his two Gazala divisions either to Tobruk, or to Egypt where they would be reasonably safe and where he could rebuild the armoured wing of his army. Therefore, at the same time as he ordered the destruction of the Belhamed dumps he instructed Gott to withdraw to the frontier while he himself held a line from west of Tobruk through El Adem to Belhamed.

Ritchie then reported on the situation to Auchinleck but failed to mention that he had already ordered Gott to send the Gazala divisions back to Egypt. He did ask, however, if the C.-in-C. wanted him to order a general withdrawal, including that of the Tobruk garrison, or to accept the risk of a short siege in the hope that it would soon be possible to relieve the fortress. Several hours of confused and contradictory telegrams now passed between the army commander and the C.-in-C. but ended with Auchinleck giving firm instructions to Ritchie to hold the Acroma-El Adem-Bir Gubi line, and expressly forbidding either the evacuation or the investment of Tobruk.

About the same time the Prime Minister intervened and signalled to Auchinleck that he presumed that Tobruk would not be given up as its possession would prevent any large scale advance into Egypt. In his reply Auchinleck explained his appreciation of the situation and the orders which he had given, and stressed the difficulties confronting Rommel. He also wrote of his plans for the future, including the building up of a reserve on the frontier ready for a counter-offensive, and sent another order to Ritchie telling him to place in Tobruk a force capable of holding the base even if it was temporarily surrounded. In the meantime the 8th Army's remaining mobile forces were to prevent the enemy from moving east of El Adem or Tobruk.

While these discussions were taking place Rommel tried to cut the coast road behind Gazala but his troops were too tired and the defence too good, and on the night of 14th/15th June the British and South Africans broke out eastwards, and not long after were re-assembling on the frontier.

Thus by the evening of 16th June the 8th Army had been defeated and driven some 80 miles eat of its chosen battlefields. It still held Tobruk and had small forces at El Adem and Belhamed, but its armour consisted of only one weak armoured brigade, the 4th, and there was no coherent infantry organization and no large reserves. Rommel on the other hand had smashed Ritchie's armour, captured great stocks of supplies, and cleared the way to Tobruk, his main objective, whose investment and capture was to form the fourth phase of the Gazala battles.

While he was waiting for Auchinleck's final word on Tobruk, Ritchie had concentrated on preventing XIII Corps from being outflanked and cut off, to perform which task he had the remains of Norrie's XXX Corps, a totally inadequate force. Nome's effective command on 15th June consisted of the 7th Armoured Division, in reality the survivors of the 4th Armoured Brigade; the 29th Indian Brigade at El Adem; and the 20th Brigade at Belhamed. And with the evacuation of El Adem 36 hours later the southern corner of Tobruk's forward defences had gone, and with it much of the possibility of holding the fortress. The 20th Brigade at Belhamed meanwhile continued to fight on, but after a clash between his armour and the DAK on its way to cut the coast road near Gambut Norrie ordered the brigade to withdraw to Solium under cover of darkness. Then, on 19th June, the 58 tanks of the 4th Armoured Brigade, which had regrouped near an FMC south of the Trigh el Abd, were also ordered back to Egypt.

During these few days the DAF's support of the army had greatly improved and it was not until the 17th, with El Adem in German hands, that Coningham evacuated Gambut and ordered his squadrons back to the frontier. Two days later, with the army unable to protect the Sidi Azeiz airfield the fighters had to retire again, this time to Sidi Barrani, and only one squadron, armed with long-range Kittyhawks, remained capable of giving any cover to the Tobruk garrison.

Tobruk itself was surrounded on 18th June and that day Auchinleck, who was still hoping to be able to hold a line west of the frontier, flew up to Ritchie's HQ at Maddalena. There Ritchie explained his predicament. His forces were not nearly strong enough to carry out the tasks he had been given and he wanted a new directive. This was shortly forthcoming. Auchinleck announced that Army HQ would henceforth be responsible for the conduct of the defence of Tobruk while XIII Corps held the frontier and gave what help it could from outside. XXX Corps was to go into reserve near Matruh where it would reform and retrain.

At Tobruk itself the defences were in a sorry state. The February decision that the port would not be held; the "Crusader" successes; and the build up of the major base, all meant that little care had been taken to maintain the fortress. Minefields had been partly cleared, anti-tank ditches had been filled in or allowed to collapse, maps were non-existent, and there was no satisfactory fire plan for the defenders' guns.

The garrison ordered to hold this almost impossible position with its 30 mile perimeter consisted of 2 brigades of the 2nd South African Division; the 32nd Army Tank Brigade with 61 Valentines and Matildas; the 201st Guards Brigade; the 11th Indian Infantry Brigade, and some administrative units. It was commanded by Major-General H. B. Klopper who had little battle experience having just come from a training command in the Union, and who made matters worse when he chose to ignore the sound advice proffered by his more experienced brigadiers. There were no aircraft and very few anti-aircraft guns but other supplies were present in enormous quantities. There were 3 million rations, 7,000 tons of water, 1.5 million gallons of petrol, and nearly 300,000 rounds of assorted field, medium, and anti-tank ammunition.

On the 20th June Rommel attacked the south-east sector of the defences with all his armour and 150 bombers, and on the 21st the garrison surrendered. The unprepared defences had collapsed in utter confusion and the unfortunate Klopper had little alternative but to capitulate. On the 20th Ritchie had tried to divert the Germans by sending the 7th Armoured Division to Sidi Resegh, and when this attempt failed, offered to keep an escape route open between Harmat and El Adem. It was a pointless suggestion because Klopper had hardly any mobile units and in any case there were great differences of opinion inside Tobruk as to whether a breakout was a practical proposition. Klopper did give orders at one stage for those who could to break out while the rest fought on but he subsequently decided that continued resistance would be of no value to Ritchie and signalled that he was proposing to surrender to save useless loss of life.

Among the few bright spots in the Tobruk calamity were the resistance of the 2/7 Gurkha Rifles and 2nd Cameron Highlanders who refused to surrender and fought on, the latter until the 22nd; and the performance of the 2nd Coldstream Guards and other units which, led by Major Sainthill of that regiment, fought their way out and escaped.

Altogether the British losses amounted to 33,000 men, of whom nearly 9,000 were South Africans; 1,400 tons of petrol; 2,000 serviceable vehicles; and 5,000 tons of food, and the surrender, which came as a shattering blow to the UK and South Africa, led to a motion of censure being tabled in the House of Commons.

The battles at Gazala and Tobruk were a humiliating experience for the 8th Army. It had met the enemy on ground more or less of its own choosing; it had begun by possessing a considerable numerical advantage, particularly in armour; at one time it had had Rommel at its mercy, and yet in the end it had once again been defeated in detail.

The Gazala position did in fact suffer from certain important defects. The forward defences were too close to the administrative areas at Belhamed and Tobruk, and as has been shown this was one of the reasons why no effective counter-stroke was ever launched against Rommel. It was also a reason for extending the British position as far south as Bir Hacheim, and for the tying up of so many of our infantry brigades in "boxes" which could be easily isolated by the enemy. Nevertheless, while a strong and mobile XXX Corps remained in being the 8th Army was always in a position to win the battle, and its failure to do so was undoubtedly due to a weakness in command at Army, Corps, and Divisional levels.

The turning point of the battle came in the last days of May, when, with Rommel at his mercy, Ritchie allowed him to regroup in the Cauldron without making a serious effort to destroy him. And it can be argued that the smashing of XXX Corps a fortnight later was a direct consequence of this failure by Ritchie to take advantage of a splendid opportunity to destroy the DAK. The British commander's inactivity during this early period is another example of his then inability to fight a battle of opportunity and also serves to emphasize Rommel's talent for such operations. And even when he did attack Ritchie persistently used forces which were too small to be effective, and by permitting his armoured brigades to fight individually instead of concentrated he wasted the advantage of the Grants' superiority. The battles, it would seem, were fought by committee, Ritchie having less than full control over Norrie and Gott, and they too little over their divisional and brigade commanders, with the result that the battles degenerated into a series of private actions fought by divisions and brigades, whereas Rommel fought always with the DAK concentrated and under his personal control.

Perhaps the greatest measure of the British failure to fight a cohesive battle, however, lies in the fact that the 8th Army suffered a crushing defeat without XIII Corps playing any real part in the battle.

So far as the loss of Tobruk is concerned the causes of the defeat are clear enough and neither Churchill nor the Middle East commanders are free from blame. It is less than fair to put all the blame on the Prime Minister though he certainly went too far in ordering the port to be held, and some of his reasons for doing so are not strong. For example he must have been told, though he disclaims it, that Tobruk was in no state to withstand a siege and that ever since February it had been understood in the Middle East that no attempt would be made to hold the port if it was strongly attacked. On the other hand the war was going badly for the allies and he undoubtedly feared the effects that the loss of Tobruk might have on home morale, on South Africa, on Turkey, and on the USA, where there was a growing desire for the projected North and West African campaigns to be dropped. The political reasons for holding Tobruk were thus very powerful indeed and it was up to Auchinleck and Ritchie to say it was an impossible military undertaking.

They had long since decided that Tobruk would not be held and it is not surprising that the defences had been allowed to run down. They then failed to realize the extent of the Gazala defeats for they would not otherwise have tried to do so many things at once, defend Tobruk, fight on the frontier, and organize a counter-offensive, it was Auchinleck too who appointed Klopper to command in Tobruk, another example of a choice that was unfair to everyone concerned. Whether anyone could have held Tobruk, especially in view of the devastating air attacks to which the garrison was subjected, is extremely unlikely but it is possible that a more experienced commander would have produced a better defence and perhaps prevented the enemy from capturing so much valuable materiel.

It was Rommel's greatest single prize and his reward was promotion to Field Marshal.

Chapter 15

The Retreat to El Alamein

The Axis powers had intended for some time that the fall of Tobruk should be followed by the capture of Malta, which thanks to the timely arrival of air reinforcements had regained its offensive capability, and by the end of June was once more threatening the supply routes from Italy to North Africa.

Rommel, however, was most anxious to exploit his Gazala successes before Auchinleck could form a stable front and reinforce the 8th Army, and he argued that with the way to the Delta almost clear the advance should be continued. He put his case to Hitler and to Mussolini and the Führer, by working on the Duce's cupidity, persuaded him to agree to an advance to El Alamein which would then become a jumping off place for the final thrust to gain the prizes of the Nile valley. Hitler had by this time become disenchanted with the proposed operation against Malta which he thought might develop into a serious drain on his resources, and was in fact very pleased to have an attractive alternative ready to hand.

Immense difficulties still faced the German and Italian armies in the desert, however, as both Cavallero and Kesselring realized. With Malta once more functioning as a British naval and air base a supply crisis in North Africa was inevitable, and they pointed out to Rommel that while every effort would be made to run convoys into Cyrenaica for some time to come the army there would have to live off its captures. In addition it was now more than ever necessary to continue the air offensive against Malta and this would have the effect of reducing the Luftwaffe's support for Rommel at a time when the DAF could be expected to grow in strength as it drew closer to its main bases.

Rommel, buoyed up by his victories, refused to be restrained and in an over-optimistic mood told Cavallero and Kesselring on the 26th of June that with reasonable luck he would reach Alexandria on the 30th. Mussolini, dreaming of himself as an eastern potentate, confirmed this aim the following day. Kesselring remained far from sanguine, however, and though as Hitler's representative he agreed to the advance to El Alamein, it was not long before he came to regard this decision as a mortal blow to the Axis designs in North Africa.

It was, perhaps, only a matter of time before Hitler elected to override his professional military advisers in the Middle East as he had already done in other theatres, but he chose a bad time to do so and Rommel was to pay for it as well as for his own unduly optimistic attitude. The desert was the last place in the world where military operations could be left to chance, as Rommel should have known.

Curiously enough the collapse at Tobruk may have had some indirect advantages for the British cause. It may have saved Malta, and it definitely helped Auchinleck and Montgomery, for on receiving news of the surrender Roosevelt immediately sent 300 Sherman tanks, 100 105 mm self-propelled guns, and many aircraft to reinforce the army and RAF in Egypt and the Middle East.

Meanwhile Ritchie had decided to fall back on Matruh where he thought he could offer battle once more with a fair chance of success. At Matruh there were some partially prepared defensive positions which could be manned by infantry, and the 120 miles of waterless country between there and the frontier would be a great embarrassment to Rommel and would give the DAF an excellent opportunity to attack his advancing columns.

In London the Defence Committee was not very sure of the correctness of the decision to let the frontier go after a delaying action, and said so, but Auchinleck was firm in his resolve to withdraw and very wisely did so. He and Ritchie then produced a plan for a defensive battle in the Matruh area while Gott waited on the frontier with orders to delay the enemy as much as possible without risking his command. The purpose of this delaying action was to give the DAF as much time as possible to operate from advanced airfields; to allow Ritchie a fair chance of preparing for his big battle; and to ensure that the forward dumps were destroyed before Rommel could reach them. To achieve this Gott was given the weak 7th Armoured Division, 5 armoured car regiments, and the 50th United Kingdom and 10th Indian Infantry Divisions. Further back the 8th Army had begun to receive reinforcements in the shape of the HQ of X Corps, the 10th Armoured Division, and the New Zealand Division from Syria. The 10th Armoured Division was a paper force having lost the tanks of its one armoured brigade to the refitting 1st Armoured Division as soon as it reached Egypt, but the New Zealanders were an invaluable acquisition. The 1st South African Division meanwhile was sent back to El Alamein to refit, and to help with the preparation of the defences.

Gott, however, had no time to organize his delaying action before Rommel advanced again, and on 23rd June he began to withdraw taking good care to destroy dumps and installations as he went. This part of his administrative plan was very successful and must have hindered Rommel considerably, and though the Germans met little opposition on the ground they now began to suffer heavily as the bombers of the DAF at last came into their own.

Tedder and Coningham had quickly learnt that the only way to give continuous support to the army, either in advance or retreat, was to have a series of landing grounds in depth, and during the Gazala battles Coningham had arranged for several Egyptian airfields to be made ready to receive his squadrons at very short notice. This precaution was to prove its worth again and again as the army retreated and the DAF assumed more and more of the burden of defending Egypt. The rapid build up of the RAF now became an immediate priority and aircraft were called in from all over the theatre, including Malta; the Delta was denuded of fighters; and other squadrons, including heavy bombers, were sent out from the UK or diverted from India and Australia. The American Liberator squadron was now permanently stationed in Egypt and plans were made to move in 35 more Liberators, 57 Mitchells, 80 Kittyhawks, and 27 Hudsons by early July.

In the last week of June the aircraft available to Tedder as AOC-inC in the Middle East were 463 in the DAF and a further 420 variously spread around the theatre. As the Axis had 421 in North Africa and 674 elsewhere in the Mediterranean the immediate advantage lay with the British, and when the 8th Army left the frontier the light bombers of the DAF turned on their maximum effort and kept it up as Rommel moved forward. They were more or less undisturbed by the Luftwaffe which was again finding out how difficult it was to keep pace with a rapidly advancing army. The enemy air forces had also been taken completely by surprise by the sudden switch of the air offensive from Malta to the desert and in consequence the dense columns of Ritchie's retiring army were never seriously attacked.

The choice of Matruh as the site for the battle for Egypt was dictated partly by the political need to check the enemy while he was still some way from the Delta, and partly because in 1940 much time and effort had been spent in preparing its defences. Subsequently, as the town became a major supply base these works had been allowed to decay, but some still remained and although it was not a naturally strong position it seemed to Ritchie and Auchinleck to be the best place in the circumstances at which to halt the German advance.

The coastal plain in this area was between 10 and 15 miles wide, and to the south of it the land rose in two stages marked by the northern and southern escarpments. The formal defences of the district in June 1942 consisted of a ring of dilapidated works round Matruh itself and minefields stretching from the coast to Charing Cross, the point where the coast road and the Siwa track crossed the northern scarp. Other but shallower minefields were placed between the scarps, and more works had been planned for Sidi Hamza above the southern ridge, though little or nothing had been done to develop them.

Ritchie, determined that this time there would be no retreat and that the 8th Army would stay where it was, alive or dead, planned a straightforward battle. While X Corps held Matruh and XIII Corps Sidi Hamza, Norrie with the HQ of XXX Corps would collect a reserve and in the safer rear areas form a striking force for a counter-attack. If by chance Rommel pushed between the two forward corps he would be crushed between them, and if he swung south Gott would take him in flank. It sounded simple and reasonably easy, and by 24th June the army was getting into position. In the coastal sector the 50th Division was established at Gerawla and the 10th Indian Division at Matruh, while Gott was preparing to send the 5th Indian Division to Sidi Hamza and Freyburg's New Zealanders to Minqar Qaim where there was a way down the southern scarp. The 1st Armoured Division was posted out in the desert to the south-west. Freyburg had originally been placed in Matruh but he protested so strongly at being "shut up" that Ritchie transferred his division to XIII Corps and the open country. The space between the corps areas was to be guarded by two small mixed columns provided by the 5th Indian Division, while the very weak 7th Armoured Division (two motor brigades and an infantry brigade) acted as a general covering force.

The next day, 25th June, Auchinleck drove up to the front, took over command of the army, and announced a change in plan. The C.-in-C. felt that with the fate of Egypt and the Suez base, and perhaps the whole of the Middle East in balance, it was only right that he should bear the responsibility for the coming battle, and he relieved Ritchie who returned to Cairo.

Auchinleck's change in plan stemmed from the belief that he was too weak in guns and armour to be certain of holding either Matruh or Sidi Hamza or of preventing a southern sweep by Rommel from enveloping the whole of the 8th Army. Either contingency could lead to defeat in detail which was a risk far too great to be accepted. This being so he issued new orders on the 26th in which he stated that the enemy were to be fought between Matruh and El Alamein; that all units were to be kept fully mobile in order to be able to strike continually at Rommel from all sides; and that the armour was not to be committed except in very favourable circumstances. Above all, the army was to be kept intact and isolated localities were not to be defended. At the same time all the infantry divisions were to reorganize themselves into Brigade Battle Groups based on their artillery units.

Ritchie had begun to form mobile columns of this sort during the later stages of the retreat from Gazala and Auchinleck endorsed the idea when he changed the army's role from one of static defence to fluid defence. In the event Rommel attacked before the changes could be put fully into effect but it is doubtful whether they could have had much prospect of success at this stage as the tactics involved were entirely new and unpractised, and were just one more problem for the army to contend with. For years past British doctrine had asserted that running fights in retreat were to be avoided and now the 8th Army, retreating before an aggressive enemy after a series of heavy defeats, and having just changed its commander, was told to reorganize, change its tactics, and fight a battle very different from that for which it had been hurriedly trying to prepare. It is not to be wondered at that a tiny element of despondency began to creep into the dogged and determined minds of the soldiers.

Rommel, whose progress had been slowed up by the round-the-clock bombing of the DAF, advanced against Auchinleck late on the 26th June. His intention was for the 90th Light Division to drive between the scarps and cut the coast road well to the east of Matruh while the DAK, with 21st Panzer moving below the southern scarp, and 15th Panzer and the 20th Corps above it, kept the 1st Armoured Division out of the battle. The 10th and 21st Italian Corps were ordered to contain Matruh itself.

By midnight the two small columns in the British centre had been scattered and the way was open for 90th Light to move on behind Matruh. The next day this division continued its advance until noon when it was checked near Bir Sarahna after a fierce battle with the Durham Light Infantry and some guns.

On other parts of the battlefield an attempt by the Matruh garrison to hit at Rommel's left rear ended in failure but the DAK also achieved little, the 15th Panzer Division being held up by the 4th Armoured Brigade above the southern scarp, though the 21st continued to move forward below it in an attempt to close the escape route down the Minqar Qaim cliff.

It was not until this point had been reached that Rommel realized that the New Zealanders were present in strength and he reacted by ordering the 21st Panzer Division to attack them immediately while he led the 90th Light on towards the coast, insisting that the road be cut before dark. He was now in a very dangerous and vulnerable position having thrust between two relatively powerful British forces, and may have survived only because Auchinleck's battle plan disintegrated.

This came about partly because Auchinleck was unable to retain control of the whole battle, and partly because of the solid resistance offered by the Italians to the attacks of the 50th Division. Yet again the failure of the British command to obtain reliable and up-to-date information led to an incoherent action or series of actions. During the morning of the 27th Auchinleck had given instructions that X and XIII Corps were to withdraw to a line from Fuka to Minqar Omar (Operation "Pike") if it was necessary to do so to preserve a connected front, and Gott acted on these orders that night without telling anyone of his intentions when it seemed that the enemy's encirclement of the New Zealand Division was likely to split his corps. He was undoubtedly bearing in mind Auchinleck's orders not to allow any formation to become isolated, and for the same reason ordered the 1st Armoured Division to fall back as well. In due course the New Zealanders broke out through the 21st Panzer, creating fair havoc as they did so, but then, not having received any clear directive did not stop until they reached El Alamein, the area appointed as the second stage position of the withdrawal. The 1st Armoured Division meanwhile had halted at Fuka on the morning of the 28th.

The news that Gott had begun Operation "Pike" first reached Holmes, the commander of X Corps, about the same time, when he received orders from Auchinleck to break out that night covered by XIII Corps, through the enemy forces that were believed to have surrounded Matruh. Unfortunately when that time came it was far too late for Gott to help, his orders to cover the break-out not having arrived until 9.30 pm on the night in question, but Holmes still managed to extricate most of his men who battered their way through the Germans and reached Fuka. There they found more enemy troops and so continued their retreat to El Alamein where Auchinleck was reorganizing the army. He gave XXX Corps (1st South African, 10th Indian and 50th UK Divisions) the task of holding the northern sector, and XIII Corps (the New Zealand and the 5th Indian Divisions) the southern. The 1st and 7th Armoured Divisions were held in army reserve and the HQ of X Corps was sent back to organize the defence of the Delta.

Battlefield confusion, dust, and bad weather prevented the DAF from taking much part in these actions but they continued to bomb the enemy's rear areas and landing grounds with some success, and severely shook up the 90th Light Division. They also mined the harbours at Solium and Matruh and contaminated the water supplies at that place.

The battle of Matruh was Rommel's last desert victory and a very good one although it was not conclusive. With 104 tanks and a few thousand infantry he had routed the remains of two British corps supported by 174 assorted tanks, and taken many prisoners. The 8th Army, however, still remained in being, disorganized and bewildered though it was, and with its basic structure little impaired it was yet capable of determined resistance as Rommel was to discover. And Auchinleck had at last formed his front, even if it was in the last ditch position.

The defeat of the 8th Army at Matruh was to a large extent the result of bad planning and poor communications. When Auchinleck took over from Ritchie it was too late to alter the battle plans in detail and Rommel exploited their inherent weaknesses to the full. Once again signals breakdowns meant that Auchinleck was unable to maintain contact with Gott and Holmes and corps, divisions and brigades again found themselves fighting their own private battles. Inevitably the British weakness in armour contributed much to their defeat. Just as on the frontier, an active defence at Matruh was impossible without a strong armoured reserve, and that Auchinleck did not have.

It is a moot point whether, having resisted the temptation to fight on the frontier, he should not have withdrawn immediately to El Alamein, or insisted that Ritchie did so. Certainly El Alamein was the stronger natural position and it would have added to Rommel's difficulties to make him attack there, but it was barely sixty miles from Alexandria and the three Commanders-in-Chief could hardly allow the enemy to get so close to the Delta without making some attempt to stop him. A comparison with Rommel's problem in December 1941 is misleading because the El Agheila defences were nearly 300 miles from the city of Tripoli, his equivalent of Cairo.

Ritchie's replacement was characteristic of Auchinleck. He had been tempted to relieve Ritchie in March when there was widespread dissatisfaction in the higher levels of the army with his performance as Army Commander, and when Godwin Austen had asked to be relieved, but at that time the C.-in-C. was put off from doing so by personal loyalty to the man he had picked; by the possible bad effects that another change in command might have had on morale in the army; and perhaps by the chance of being saddled with an unsympathetic army commander. Besides which he undoubtedly thought that Ritchie would have learned by experience and would improve as time passed, and in any case he, Auchinleck, could continue to hold a watching brief over his subordinate's command.

As things turned out the Gazala battles only emphasized Ritchie's shortcomings, and his plans for a final battle at Matruh which was almost certain to be lost, and possibly the Middle East with it, probably helped Auchinleck to make up his mind to remove him. At the same time the decision to assume full responsibility for whatever might arise in an extremely perilous situation was typical of Auchinleck. At no time was he a man knowingly to shirk his responsibilities.

Ritchie had been an unfortunate choice as Army Commander though he was later to become a successful Corps Commander under Montgomery in north-west Europe. In the desert, moreover, he had been placed in a singularly difficult position by his Commander-in-Chief. His original appointment at a critical stage in "Crusader" was understandable as a temporary measure but his subsequent retention had unfortunate consequences for which Auchinleck must share the blame.

Ritchie was both vigorous and able, and was an excellent staff officer, but in November 1941 he had never commanded more than a battalion. He then knew nothing of armoured warfare, very little about his subordinate commanders or his troops, and as Army Commander was even less happily placed than Cunningham had been because his Corps Commanders were not only vastly more experienced in command, but were his superiors in rank. Nevertheless he was generally popular and his confidence was badly needed by the army after the Sidi Resegh defeats and the removal of Cunningham.

His new relationship with Auchinleck had also begun well, perhaps because the Commander-in-Chief gave most of the orders, but it was later to become less happy. From being Auchinleck's principal staff officer Ritchie found himself in a situation where he had to give the orders at a time when he was unprepared for such a responsibility, and Auchinleck was probably unfair to himself, to Ritchie, and to everyone in the army, when, having pitchforked Ritchie into a difficult military situation, he left him there, the fact that his performance in "Crusader" was adequate, and that his replacement would have been hard to explain to the nation and the army notwithstanding.

As long as Ritchie remained in command of the army his lack of experience and tactical skill prevented him from improving his standing with his senior subordinates, who remained his superiors in battlefield knowledge. It was an all but impossible situation and it is to Ritchie's credit that he retained his popularity as a man among his colleagues. On the one hand were Auchinleck, Gott, and Norrie, with a wealth of command experience, and on the other his own imperfect knowledge and the responsibility for taking the vital decisions. A less robust character than Ritchie's would have crumpled as he tried to resolve these conflicting pressures, and the changed relationship with Auchinleck which brought its own special problems. As army commander it was essential that Ritchie should be seen to be capable of independent decision, if only for his own private peace of mind, and although towards the end he relied increasingly on Auchinleck for advice, he had already chosen an unfortunate time to demonstrate his independence when he disregarded the C.-in-C's. eminently sound recommendations for the use of armour in the Gazala battles. Ritchie's experience as commander of the 8th Army may be compared to that of a learner driver in a high-powered and unfamiliar car with an oversize instructor beside him and passengers with greater experience than his own offering advice from the back seats. Confronted by problems similar to those of the "Rush Hour" it is not surprising that he crashed.

In the final analysis, however, the fault must lie with Auchinleck. In the first instance Ritchie's appointment was meant to be temporary and Auchinleck could have replaced him without excessive difficulty, either after "Crusader" or the retreat to Gazala, instead of which he not only chose to leave him in command but failed to see that his own wishes were carried out. Had Auchinleck insisted more firmly on the line to be taken at Gazala the story might have ended differently. The C.-in-C's. reasons for retaining Ritchie as army commander after events had shown that he was unready for the task deserve consideration but were not good enough to justify the action he took.

Chapter 16

The Fighting in the El Alamein Positions in July 1942

After the defeat at Matruh Auchinleck increased his efforts to plug the gap between El Alamein and the Qattara Depression while Rommel strove to prevent the 8th Army from settling into a firm and strong defensive position. The latter felt that if he could only carry the El Alamein area the Delta would be his for the taking and he drove his men on, allowing them no respite. Having reached El Alamein this was without doubt the course to adopt, for the longer the British stayed there the harder would it become to turn them out, but as his supply position deteriorated Rommel must have wondered whether he should not have paused after the capture of Tobruk.

The original policy of the Axis Powers had been to follow the capture of Tobruk with a six weeks' pause for consolidation and re-supply, and when the Gazala successes led to approval being given for Rommel to advance into Egypt the German and Italian supply and transport organizations were taken completely by surprise and found it impossible to satisfy the needs of the Panzerarmee. By the beginning of July Rommel's service system was unable to cope with the requirements of even the spearhead units and the rest of the army suffered accordingly. The huge stocks of captured British material were of immense value and were put to good use but time was needed to sort out and distribute these spoils, and time was at a premium as Rommel drove relentlessly eastwards. Fuel, water, and ammunition were sources of constant anxiety to the German commander but his greatest problem was the lack of serviceable transport vehicles without which no army could survive for long in the desert. The British had discovered this months earlier and had been able to build up a vast transport organization but Rommel was unable to do this and could not use the railway along the coast as Gott's retreating forces had spiked all the locomotives. Nor could he make use of seaborne transport in the face of the Royal Navy's command of the Eastern Mediterranean.

Nevertheless he pressed on with great determination and on 30th June his forward elements were in contact with the Alamein defences.

Between the sea at El Alamein and the Qattara Depression lay 38 miles of desert which rose imperceptibly from the coast to the 700 ft. hills forming the depression's northern rim. The intervening area was diversified by the presence of several low ridges, of which those at Miteiriya, Ruweisat, and Alam Haifa were to become famous; some "Tels" or mounds; and many saucer-shaped depressions known as "Deirs". Among these features patches of loose sand alternated with areas of firmer ground which permitted easy movement of men and vehicles. The ridges were normally formed of very hard rock in which the excavation of defensive positions was unbelievably difficult.

The area had been recognized as a likely position from which to defend Egypt since before the war and some work had been done on the construction of permanent defences, but no great progress had been made and all such activities came to a halt when the Middle East Command had to meet the needs of the "Crusader" and Syrian campaigns.

The original plan had been for defended localities to be created at El Alamein, Bab el Qattara and Naqb Abu Dweiss, each about 15 miles from its neighbour. At El Alamein the positions had been dug and partly mined and wired; and at Bab el Qattara the works had been dug and wired but there was no minefield. The southernmost locality was a defensive position in name only. Nome especially was very anxious about these positions and wanted to create other "boxes", in particular at the western end of the Ruweisat Ridge, but work on these had hardly begun when Rommel attacked once more.

It can be seen, therefore, that in July 1942 the British positions at El Alamein were anything but strong and Auchinleck framed his tactical plan accordingly. He proposed to hold the defended localities with part of the army and to canalize the enemy's advance so that the rest of his command, now in the process of forming itself into a mobile striking force, could hit at the attackers' flanks and rear. He ordered the reorganization of the army into Battle Groups to continue and directed the Corps Commanders to ensure that the maximum forces were concentrated at any decisive point irrespective of sector responsibilities. At the same time all those who did not have a specific front line job were sent to the rear.

Auchinleck has been criticized for not issuing a "backs to the wall" directive at this time, and had such an order been issued it would undoubtedly have removed much of the uncertainty and confused thinking that existed in the army where many of the troops found the new measures inconsistent with a

were undertrained. The supply situation was also extremely grave, the captured stocks of fuel and food being sufficient for defensive operations but quite inadequate for a major offensive. Lorries were numerous enough but the lack of British spare parts and the activities of the RAF were rapidly reducing the effectiveness of his transport system. In fact nothing was safe from the attacks of the DAF which were having a very serious effect on his administrative build-up and he sought urgent air reinforcements both to protect his army and to attack the British bases and supply centres. For the army he wanted German troops, anti-tank guns, recovery vehicles, and more tanks capable of outfighting the Grants.

Nevertheless the German Commander had no immediate fears of a major breakthrough by the 8th Army although the situation would remain dangerous until the 164th Afrika Division arrived, and until a mobile reserve had been formed and the front thoroughly dug and mined for defence.

The difficulties enumerated by Rommel in this report were almost exactly the same as those listed by Kesselring and Cavallero when they were pointing out the consequences of a failure to break through quickly at El Alamein. Kesselring especially found himself in a most unsatisfactory position, being faced with demands for more air support from Rommel at a time when he had already been obliged to divert much of his strength for the renewed assault on Malta.

July 1942 was a very good month for the RAF in the Middle East and Auchinleck gave them much of the credit for stopping the enemy advance at El Alamein. On average some 500 sorties a day were flown in operations against the enemy air forces, supply lines, and in support of the army, and though the losses were high, 113 aircraft, they were not exceptional in view of the amount of work that was done, which was usually in the nature of continuous operations throughout each 24 hours. 98 enemy aircraft were destroyed during the same period and the German soldiers complained bitterly about the effect of this continuous air offensive and the inability of the Luftwaffe to protect them. Despite these successes, however, the co-operation between army and RAF was not as good as it might have been. The machinery for co-operation had been dislocated during the retreat and it was to be a long time before it was again working properly, and in the meantime close support was something of a hit and miss affair with the mistakes inevitable in such circumstances.

Much of the responsibility for this must lie with Auchinleck who removed the first essential for satisfactory co-operation when he set up a Tactical HQ at El Imayid, 40 miles west of the permanent Army and DAF HQs at

Amiriya. The situation gradually improved however, and by the end of the month the DAF was able to operate very close to the men on the ground, to the army's immense satisfaction.

The Fleet had left Alexandria during Rommel's advance when plans had been made for the destruction of the harbour and dockyard installations, but it was not long before the ships returned to the fighting. Four times in July cruisers and destroyers bombarded the Matruh area with the result that that port ceased to be of much value as a supply centre for Rommel's army, and thereby increased his already fantastic administrative difficulties.

By the end of July both armies had fought themselves to near exhaustion and on the 31st Auchinleck gave orders for the Alamein positions to be strengthened while the army rested and retrained. He was not very worried about the likelihood of an enemy attack in August but at the same time gave mid-September as the earliest date for a renewal of the British offensive, by which time new tactical problems would require solution. With the El Alamein-Qattara region being developed for defence by both sides, stalemate seemed about to set in as minefields were sown and room for the manoeuvre of armoured formations was removed.

The July fighting ended with a British success of a somewhat strange though characteristic sort. The 8th Army, though fighting in demoralizing conditions of extreme personal discomfort, heavy casualties, few gains, and constant changes of plans and tactics, nevertheless succeeded in halting and outfighting Rommel. This was a tremendous boost to British morale and with the cheering sight of the RAF constantly attacking the enemy and the knowledge that new formations were arriving, the army slowly began to recover its poise and confidence.

On the other hand there were a number of disconcerting features about the British performance in these battles. As usual the troops fought bravely on all occasions but their commanders were no more successful than hitherto. It was normal for signals to break down and for contact between formations to be lost, and there arose a sad loss of confidence between infantry and armour as a result of the Ruweisat battles where the New Zealanders felt that the 1st Armoured Division had not supported them properly.

Time and again plans were made and put into effect without sufficient care having been taken to ensure that they had a real chance of success, and attacks were frequently uncoordinated, infantry and armour fighting individually and being committed in penny packets. To some extent this was unavoidable in view of the British weakness in armour but Auchinleck, who knew the limitations of "Jock Columns" well enough, did not insist on the best use being made of such strength as he did possess. The 8th Army, therefore, continued to pay for the bad habit of employing armour and infantry as separate entities, there having been no time to train and practise the new and debateable methods of tactical co-operation that Auchinleck was trying to impose on his command.

On the German side too, the troops had fought wonderfully well under no better conditions except that they had appeared to be winning. Victory is an incalculable stimulus and it was this and their superb training and discipline that enabled them to carry on for so long, but by the end of July even the DAK was showing signs of reaching its limit. Rommel recognized this when, on the 17th, he wrote to his wife that he could not fight much longer without his front cracking, and it is this comment of the enemy commander that is the best justification for Auchinleck's persisting with his hurriedly prepared and expensive attacks. Had it succeeded any one of these might have led to a massive enemy collapse and although there would have been no prospect of exploitation Egypt would have been made utterly safe.

Chapter 17

The Arrival of Montgomery

Meanwhile, as the fate of Egypt and the Allied position in the Middle East seemed to hang in the balance, Churchill and Roosevelt were making vital decisions about the conduct of the war as a whole. Chief among them were the conclusion that there would be no cross-Channel operation in 1942, and the decision to make an allied landing in French North Africa (Operation "Torch") not later than 30th October that year. This last was bound to have important effects on the Mediterranean theatre and the Prime Minister gave increasing attention to events in that area.

The defeats of the first six months of the year had led public opinion at home and in the USA to question the performance of the Middle East High Command, and it was widely felt that Auchinleck and his subordinates were tactically outclassed by the Germans, that army/air co-operation left much to be desired, and that our tanks and anti-tank weapons were inferior to those of the enemy. These attitudes, and the need to establish closer relations with Stalin, now faced with a German offensive in the Caucasus, led Churchill to decide to visit both Moscow and Egypt. He landed in Cairo on 3rd August, and was joined there by Brooke, the CIGS, Wavell, and Smuts. His immediate concerns were two: to decide on future British policy in the theatre and to examine the conduct of the war there up to that time.

After discussions which left many questions unanswered, particularly about the northern front which had so worried successive commanders-in-chief, it was decided that the best possible contribution to the security of the Middle East would be the defeat of Rommel, the recapture of Cyrenaica, and an advance into Tripolitania. Auchinleck agreed with this conclusion and repeated his confidence in the 8th Army's ability, once it had been reinforced and retrained, to smash Rommel absolutely though he emphasized that this would be impossible before the middle of September.

Churchill, however, exasperated by Auchinleck and the subordinates with whom he had surrounded himself, decided to sack him and offered his job to Brooke. Brooke refused on the grounds that he was needed as CIGS and the choice finally fell on General Sir Harold Alexander, with Gott as the commander of the 8th Army. Gott was then killed in an air crash, his death coming as a grievous blow to the army, no other commander in the desert having so gained their affection and confidence. Nevertheless, it was probably fortunate that Gott did not succeed to the army command, for there is little doubt that his influence had been important in the development of tactics which had led to many brilliant exploits but which in the sum had resulted in defeat in battle. Gott himself knew that he had served too long in the desert, and that the need was for fresh and unprejudiced leaders capable of inculcating the army with a new sense of purpose and confidence. As it transpired Montgomery, the man selected to replace him, was to prove himself a master in battle and in he and Alexander the hour most certainly produced the men.

Auchinleck was told of these changes on 8th August and offered the new Persia and Iraq Command, but this he was unable to accept, believing it to be strategically unsound, and on the 15th Alexander formally assumed command in the Middle East. Montgomery who had taken over the 8th Army on 13th August, two days before he was ordered to do so, then asked for Lieutenant-General B. G. Horrocks to come out from England to take command of XIII Corps, and Auchinleck returned to India as C.-in-C. under Wavell, who became Viceroy.

Auchinleck had then been C.-in-C. in the Middle East for 13 months, had made the "Crusader" victory possible, and had saved Egypt by his determined fighting at El Alamein. He was also much liked and greatly admired in the army, but except for his own sake there were few who were sorry to see him go, it being generally felt that a change was needed. As a battlefield commander he could be outstanding but in the later period of his command his efforts to improvize organizations and tactics while fighting was in progress had little success and caused him to lose the confidence of many of his senior officers. Often, it seemed, he had the right ideas but was as ill-advised in choosing a time to apply them as he was in choosing subordinates.

His appointment of Ritchie to command the 8th Army was understandable, although he could have taken command in person, as indeed he was to do later, but his remaining at Army Headquarters to advise Ritchie is hard to justify. By making Ritchie the Army Commander, Auchinleck undoubtedly gave himself more time to deal with other Middle Eastern problems, though perhaps not much more than he would have had if he had retained open control of the army with Ritchie as his Deputy Chief of Staff, and it is open to question whether, although Auchinleck did not directly interfere with Ritchie, there can have been much difference at first between "advice" and "orders". Later the situation changed, and it may be asked why Auchinleck did not insist on his ideas and plans being carried out when they were so much better than those of his advisers and ill-chosen subordinate commanders. All in all he was a fine and very brave man, and a commander loved by his troops, but perhaps not prepared to be as tough and ruthless with other people and their ideas as he was with himself and his own. There is no doubt, however, that Auchinleck's intervention at Matruh and in the subsequent battles at El Alamein saved the day for the 8th Army and paved the way for Montgomery's brilliant action at Alam Haifa and his later victory at El Alamein.

Alexander now gave Montgomery the task of destroying Rommel at the earliest opportunity and he set about it with vigour. His first concern was with the army's morale which was at an unsatisfactory level, the 8th Army being indeed "Brave but Baffled". The continuous retreats had not been explained and so were not understood, and with this lack of understanding in the army ran scepticism about the quality of the high command and a lack of confidence in its weapons. This situation had to be put right very quickly, Alexander's contribution being to give Montgomery a free hand in doing so and all the support and encouragement he needed. The new army commander's first move, taken very promptly, was to let it be known that there would be no more retreats, that Jock columns and other idiosyncrasies of the desert were things of the past, and that henceforth the Division would become the basic fighting formation of the army; and so successfully did he develop this argument that the army took on a new lease of life.

He also set out to impress his personality on his command with the aim of giving it fresh confidence in its leaders. He did this by a series of visit and talks, and in a relatively short time not only convinced the army of his ability to lead it to victory, but imbued it with some of his own aggressiveness of spirit and sense of purpose. His decision to set up his HQ alongside that of the DAF was another extremely important move, and showed immediate results in improved interservice co-operation.

The RAF meanwhile was fully occupied with problems of its own, though fortunately its commanders were left unchanged. Tedder and Coningham had to decide how best to divide the air effort between cover for the army and the defence of the Egyptian base areas which were now uncomfortably close to the enemy's growing air forces, and to guard against the possibility of airborne landings by Axis parachute troops on airfields and other vulnerable points. New landing grounds were another immediate need as was the creation of an airfield construction force capable of providing landing grounds during a long and rapid advance by the army. The strength of the fighter squadrons was a further source of anxiety which increased as an independent USAAF command was set up in Egypt and American replacements for the DAF squadrons declined. Eventually the allied air strength in the theatre would be greater than ever but in the meantime the DAF squadrons were well below strength, many were still armed with obsolete Hurricane Is and Tomahawks, and the American squadrons were far from battleworthy. It was the latest example of the Chiefs of Staff's habit of regarding total numbers as the equivalent of effective fighting strengths and the DAF had to work tremendously hard to maintain its operational superiority.

Alexander and Montgomery were fortunate to arrive in the Middle East when the tide was beginning to swing strongly in the British favour after the stabilization of the front at El Alamein, but in the Axis camp the situation was far from happy and friction between the allies was growing. Throughout July Rommel had complained that the supplies reaching his army were sufficient only for its daily requirements and that an unfair share of cargo space was being allotted to Italian needs, and he repeatedly asked for more German troops, albeit with little success. The main troubles were that the Axis powers lacked the shipping and sea power to ensure a steady flow of supplies and men to North Africa and that the ports of Tobruk, Bardia, and Matruh were not capable of handling the large cargoes involved. There were men and vehicles enough in Italy to satisfy many of Rommel's needs but they could not be shipped to Africa where in any case there was barely enough transport to carry those that did arrive up to the front, quite apart from the difficulties of coping with the incessant attacks of the DAF. Rommel put the blame for his parlous supply situation squarely upon his Italian allies, and Cavallero reorganized the whole administrative system for the Axis forces in Africa on a basis which might have improved matters had it had time to get into its stride before Montgomery began the offensive which was to lead him to Tripoli.

Chapter 18

Montgomery's Doctrine of War and Command, and the Battle of Alam Halfa

The new commander of the 8th Army was one of the most intensely professional officers in the British army and has favoured posterity with a clear recital of the doctrine on which he based his practice of war. His general military creed, evolved after many years of thought and study and practised as a Divisional Commander in France in 1940 and later in England between 1940–42, was founded on the beliefs that fighting was everybody's business be they commandos or cooks,, and that no one could be a successful soldier unless he was physically fit. To this end he insisted on rigorous training in his commands and ruthlessly weeded out any who fell short of the high standards he set. He would allow nothing to distract his men's attention from the business of fighting and killing the enemy and in England had cleared wives and families out of the forward areas of his command. He was also utterly opposed to any practice which savoured of a "defensive" mentality and went to great lengths to ensure that his men were imbued with a spirit of offensive action akin to his own. In his view a defensive action was only to be regarded as a step towards the mounting of a crushing counter-attack, and for this reason had preferred to plan for the defence of the UK with a light defensive screen behind which lay a powerful counter-strike force, a doctrine which was not very popular at the time.

At the same time as he developed physical and mental toughness as the corner-stones of his policy for battle, he fully recognized the complementary needs for comfort and high living standards during periods of relaxation, and made every effort to ensure that his troops were as comfortable as possible in their billets, were well fed, and had regular periods of leave.

His doctrine of command followed similar lines of robust offensive mindedness to which he added a requirement for absolute confidence between men and commanders at all levels. He required of any commander that he should have confidence in himself and his men and that he should carry out his orders wholeheartedly. He should know exactly what was required of him and his men as individuals and should never be given any task that was beyond his or their abilities.

For those with high responsibilities additional qualities were required. A senior commander should be able to do everyone else's job at least as well as they could and should insist that his plans were carried out to the letter. This meant that a commander should keep a firm grip on his subordinates, especially as operations developed in battle, and avoid anything in the nature of councils of war. Conferences, said Montgomery, were the means by which a commander gave his orders and made sure that they were understood, procrastination and uncertainty being sure to wreck the most skilful tactical plans ever made.

For an army commander the selection of subordinate commanders was of exceptional importance and if, as Montgomery claims, he spent a third of his time on it, there is no doubt that it was time well spent. Having chosen an officer for a particular job Montgomery saw that he was properly trained for it and then gave him full responsibility and backed him to the limit. He knew how important training was at high level as well as at low and acted in accordance with this belief.

For his own conduct as Army Commander Montgomery laid down yet more rules. Past victories were to be studied for the lessons they taught but were never to be used as blueprints for new actions, and it was essential to plan two battles ahead. The making of plans was the Army Commander's responsibility alone and in order to relieve him of the routine tasks of command a Chief of Staff was needed, in Montgomery's case, Brigadier F. de Guingand. The Staff existed not to plan operations but to provide the commander with information and to issue the executive orders for putting his plans into effect. The need to maintain high morale, the importance of the spiritual factor or belief in the cause for which he was fighting, and immense faith in the British soldier's ability to respond to good leadership completed Montgomery's philosophy of command in general terms, and it never let him down.

Underlying everything was the factor of morale and he spent as much effort on securing a satisfactory standard in this matter as on anything else. He knew well enough that battle success was the surest way of achieving a high level of morale in his command but until this was possible other means had to be employed. Hard work and the knowledge that the well-being and professional performance of the individual soldier were of vital importance to his superiors were essential ingredients of his policy, to which he added physical fitness and belief in a cause. Men would fight much better, he thought, if they believed in the justness of their struggle but above all if they had confidence in their own skills and those of their commanders. He applied this doctrine by insisting on the importance of thorough training and by giving units and commanders tasks suited to their particular talents. Thus one formation might be given a mobile role and another, whose skills were different, a part in a set-piece battle.

In the tactical sphere Montgomery was equally precise, the concept of what he called "balance" underlying all his actions, at least in their initial stages. Balance was a word much used by Montgomery and his own definition is to be found in his Memoirs, but the concept on which he based his actions is perhaps better described as that of the Tactical Advantage. By this is meant the occupation, by seizure or defence, of a position whose possession guarantees the retention of the initiative because the ensuing battle must be fought on grounds of one's own choice. (Cf. Slim at Kohima-Imphal.)

When he arrived in Egypt to take command of the 8th Army Montgomery had already made a general appreciation of the situation in the desert. The aim was straightforward enough, namely, the destruction of Rommel's army at the earliest opportunity and an advance into Tripolitania, but there were some other factors that also required careful consideration. If Tripoli was to be reached it was essential that Rommel be smashed at El Alamein, for if he withdrew and established himself in strength in the Jebel or at El Agheila he could pose a constant threat to any British force in Western Cyrenaica or Western Egypt, and such a condition was not to be tolerated.

Second on Montgomery's list was the need to create a mobile armoured force capable of outfighting Rommel's German armoured divisions, and for this purpose he made up his mind to give the 8th Army its own Panzerarmee in the form of an Armoured Corps of three or four armoured divisions.

His personal position, too, merited careful examination. He had somehow to restore the army's confidence in itself and in the High Command, and to establish his own position as Army Commander in the presence of a number of generals who had a great deal of desert experience whereas he had none at all. On the other hand he knew and liked Alexander and knew that the C.-in-C. would support him so long as he was successful. His lack of desert experience gave him no concern as he was sure of his professional ability and believed that so long as he planned correctly he would win.

In his books Montgomery makes no mention of the administrative position in North Africa though it is inconceivable that he did not consider it when making his appreciation. The British prospects in fact were excellent. In the Nile valley a miniature war economy had been developed, reinforcements were arriving almost daily, and the army's needs were well understood by experienced and skilful planners who had learnt a great deal from the previous year's campaigns.

Rommel, however, was in a very difficult situation. His bases at Benghazi and Tobruk were 680 and 330 miles behind the front, he was desperately short of transport, fuel, and spares, and while Malta held out no improvement could be expected. As it was, with the RAF keeping up its attacks on his ports and supply lines it was only by using captured stocks that Rommel was able to maintain himself at El Alamein. He had accepted the risks inherent in over-extending his administrative resources in the hope of an early breakthrough at El Alamein in July, and when this failed it was not long before a difficult situation deteriorated into one of very real danger.

When Montgomery reached the 8th Army he at once began to put matters right. He removed any uncertainty about future policy by announcing that the army would stay where it was alive or dead, and ordered all plans for further retreat to be burnt. Then, in order that the army should have a focus on which to concentrate the new sense of urgency that he hoped to induce in it, he set out to establish himself as its mascot. He did this by visiting units, talking to all and sundry, and identifying himself with the interests of the common soldier. At the same time he left the army in no doubt that its new chief was a man who knew his own mind and was determined to have his own way, including victory over the redoubtable Rommel.

His arrival produced many changes at all levels although it was not until after the battle of Alam Haifa that he was able to devote much of his time to the basic reconstruction of the army. Then, however, he completed the command and staff changes he had begun as soon as he reached the desert, replacing many tired and unimaginative officers and choosing to succeed them men who thought as he did and on whom he could rely to carry out his orders without quibbling. Horrocks had already come to take over XIII Corps and in due course he was followed by Lieutenant-General Sir Oliver Leese who was given XXX Corps; the Rev. F. W. Hughes who became Chaplain-General; Kirkman as Brigadier Royal Artillery (BRA); and Robertson, Graham, and Belchem in the Administrative and Operations branches. De Guingand had already been made Chief of Staff and it was not long before Major E. T. Williams was promoted to head the Intelligence Branch of the army. Notable among the officers whom Montgomery retained were Lumsden who was given X Corps and the then Brigadier John Harding who after taking the first steps to create the new X Armoured Corps became the commander of the 7th Armoured Division.

With his own nominees firmly settled in Montgomery was able to develop his plans at a rapid pace. He stamped out the tactical heresies of Jock Columns, Brigade Groups, and "boxes" and laid down that divisions would be fought as divisions. Auchinleck who had said something similar before Gazala had then not insisted on its application, but no one doubted that Montgomery would insist, or that he would hesitate to sack any who carried out his instructions less than wholeheartedly.

Among his earliest actions had been the move of his HQ to Burg el Arab where the army and RAF could co-operate closely and where the staffs could enjoy relative peace and quiet in which to do their work. This had the indirect effect of encouraging the army, who saw things returning to normal with their commander living in reasonable comfort. While they were always glad to see their generals well forward in battle it seemed unnatural for them to live habitually as private soldiers and Montgomery's return to Burg el Arab took some of the edge out of the feeling of desperate crisis.

The retraining of the army which had been begun by Auchinleck was continued by Montgomery, especially after Alam Haifa, though on lines which accorded with his own ideas of tactics; and as more new weapons arrived he was able to build on the Alam Haifa success to restore his men's confidence in themselves and their equipment. Since 1940 the desert army had fought continuously and had had all too little training, and the first could never take the place of the second.

Meanwhile Rommel, unable to forget his July failure to break through at El Alamein, and knowing that with each day that passed his strength relative to the British was growing less, soon decided that if he was to retain the initiative he must attack before the 8th Army could gain the full benefit from the convoys due to reach Egypt in early September.

Therefore, after inspecting the El Alamein defences with some care, he concluded that the relative weakness of the British line between Alam Nayil and the Qattara Depression offered him an opportunity to break in and drive north behind Montgomery's rear, the classic German tactic in the desert. North of Alam Nayil the defences were so strong as to preclude any chance of success except for an attack in overwhelming numerical superiority, and that he did not have.

As the proposed attack involved a night march by his armour Rommel planned to begin on 30th August, in a period of the full moon. This done, he found himself shockingly short of supplies. The tonnage reaching the Axis army was far below its needs and on 22nd August he reported that if the attack was to go as planned he would require 6,000 tons of fuel and

2,500 tons of ammunition between the 25th and 30th of the month. Rome promised to do what it could but thanks to the RN and RAF only 1,500 tons of fuel had reached Tobruk by 29th August and the German commander was faced with the necessity of attacking without sufficient fuel for his tanks and other transport. As Ritchie had discovered in western Cyrenaica, the need to carry supplies 350 miles overland from Tobruk imposed very severe restrictions on the mobility of an army already seriously short of transport vehicles, and for this reason Rommel advised OKH that the offensive would have to be confined to the El Alamein area only.

He was at this time seriously ill with a stomach disorder and on 22nd August had asked for Guderian to take over the coming battle. That general was not available, however, and Rommel agreed to continue in command under medical supervision until he could go to Germany for a long cure.

As always his plan of attack was simple and bold, as it needed to be with his administrative weakness making victory entirely dependent on the rapid success of his first blow. While the 21st Italian Corps, the 164th German Division and a Parachute Battalion held his left and raided the British to make them think an attack was coming in the north, Rommel, with the DAK, 90th Light, various recce units and the Italian 20th Corps under command, would assemble in secret between Bab el Qattara and El Taqa and drive eastwards. Then, protected by the Luftwaffe, the German armour would wheel into line and face north before advancing towards the coast behind the main British positions. (Cf. Gazala, Matruh.) The Luftwaffe was ordered not to attack the British positions in the southern sector in the hope that surprise would then be complete.

Risks there were in plenty, not least among them the fact that the DAK would be required to advance 30 miles in darkness on the night of 30th August over unreconnoitred and probably mined ground, and to be ready to attack only 7 hours later. Rommel knew neither the strength of the British in the southern sector nor the extent of the defending minefields and having failed to allow enough time for these to be cleared was to find that his advance took a dangerously long time to get under way.

Nor was he to achieve the advantage of surprise, the DAF having discovered in mid-August that an enemy build-up was taking place in the south and thereafter attacking it continuously. The DAF's assault caused immense damage to enemy equipment and seriously affected the morale of both German and Italian troops long before the battle started, and by its sheer weight bore down the enemy air, despite the substantial reinforcements that had arrived since July.

While these preparations were being made Montgomery had divined Rommel's intentions exactly and made plans to counter them. He had realized as soon as he reached the desert that he would need time to prepare for a big offensive but that so long as the 8th Army held the Alam Haifa and Ruweisat Ridges, particularly the former, Rommel could achieve no decisive success as he did not have the strength to succeed in a frontal assault against the strong defences of the British right. This being so Montgomery decided to hold the ridges and to prepare to defeat the right hook against the British left that was the only course open to the enemy commander.

He proposed to do this by using artillery and mines to protect his right so that it could be held with the minimum number of troops and by holding the vital ridges in the greatest possible strength to threaten any advancing force which neglected to occupy them with complete and utter destruction. He then conceived a battle in which the German attacks were to be allowed to break up against a firm defence based on dug-in tanks, powerful artillery, and the fresh though inexperienced 44th Infantry Division, which he called up from the Delta for this purpose. Auchinleck had also arranged for a defensive position to be developed on the Alam Haifa Ridge but there the similarity ended for he had envisaged a fluid battle with armour being used in the traditional British fashion as a mobile force.

On 30th August the 8th Army still consisted of two Corps, XXX Corps under Ramsden with the 9th Australian, 1st South African, and 4th Indian Divisions under command, and the 150 Valentines of 23rd Armoured Brigade in reserve, disposed in depth to the north of the Ruweisat ridge; and Horrocks' XIII Corps to the south, with the New Zealand Division holding the Ruweisat-Bab el Qattara corner. The 7th Armoured Division provided a screen between the New Zealanders and Qarat el Himeimat and the 8th Armoured Brigade, from 10th Armoured Division, waited south-east of Alam Haifa on the flank of Rommel's probable advance. The ridge itself was held by the 44th Division with the tanks of the 22nd Armoured Brigade dug in on its western end where their guns could be united with those of the divisional artillery.

Herein lay the key to Montgomery's defensive battle. No longer were British tanks to be lured on to enemy armour and guns in prepared positions and there destroyed. If Rommel wanted a victory he would have to advance to achieve it without being able to rely on the British contributing materially to their own defeat, and Montgomery, who was far from confident of the ability of his armour to fight a successful mobile battle, gave Horrocks strict instructions to fight all the time in his prepared positions and not to allow his tanks to be mauled before they were required for his coming offensive.

His battle plan was clear and uncluttered. The New Zealand and 44th Divisions were to hold their ground while 7th Armoured gave way before the German advance and harried its flanks. Then, when the enemy turned north, they would find Gatehouse's 10th Armoured Division deployed in hull-down positions at the western end of the Alam Haifa feature and, covered by the artillery of the 44th Division, completing the barrier against which Rommel was to waste his strength. It was the Germans' turn to be drawn into a curtain of gunfire and in order to ensure that Rommel would attack rather than by-pass Alam Haifa Montgomery had a dummy map showing the ground to the east of the ridge as impassable "planted" in the desert where the enemy were sure to find it.

The DAF too had an important part to play in this battle, and after discussing the matter with Montgomery, Coningham ordered his squadrons first to plaster the enemy's forward areas, and then to keep the Luftwaffe out of the battle itself. This was no easy task for the enemy air had regained much of its strength and at the end of August had a distinct superiority in fighters, most of the British fighters being Hurricanes of early marks, whereas the Germans had many Me 109s. Otherwise the numerical strengths were roughly equal, each side having some 450 serviceable aircraft.

Rommel's advance began late on 30th August with heavy raids against the XXX Corps front while the DAK moved south and east. There his armour quickly became entangled in the XIII Corps minefields and under heavy air attack made only slow progress. Surprise and speed, the two factors on which he depended so much, were thus lost to Rommel from the outset, and when he joined the DAK at 9 a.m. on the 31st he considered calling off the attack altogether. However, after discussing the situation with Colonel Bayerlein, temporarily commanding the DAK, he decided to continue the advance with the aim of capturing the Alam Haifa ridge, where unknown to him, the 92 Grants and 34 Crusaders of the 22nd Armoured Brigade were waiting behind their 6-pounder anti-tank screen.

During the afternoon the DAK battered at the British facing them without success but when darkness fell they were still in line between Bab el Qattara and Alam Haifa ready to drive north again when Rommel gave the word.

The British in the gap between the ridges had meanwhile been rein-forced, Montgomery having waited until the enemy armour was committed at Alam Haifa, and then sending 100 Valentines from the 23rd Armoured Brigade to help Gatehouse's 10th Armoured Division.

During the night the DAF attacked the enemy's leaguers, doing great damage and preventing the soldiers from getting any rest, but early on 1st September Rommel renewed his assault. No significant gains were made, however, and about noon the Field Marshal announced his intention of going over to the defensive where he stood, an important factor influencing this decision being the shortage of fuel and his inability to bring more forward.

By this time Montgomery had called up a South African and an Indian Brigade from XXX Corps and another from the 50th Division where it had been guarding rearward airfields, and had warned Freyberg to be ready to counter-attack southwards towards Himeimat with the aim of closing the minefield gap behind Rommel's armour.

The following day Rommel ordered his army to withdraw slowly to positions just beyond the British minefields. His big effort had failed, and with no chance of renewing it he decided to disengage. The reasons he gave to OKH to explain this withdrawal were the loss of surprise; delays by mines; the irregular start of his attacks; incessant bombardment from the air; and a desperate shortage of fuel. No mention was made of British tactics and his explanation would seem to have been less than the whole truth, although Montgomery gives the DAF the credit for preventing a resumption of the attack on 2nd September by its attacks on Tobruk the previous night which cut off the supply of petrol to the enemy's mobile forces.

Montgomery was now pressed by his armoured commanders to lose his tanks in a counter-attack against the retreating Germans. He resisted this temptation, which had never been part of his plan, on the grounds that the army was in no condition to engage in a mobile battle with the still powerful DAK, but he did order the New Zealand attack to close the minefields to go in on the night of the 3rd/4th September, with the 7th Armoured Division coming up from the south to help bar any escape routes.

The New Zealanders and the 132nd Infantry Brigade duly advanced but when after three days' sharp fighting they had made little progress and had failed to gain their objectives Freyberg, seeing nothing to be gained from leaving his men in very exposed positions, asked Montgomery to call the attack off.

Thus the main battle ended with the Germans beaten off and the British positions south of El Alamein still essentially intact although the enemy were not completely cleared from the southern end of the defenders' minefields. This apparently was not displeasing to Montgomery who was more than ready to leave the enemy in some strength on his southern front while he prepared a major attack of his own in the north. For this reason he overruled

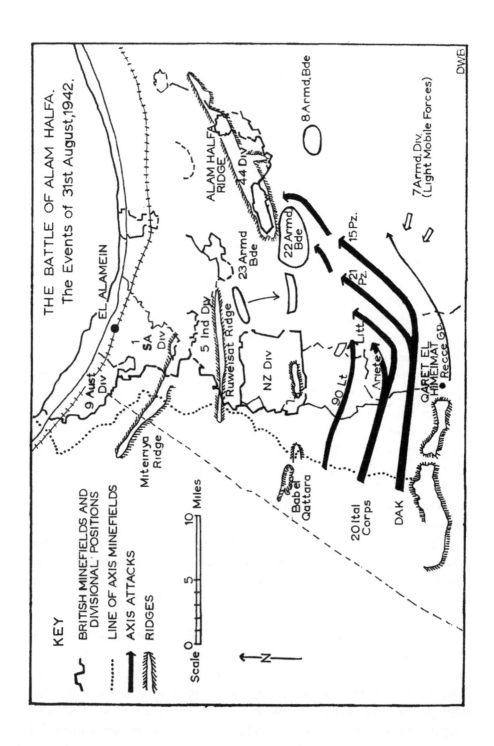

THE BATTLE OF ALAM HALFA.
The Events of 31st August, 1942.

KEY

BRITISH MINEFIELDS AND
DIVISIONAL POSITIONS

LINE OF AXIS MINEFIELDS

AXIS ATTACKS

RIDGES

Scale 0   5   10
              Miles

EL ALAMEIN

9 Aust Div

1 SA Div

5 Ind Div

Miteirya Ridge

Ruweisat Ridge

NZ Div

23 Armd Bde

22 Armd Bde

ALAM HALFA RIDGE

44 Div

8 Armd Bde

7 Armd Div
(Light Mobile Forces)

15 Pz.

21 Pz.

90 Lt

Litt.

Ariete

20 Ital Corps

DAK

Bab el Qattara

QARET EL HIMEIMAT

Recce Gp.

DW⁶

a request by Horrocks to seize the high ground at Himeimat, preferring to leave that vantage point in enemy hands as part of the deception plan for his big attack at El Alamein.

Coningham was no less pleased than Montgomery with the success of the battle which in the air was a great victory for the DAF. They had beaten down Kesselring's attempts to protect Rommel's army and had done untold damage to the equipment and morale of the enemy troops by their continuous onslaught. With the 8th Army in well-defined defensive positions the DAF had found itself at liberty to attack anything that moved and made excellent use of the opportunity. The encouragement thus given to the army was immeasurable and inter-service goodwill reached a new high level.

For its importance Alam Haifa was not a costly battle. Rommel lost altogether 2,910 men killed, wounded, and missing; 55 guns; and 49 tanks; and Montgomery 1,750 men, 67 tanks, and 15 guns. 41 enemy aircraft were destroyed and 68 British. It is important to remember, however, that whereas the 8th Army was enjoying very rapid reinforcement the loss of 49 tanks was a very heavy blow indeed to the Panzer-armee where replacements were very few and far between.

The battle of Alam Haifa was chiefly important because a major German thrust had been effectively halted, and the 8th Army and the DAF had jointly won an easily recognizable victory which had the immensely valuable results of restoring the army's faith in itself and the RAF, and of giving it real confidence in its new commander, who had predicted exactly the course that the battle would follow. At last it seemed that the 8th Army had found an answer to Rommel and morale rose to an unprecedented height.

It was a combined services victory in the very best sense, the land battles of 31st August to 7th September having completed the earlier work of the Navy and RAF in so weakening the enemy that his attack had had to be mounted on an inadequate administrative base.

In the tactical sphere Montgomery had ensured that the battle was fought on ground of his own choosing, and had amply demonstrated the advantages of strong central command and of concentration of force. And although XXX Corps had done little fighting it was generally known and understood that the army had fought as a whole under a comprehensive plan. (Cf. Ritchie at Gazala.)

There is no doubt whatever that it was a great personal success for the new Army Commander, and the argument that Montgomery fought on a plan made by Auchinleck has little substance. Quite apart from his orders to De Guingand to burn all existing plans, Montgomery was never a man to copy another's ideas, being supremely convinced of his own ability and determined to act according to his own beliefs. That Auchinleck appreciated the importance of the Alam Haifa area and proposed to fight there is also beyond question but the manner in which the battle was finally fought was all Montgomery. It was his decision alone that led to the 44th Division being used to hold the Alam Haifa ridge in strength and to the armour being fought from fixed positions, a method hitherto unknown in the 8th Army; and it was his firm control that saw the battle fought by divisions and not by Brigade Groups. It has already been remarked that Auchinleck's plan, by contrast, provided for a fluid defensive battle in the Ruweisat-Alam Haifa region.

Criticism of Montgomery's failure to counter-attack across Rommel's line of retreat after 3rd September would similarly seem to take too little note of the strategic situation and of the condition of the army, as well as the fact that the attempts by the New Zealand and 44th Divisions to close the minefield gaps had been unsuccessful. Moreover with "Torch" due to begin at the end of October it was important both to prevent Rommel from concentrating his strength by a retreat to El Agheila, and to force him to continue to fight where he was at the end of long and difficult lines of communication and supply.

At the same time the 8th Army was still badly in need of training and reorganization and in no shape to start a major offensive for which the administrative preparations were themselves incomplete. The DAK had been badly hit at Alam Haifa but it was nowhere near the end of its effectiveness, and among its tanks were many that were far superior to any that the British could put into the field. In addition, Montgomery's reformed X Corps was not ready for battle and he was determined that nothing should be done which might reduce the chances of winning a decisive victory in the near future. Had he believed on 3rd September that his army was capable of delivering an annihilating blow at Rommel he might well have acted differently but as in the strategical and tactical circumstances of the time anything less was unacceptable he stood firm in his existing positions.

From the Axis view point Alam Haifa simply emphasized the significance of Rommel's failure to pause and consolidate after the capture of Tobruk or even on the Egyptian frontier. As he advanced more and more aircraft were diverted from their attacks on Malta to cover his army, and when that island recovered its offensive power Rommel was immediately in difficulty. With his front some hundreds of miles from his bases, and these impossible of supply, while the British on short lines were building up rapidly, it was only a matter of time before a precarious supply situation declined into one of acute danger. (Cf. Ritchie, January 1942.) Perhaps after all the loss of Tobruk and the retreat to El Alamein were blessings in disguise to the British, Kesselring being right when, after the capture of Tobruk, he wanted to halt the German advance and concentrate on the reduction of Malta. As it was, Hitler chose to back Rommel and Malta survived.

Chapter 19

The Battle of El Alamein (1)—The Plans

The Alam Haifa victory had two particular results for General Montgomery. It confirmed his position as a commander who could win against Rommel, with all that that implied for the confidence and morale of his army, but it also imposed a delay on the preparations that he and Alexander were making for a new British offensive.

These preparations had been going forward since early August, it being essential to hold Rommel in Egypt while the "Torch" landings were taking place in Algeria, but in view of the fortnight's hold-up in training and re-equipment caused by Alam Haifa, Montgomery and Alexander decided to wait until the last possible moment before attacking. Two factors influenced this decision, the putting back of "Torch" until 4th November, and the need to wait for a moonlight period. This last was especially important as a night assault by infantry was the only sure and speedy way of breaking through the minefields and defended localities with which Rommel was developing his front.

Churchill, becoming increasingly anxious about "Torch", pressed for the offensive to start at the end of September but Alexander, mindful of the need for thorough preparation, supported Montgomery's decision that the full moon period of October was the earliest possible time if success was to be assured, and D-Day was finally set for 23rd October. This date had the advantage of being within 14 days of the "Torch" landings so that even if things went badly for the 8th Army, at the end of the period for which Montgomery estimated the battle would last Rommel would find himself threatened from two sides.

The objects of the El Alamein offensive were two-fold. There was the immediate military need to destroy Rommel before he could retreat to a strong position at El Agheila, and there were the important political advantages to be gained from victory. First among these came the need to persuade the French not to oppose "Torch", and an allied success in Egypt was the argument most likely to induce them to come in on the winning side. The other considerations were the needs to encourage the Russians and other allies, to raise civilian morale at home, and to demonstrate to the uncommitted nations where ultimate victory was certain to lie. One other possible consideration perhaps was the knowledge that El Alamein was likely to be the last all-British victory in the German war, a victory that was badly needed if British as distinct from allied prestige was to be restored.

Montgomery meanwhile had resumed his reorganization of the 8th Army and in September 1942 was at last able to introduce his own tactical theories and techniques of command, in which he was greatly helped by the arrival of 300 Sherman tanks from the USA. It was at this time too that he completed the selection of his senior officers, bringing Leese to command XXX Corps and Kirkman to join the army staff as BRA.

On the other side of the minefields Rommel gave little thought to another strategic withdrawal, although Alexander was for a long time fearful that he might fall back to Matruh or Solium and thus shorten his communications with Benghazi by more than 200 miles. Rommel may have decided in any case that with a still powerful army it was as well for him to fight at El Alamein as it had been for Auchinleck and Montgomery, besides which Hitler was in no mood to countenance strategic retreats. Furthermore there was always the chance that he would be able to fight off the British attack, and he set about the task of creating a very strong position between the sea and the Qattara Depression. Here both flanks were secure and the whole history of the desert war had shown how armoured thrusts had collapsed against firmly manned infantry and anti-tank guns. His fuel supplies were still extremely precarious and a great worry but in a defensive battle even these would be less of an anxiety than in an attack.

Apart from the shortage of petrol his main worries were the fighting ability of the Italians and the scale of the British air attack. The air he could do little about beyond asking the Luftwaffe, itself embarrassed by a lack of fuel, for the greatest possible support, but he disposed his troops so that the line was held alternately by Germans and Italians in the hope of securing greater stability. Even then he was not entirely happy. Lacking fuel and really large numbers of tanks it was impossible to achieve rapid concentrations of armour over the long distances involved and to create an armoured force to be held in reserve, and he was obliged to spread his armoured divisions along the whole front with many tanks undesirably close to the forward positions. At this time 15th Panzer, 90th Light and the Littorio supported the northern sector and 21st Panzer and the Ariete Divisions the southern.

With his defensive plans set in motion Rommel left for Germany to undergo medical treatment and the Axis command devolved upon General Stumme.

Three problems faced Montgomery at this juncture. He had to discover first how to blow a hole in Rommel's defences, secondly how to push X Corps through it, and thirdly how to destroy the Axis army before it could escape westward in effective strength.

His first plan, made in September, was for simultaneous attacks on both flanks with the main thrust in the north where XXX Corps would blast two gaps in the defences through which X Corps would drive to place itself across Rommel's L.-of-C. This would force Rommel to attack X Corps with his own armour which would presumably be destroyed. (Cf. "Crusader".) In the south XIII Corps would meanwhile mount diversionary operations while holding the 7th Armoured Division ready for a destructive pursuit.

The main attack was to go in slightly to the right of centre thus creating opportunities for flanking moves to right or left and giving greater flexibility than a heavy blow in the south which had a left hook as its only possible development.

It was an excellent plan but Montgomery discarded it on 6th October as being too ambitious for his still partly-trained army, and because he had no intention of risking failure by giving his formations tasks which might be beyond their powers.

His second plan, on which the battle was finally fought, was very different. Under cover of an elaborate deception plan designed to lead the enemy into believing that a typical southern swing was to be made by XIII Corps, XXX Corps would drive two corridors through the Axis positions in the north. X Corps would then move through these corridors and establish itself in a position from which it could cover the XXX Corps infantry as it set about the methodical destruction of the infantry divisions which held Rommel's defences together. The key to the battle lay in getting X Corps quickly into the open country beyond the German minefields where it could protect XXX Corps and draw the enemy tanks into counter-attacks on itself.

This plan involved certain departures from established desert practice. Hitherto the policy of both sides had been to destroy the enemy's armour first and then his infantry, an unsound practice in Montgomery's opinion in view of the German superiority in mobile warfare, an advantage which he was at pains to reduce. He believed that the way to defeat Rommel was again to force him to weaken himself in attacks against the British armour securely established on ground of his, Montgomery's, choice, while XXX Corps set about the systematic destruction of the enemy infantry and thus removed the backbone of the Axis army. To achieve this he proposed to drive a hole through the enemy's defensive positions through which he would pass the armour of X Corps, a manoeuvre designed to secure two advantages. In the first place, unless he was willing to accept the impossible condition of seeing his infantry destroyed Rommel would have to attack the British armour on its own ground and across his own minefields, and secondly, safe behind its armoured screen, XXX Corps could set about the task of reducing the enemy's infantry defences by the "crumbling" process. Such a plan would also enable Montgomery to make good use of his superior numbers of tanks and to obtain a degree of tactical surprise by a change in battle technique. The attack itself was to consist of a steady infantry advance under cover of darkness, the infantry clearing the anti-personnel mines but leaving the armoured formations to clear their own lanes in the antitank minefields. The choice of sector for the main breakthrough by XXX Corps was made after Williams had pointed out the alternate dispositions of the Germans and Italians and how an Italian front was likely to be the more susceptible to a heavy frontal assault.

Strategic surprise being out of the question, great efforts were made to gain tactical surprise by leading the enemy to suppose that the main attack would come in the southern sector. By using dummy vehicles and buildings to create an impression of a steady high density in the northern assembly areas and by replacing these models overnight with the real thing as the date for the attack drew near, the enemy were prevented from discovering the imminence of the assault as no sudden concentration was apparent. Other stores were camouflaged and dumped in the open desert, and as in 1940 also escaped discovery. In the southern sector the bases of the visual deception plan were the building of a dummy pipeline, and the establishment of large but incomplete concentrations of troops, stores, and vehicles, all of which could be clearly seen from the high ground at Himeimat.

Secrecy was obtained (Cf. Wavell) by a gradual stopping of leave without general orders on 21st October, by which time everyone in the army except the men in the most advanced positions had been told what was afoot and what their specific tasks would be.

When the battle started late on 23rd October the 8th Army was disposed as follows. On the right was Leese with the five infantry divisions of XXX Corps, 9th Australian, 51st Highland, 2nd New Zealand, 1st South African, and the 4th Indian; and on the left Horrocks' XIII Corps with the 50th and 44th Divisions, and the 7th Armoured Division. In the rear, waiting for room to move, was Lumsden with X Corps, consisting of the 1st and 10th Armoured Divisions, with the 8th Armoured Division in reserve. The other formations available to Montgomery included three allied infantry brigades

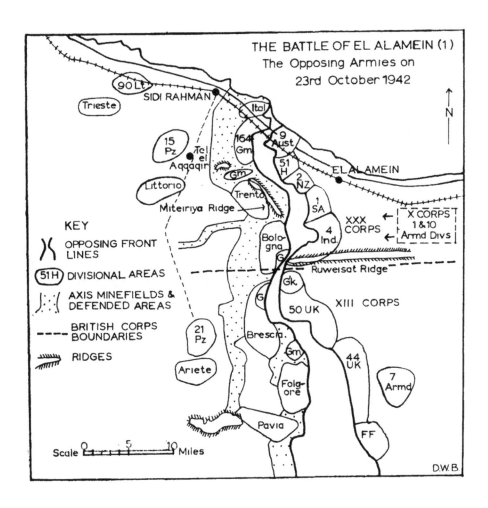

and two additional armoured brigades. Altogether he had some 200,000 men; 470 Grants and Shermans, and 700 British cruisers and I tanks; 100 American 105 mm SP guns, 832 25-pounders and 750 6-pounder anti-tank guns.

Rommel had the German 90th Light and 164th Infantry Divisions in the north with other German units and the Italian 10th and 21st Corps covering the rest of the front, supported in the north by 15th Panzer and in the south by the 21st Panzer, a total of about 90,000 men. As his main weapons he had 118 "Specials" and 100 other German tanks, and 24 88s. Most of his field artillery at this stage was Italian and nearly obsolete, and he also had 300 virtually useless Italian medium tanks.

Montgomery thus enjoyed an all round superiority of 2 : 1 in men and weapons, and with the DAF giving him absolute safety from air attack he felt strong enough, despite his army's lack of training and in many cases inexperience, to be certain of victory.

His battle orders provided for a preliminary bombardment by more than 1,000 guns after which 4 divisions from XXX Corps were to break in on a 7-mile front against parts of the 164th, Trento, and Bologna Divisions in the enemy's left centre. Four hours after the infantry attack had begun X Corps with 600 tanks was to advance in its turn along the two corridors opened by XXX Corps, clearing the remaining minefields as it went. It was hoped that the infantry would clear routes right through the enemy defences but if this had not been achieved by daylight on the 24th X Corps was ordered to fight its way, irrespective of cost, into the open country to the west. Meanwhile Horrocks' Corps was directed to attack in the southern sector and to work to hold 21st Panzer in the south and to draw enemy armour away from the northern corridors.

The task of the RAF was again twofold. By attacking enemy airfields and preventing reconnaissance Coningham intended to secure absolute air superiority and ground security by 23rd October. Then, as the battle began, he proposed to use all his bombers against the enemy guns in a counter-bombardment role after which they would co-operate in the land battle as opportunity offered. In each of these duties the DAF was hugely successful and so dominated the airspace that it was possible to maintain a standing patrol of fighters over each of the enemy's forward landing grounds.

Montgomery set up a Tactical HQ at El Alamein on 23rd October and there issued his last orders. At all costs the battle was to be kept moving, and the initiative retained; 12 days should see it finished.

Chapter 20

The Battle of El Alamein (2)—The Fighting

The battle itself was fought in three phases. Between 23rd/24th October came the Break In, which was followed in turn by the Dogfight phase, which lasted from 25th October to 1st November, and Operation "Supercharge", which began on 2nd November and ended with the pursuit of the beaten Rommel.

At 9.40 p.m. on 23rd October Montgomery's guns opened their counter-battery bombardment and at 10 p.m. when the barrage lifted to the enemy's forward positions four divisions of XXX Corps began to advance.

The Australian and Highland Divisions, directed on Kidney Ridge, soon forced open a gap just north of the Miteiriya feature, and the New Zealanders, with the 9th Armoured Brigade under command, and the South Africans did likewise two miles to the south. Elsewhere an Australian Brigade demonstrated north of Tel el Eisa and the 4th Indian Division made heavy raids on the positions of a German parachute battalion at the western end of the Ruweisat Ridge. These were important feints but it was in the south that the chief diversionary attack was made, XIII Corps endeavouring to cut two holes in the minefields north of Himeimat and to tie down the 21st Panzer Division.

At first the infantry attacks in the northern sector went well but against stiffening resistance the advance slowed down and although many of the corps' first objectives were reached daylight came with the minefields still unbroken and infantry and armour jammed tight in the corridors under heavy fire and counter-attack. An innate weakness of the plan was that with a huge assault force so tightly packed, manoeuvre was impossible; any unforeseen check would have the effect of throwing the whole offensive somewhat out of gear, which was precisely what had happened when Montgomery awoke on the 24th. Not only had the enemy troops resisted with uncommon determination but their defensive system had been found to be much deeper than anyone at Army Headquarters had expected.

In the northern corridor the 51st Highland Division, delayed by the need to deal with a strongly held defended locality, had held up the 1st Armoured

Division; while in the southern corridor, where the New Zealanders had reached the Miteiriya Ridge, the 10th Armoured Division came to a halt in front of an anti-tank screen, and remained east of the crest.

Thus neither corridor had been cleared sufficiently for the armour to pass through to the rear of Rommel's defence system, and Montgomery sent for Lumsden and repeated his orders for X Corps to fight its way clear if the infantry were checked.

During the day the British attacks continued and by evening the 2nd Armoured Brigade of the 1st Armoured Division had broken clear only to be counter-attacked by 15th Panzer exactly as Montgomery had hoped, his tanks occupying the attention of the enemy armour while their infantry was destroyed. The 10th Armoured Division, however, remained stuck fast at Miteiriya and Gatehouse, supported by his Corps Commander, Lumsden, sought permission to disengage until the infantry and engineers had made another attempt to clear a way through the defences on that part of the front. Leese did not agree with this suggestion and De Guingand called him and Lumsden to a conference at Montgomery's HQ at 3.30 a.m. on the 25th. Gatehouse's argument was that it would be suicidal for his tanks to force their way out across the Miteiriya Ridge and uncleared minefields covered by anti-tank batteries, and that such an attempt would end in the destruction of a major part of Montgomery's so-called Corps de Chasse. The Army Commander would have none of this and in a stormy telephone interview insisted that the 10th Armoured Division continue its advance. Anyone who disagreed would be removed. The chastened Lumsden then returned to his own HQ and Gatehouse resumed his attacks. In these his division lost heavily but by 8 a.m. one of its armoured brigades was a mile beyond the minefields and in touch with the 2nd Armoured Brigade on its right, and the other was making good progress.

Far away to the south Horrocks' Corps was fulfilling its main task in holding down 21st Panzer, but neither the 7th Armoured nor the 44th Divisions achieved more than local penetration, and on the 25th Montgomery ordered their advance to halt rather than incur heavy casualties, especially to Harding's 7th Armoured Division.

The second phase of the battle, Montgomery's "dogfight" was now well under way. This was the period in which the enemy infantry were supposed to be methodically destroyed by the crumbling attacks of XXX and XIII Corps while the Panzers broke themselves to pieces against Lumsden's armour. This plan, however, went rather astray, chiefly because X Corps was not properly clear of the defence system, and although it had no substantial

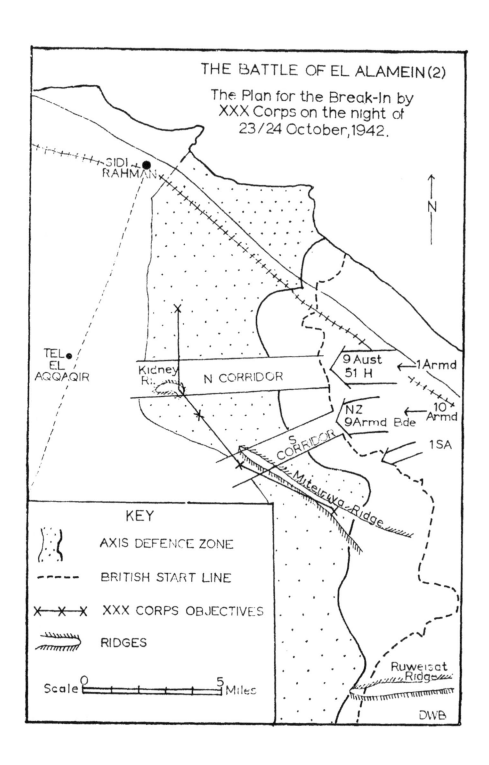

THE BATTLE OF EL ALAMEIN (2)

The Plan for the Break-In by
XXX Corps on the night of
23/24 October, 1942.

N

SIDI
RAHMAN

TEL
EL
AQQAQIR

Kidney
R.

N CORRIDOR

9 Aust
51 H

1 Armd

NZ
9 Armd Bde

10
Armd

1 SA

S CORRIDOR

Miteirwa Ridge

KEY

AXIS DEFENCE ZONE

------ BRITISH START LINE

X—X—X XXX CORPS OBJECTIVES

RIDGES

Scale 0   5 Miles

Ruweisat Ridge

DWB

success 15th Panzer was able to attack the 51st Highland Division at Kidney Ridge as well as the 1st Armoured Division.

By noon on the 25th, Montgomery, having seen the inability of the 50th Division and the New Zealanders to make progress at Munassib and in the southern corridor decided to shift the weight of the crumbling operations to the northern part of the front, and ordered the Australians to attack the enemy in the salient between the coast and the northern corridor while 1st Armoured Division moved westwards with the intention of getting astride Rommel's communications along the Sidi Rahman track. Sidi Rahman itself was the nodal point for all the Axis supply routes in the area and of obvious importance.

On the night of the 25th/26th the Australians attacked and made some headway, as did the New Zealand and South African Divisions in front of the Miteiriya Ridge, but apart from the 7th Motorized Brigade which established itself on Kidney Ridge, the 1st Armoured Division was unable to advance and the Master Plan suffered another check.

Throughout the 26th XXX Corps continued to attack but its thrusts were becoming weaker and Montgomery spent the day in his caravan thinking about his next moves. The situation was by no means unsatisfactory although it was not as good as he had hoped and predicted. His armour, though still not fully clear of the enemy defences, was in positions from which it could protect the infantry and deal with German counter-attacks which after all was its main function at this stage, and he still had 800 tanks and plenty of ammunition. His infantry meanwhile, though the break-ins were still ringed by Rommel's anti-tank screens, was gradually breaking up the enemy divisions by limited attacks on narrow fronts. In the process, however, XXX Corps had suffered some dislocation and the momentum of the offensive had fallen away. Casualties too had been heavy, particularly in the 51st, South African, and New Zealand Divisions, and with reserves for the Commonwealth divisions running short Montgomery decided that evening to withdraw Freyberg's men from the line to reform in readiness for another large scale attack. As the New Zealanders were pulled out the South Africans took over the southern corridor while the 4th Indian Division, now under XIII Corps control, assumed responsibility for the old South African section of the front.

By this time, Rommel, hastening back from Germany, had returned to the battlefield, and on the 26th he called the 21st Panzer north to the Kidney Ridge area which he attacked next day with some 150 tanks. This attack was beaten off by the Highlanders and the 1st Armoured Division with the loss of 50 tanks, a heavy blow to the German commander. Nevertheless he was preparing to renew the attempt next day, 28th October, when the DAF attacked his assembly area and destroyed his concentration.

Montgomery, however, had now made up his mind and while the Germans were battering at Kidney Ridge had issued his orders for the next stage in the battle. With the whole of the DAK facing the northern corridor no breakout there was possible and he decided to develop the Australian attacks of the 26th into a major thrust which would allow XXX Corps to drive along the road and railway axes to Sidi Rahman while X Corps guarded its left. XIII Corps was to adopt a defensive attitude but maintain pressure by a series of patrols and raiding operations. This reduction of XIII Corps' responsibility enabled Montgomery to transfer the 7th Armoured Division to Leese's command together with three infantry brigades, and he also called forward a reserve brigade of the 51st Division so that the whole of Morshead's Australian Division could be concentrated for its big attack. 21st Panzer having already moved north, it was possible to transfer the 7th Armoured Division without endangering the 8th Army's left flank.

Rommel meanwhile had guessed what was in Montgomery's mind and on the night of the 28th/29th he moved the 90th Light Division to Sidi Rahman to deal with the Australian attack, thus concentrating all his reliable armour and mobile forces in the northern quarter of the front. It also meant that the corset, whose strings had been loosened by the move of 21st Panzer, was now completely undone, and that German formations no longer held the Italians together. This was pointed out to Montgomery by McCreery, who was on a visit to the front with Alexander, and on the 29th the Army Commander ordered the breakout attack, Operation "Supercharge", to go in on an axis just to the north of the original northern corridor where the line was held by Italians alone. Some such modification of the breakout plan had been implied by the success of the Australian attack towards the coast. There Morshead had actually driven behind the 164th Division and reached the coast road between Tel el Eisa and Sidi Rahman before being counter-attacked by the 90th Light, and though he had then been forced to halt, his drive was effective in preventing a southerly regrouping of that part of Rommel's mobile force, which suited Montgomery excellently.

The plan for Operation "Supercharge" provided for the Australians to continue their attacks in the coastal sector and to occupy the 90th Light while the New Zealand Division, with the 9th Armoured and 151st and

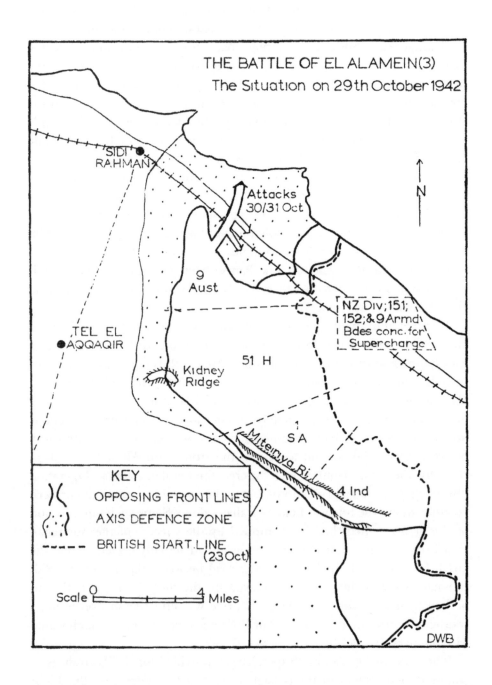

THE BATTLE OF EL ALAMEIN(3)
The Situation on 29th October 1942

Attacks
30/31 Oct

9
Aust

NZ Div; 151;
152; & 9 Armd
Bdes conc. for
Supercharge

SIDI
RAHMAN

TEL EL
AQQAQIR

Kidney
Ridge

51 H

Miteiriya Ri.

S A

4 Ind

N

KEY
OPPOSING FRONT LINES
AXIS DEFENCE ZONE
BRITISH START LINE
(23 Oct)

Scale 0 — 4 Miles

DWB

152nd Infantry Brigades under command, broke in on the night of the 31st October/1st November and cut a path by which the 1st, 7th, and 10th Armoured Divisions could reach the open desert. With the armour in the clear the DAK was to be brought to battle and smashed while armoured car regiments crossed the enemy's supply routes and isolated him by cutting off his fuel supplies. This was a definite change in tactics. The enemy had taken such a hammering that Montgomery was now prepared to use his armour in a mobile battle with the aim of destroying the DAK and getting across the L.-of-C. of the whole of Rommel's army left in Egypt. Without armoured support there could be no hope for the enemy infantry still in the Alamein positions, and these could be dealt with later.

The Australian Division duly attacked on the night of the 30th/31st and reached the coast, thereby cutting off the 164th Division. They were then counter-attacked by Rommel and after some very heavy fighting most of the Germans managed to fight their way out of the trap. This action, however, fully occupied both 90th Light and 21st Panzer, and when the New Zealanders advanced at 0100 hrs. on 2nd November, "Supercharge" having been postponed for 24 hours because of the disorganization of X and XXX Corps, they were not at first met by German tanks. By dawn that morning they had opened a 12-mile gap in the enemy defences and X Corps was clear of the minefields though not yet out in the open in strength. The break out had not been easy, however, and the 9th Armoured Brigade had lost 87 tanks in driving through the enemy anti-tank screen. Nevertheless it was able to hold open the gap for the 1st Armoured Division to deploy.

Later in the day the 1st and 10th Armoured Divisions clashed with the DAK and Rommel near Tel el Aqqaqir and were again disorganized and brought to a halt, the German commander and his 90 tanks fighting a brilliant action against greatly superior numbers. Meanwhile the 51st Highland Division supported by tanks had broken out of the salient in a south-westerly direction and by dark the 7th Motorized Brigade was beyond the Sidi Rahman track.

On 3rd November little progress was made although the 1st Armoured Division strove desperately to break through at Tel el Aqqaqir and the 51st Division tried to outflank the enemy on the south. The armoured cars, however, had been doing great damage in the Axis rear where retreating enemy columns, mostly Italians, had been reported by the DAF. Rommel, who had considered a withdrawal on the 29th but discarded the idea because he had no transport to carry back the Italian infantry, had now begun to retreat in earnest, making use of the respite won for him by the sturdy

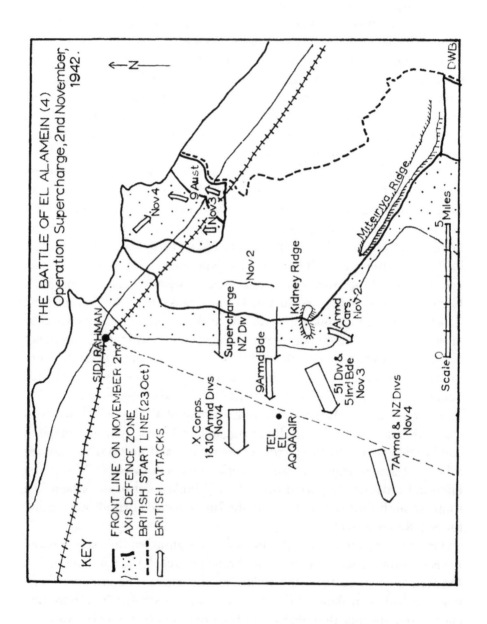

THE BATTLE OF EL ALAMEIN (4)
Operation Supercharge, 2nd November, 1942.

N

KEY

FRONT LINE ON NOVEMBER 2nd
AXIS DEFENCE ZONE
BRITISH START LINE (23 Oct)
BRITISH ATTACKS

SIDI RAHMAN

9 Aust
Nov 4
Nov 3

Kidney Ridge
Nov 2
Armd Cars
Nov 2

Supercharge
NZ Div

9 Armd Bde

Miteiriya Ridge

X Corps.
1&10 Armd Divs
Nov 4

51 Div &
5 Inf Bde
Nov 3

TEL
EL
AQQAQIR

7 Armd & NZ Divs
Nov 4

Scale
0   5 Miles

DWB

defence at Tel el Aqqaqir, and hoping to be able to make a stand at Fuka on the 4th. Hitler, however, refused to authorize a retreat and Rommel felt obliged to cancel his orders for withdrawal, though he immediately sent an ADC to OKH to explain the realities of the situation. Hitler's reply came on the 5th with permission for Rommel to act as he thought best by which time it was too late for much to be saved though Rommel had ordered the retreat to be resumed at 3.30 p.m. on the 4th. The extent to which the German retreat was curtailed by Hitler's intervention is hard to calculate but there is little doubt that the 8th Army failed to make the best use of what now appears to have been a golden opportunity.

Montgomery had given orders for the pursuit on 3rd November but it was not until the morning of the 5th that it got under way by which time Rommel's disengagement was going well. However, his anti-tank screen had by then been pushed northwards and a wide gap was open for X Corps to drive round and across his line of retreat. XIII Corps, in the meantime, had formed itself into mobile columns and was clearing up in the southern sector where 4 Italian divisions without food, fuel, or vehicles had been left to surrender by the Germans.

Montgomery's plan was to cut off the enemy retreat by sending the New Zealanders and armour to block the coast road at the Fuka and Matruh bottlenecks. Unfortunately these moves were not successful, Freyberg's division becoming entangled with the supply convoys of X Corps and advancing only 20 miles on 3rd November. X Corps was now given the 1st and 7th Armoured Divisions and the New Zealand Division and told to develop the pursuit while XXX Corps dealt with the enemy between El Alamein and Matruh. The advance moved on again on the 5th but when the 4th Armoured Brigade reached the coast after some fighting near Fuka very few enemy were found. A left hook by the 10th Armoured Division on Daba had a similarly disappointing result and the division went on a further ten miles before coming to a halt before a dummy minefield laid long before by the British. Harding then took the 7th Armoured Division on a wide sweep along the southern scarp only to run into the trucks of the New Zealand Division and later halt in his turn before another dummy minefield.

Montgomery's last big trap, at Baggush, closed on 6th November and again caught little or nothing. He had made no alteration in his orders after the enemy's escapes on the 4th and 5th, and that night heavy rain turned the area south of Matruh into a bog and stopped any hopes of a rapid cross-desert pursuit by his armour, Rommel escaping with 10 tanks and some

10,000 German troops. Many of the British commander's left hooks had been directed too close to the enemy's front and landed too late to catch his rapid retreat along the coast road. For reasons best known to himself Montgomery had decided against a long cross-desert drive to cut off Rommel with time and space to spare, and Charing Cross, perhaps the best objective of all was not reached until the enemy had made good their escape. For his part Rommel could never find a satisfactory explanation for what he always regarded as an unusually hesitant and cautious pursuit.

Although Rommel was not annihilated at El Alamein it was still a decisive victory for British arms and a second personal success for General Montgomery. He obtained tactical surprise at the start and again in "Supercharge"; by keeping up his attacks he retained the initiative throughout; and he exercised a degree of personal control without which the offensive might have degenerated into stalemate. He secured an admirable degree of co-operation with the RAF and created in his army a determination and offensive spirit without which they might never have won through the bitter battles of the "dogfight" period.

On the other hand he was fortunate that Rommel stood and fought as long as he did, perhaps as a result of his absence in Germany until the 26th October, perhaps because the British failures to break out in the early stages encouraged him to fight on, and less likely, because of Hitler's influence. Nevertheless in an attrition battle Montgomery was bound to win, and a great victory, even if costly, was what he, Churchill, and the British nation then needed above all else. His greatest problem was to ensure that Rommel did not withdraw before the battle began, and in that he was successful.

He was fortunate too that Rommel was away from the front when the British attack was launched and that General Stumme was unused to the desert. Stumme's opportune death and the capture of Von Thoma, the commander of the DAK were other instances of his good luck though they cannot have influenced the outcome of the battle. Essentially, however, it was a contest between Montgomery and Rommel with the latter suffering all the disadvantages attendant upon difficulties of supply and enemy superiority in numbers and in the air.

In the conduct of the battle itself Montgomery may perhaps be criticized on two counts: the decision to pass his armoured corps through XXX Corps on the second day, and in his management of the pursuit. The battle did not in fact go exactly according to plan, few battles ever do, and it is probably true that he gave his armour in particular too big a task in the initial break-through operations, and in his orders for the pursuit on 3rd November, though this last may be questioned. Certainly Lumsden and Gatehouse had much to commend their requests for further infantry attacks if X Corps was to remain as Montgomery had christened it, a Corps de Chasse, but he was the Army Commander and as such perfectly right to insist on his orders being carried out. It may be too, that Montgomery underestimated the infantry superiority required to break quickly through a strongly prepared defensive position. Certainly he did not possess the 5 : 1 advantage in numbers that was to be fundamental to so many successful attacks against prepared defences later in the war.

There is no doubt, however, that the decision to superimpose X Corps on XXX Corps in the corridors led to congestion and muddle when the infantry were checked, and it is worth asking whether it might not have been better to give Leese more armour to support his infantry rather than to use the Corps de Chasse as a bludgeon and so blunt it (cf. O'Connor and 7th Armoured Division at Tobruk in 1940), or to have placed the necessary force of infantry and armour under one Corps commander. Alternatively, insofar as Rommel's armour beat itself to death in unsuccessful counter-attacks, Montgomery's plan worked, and it was no small feat to break through the heavily defended El Alamein positions. There being no room or scope for manoeuvre, a frontal assault for which a club was required was unavoidable and he had the determination to wield his club until his ends had been achieved. A wide breakthrough was out of the question and with Rommel able to concentrate quickly against the narrow holes punched in his line a battering ram tactic was the only one open to Montgomery if his general plan was to succeed and his armour reach positions from which it could protect the infantry engaged in "crumbling."

His concept of an armoured Corps de Chasse is another matter altogether. X Corps was hardly the equivalent of the DAK as was Montgomery's original idea and he used it in a manner different from that implied in the name he gave it. Certainly it was far from being the integrated force of tanks, guns, and infantry that Rommel and others had used with such success in Europe and North Africa. Rather does it hark back to Marlborough's cavalry arm which slaughtered the French at Ramillies and the "cavalry" charges of British tanks before Alam Haifa, for which there was no place in modern war, the "Death Ride" of the 9th Armoured Brigade in "Supercharge" being an exception. It is true that Montgomery intended to use the Corps de Chasse to destroy a retreating enemy but then by definition it would imply a rapid and concentrated drive rather than a dispersed pursuit with no chances being taken.

Montgomery has also been criticized for being unable properly to apply his concept of "balance" to the battle at El Alamein. Such criticism is misplaced, flexibility being a greater virtue in a commander than rigidity of mind though not of purpose, and was well demonstrated in the relatively static battles of 23rd October–1st November 1942.

In more fluid fighting Montgomery shows up less well, and may perhaps be criticized for not mounting a more effective pursuit after the break-out on 2nd November. He made no change in his instructions after Rommel had escaped his clutches on 4th and 5th November and though his army was desperately tired it had been winning and with huge reserves behind it was to continue to do so, and he might have done better had he ordered his armour to drive rapidly westwards. On the other hand the Corps de Chasse no longer existed in its original form on 3rd November. It had of necessity been used in pieces and reformed, and could hardly have been expected then to carry out a role of all-out pursuit, quite apart from the facts that its organization had suffered during the battle, that there was no satisfactory routeing plan, and that supplies of fuel were slow in reaching the armoured regiments. Nevertheless British superiority was so great at the time that a more determined pursuit would have paid large dividends.

Montgomery explains his caution by repeating his determination to avoid a serious setback, though how this could have occurred is hard to see as on 5th November Rommel had no more than 20 serviceable tanks, and the 8th Army several hundred. He was of course still new to the desert and probably wary of the powers of recovery of Rommel and his seasoned veterans, and in any case felt with some justice that the battle which he had planned had been fought and won. Certainly Tobruk for supplies, and the Martuba airfields for convoy protection, were regained in time for the larger plans in the Mediterranean theatre to be in no danger. One additional point of interest lies in the fact that in the closing stages it was Freyberg and not one of the armoured commanders who was given the responsibility for launching the pursuit. It may be that by this time Montgomery had little confidence in the thrustfulness of Lumsden, and it is possible that had he known then the full quality of Harding the preparations for the pursuit would have centred round the 7th Armoured Division.

The rain of 6th November was another hindrance to the pursuers, but the last word on the pursuit probably lies with Carver when he argues that once Rommel had decided to escape along the coast road no cross-desert pursuit was really likely to catch him. There is after all no evidence of a destructive pursuit since Wavell's campaign of 1940/41 when O'Connor was able to cut a corner by sending the 7th Armoured Division through to Antelat. On every other occasion in the desert the escapers had succeeded in avoiding complete destruction. It would be churlish, however, not to pay tribute to the fighting qualities of the German soldiers and the skill of their commander. They fought at El Alamein against great odds and with little prospect of success, but they fought hard and long and with great bravery and to such purpose that Montgomery was unable or unwilling to risk an all-out pursuit even when his armour had reached the open desert.

At El Alamein the 8th Army suffered 13,500 casualties and lost 150 tanks as against German losses of about 10,000 men killed, wounded, and missing, and 17,000 Italians; nearly 500 tanks, and hundreds of guns. Superficially the cost might appear to be high but 4 crack German Divisions and 8 Italian Divisions no longer existed, and Rommel fought no more great battles in North Africa.

In the air the DAF had done all that was asked of it, and as at Alam Haifa had played an indispensable part in the British victory.

Above all, however, it is to Montgomery and his army that the greatest credit must go for a victory that placed the British people firmly on the road to ultimate success. First and foremost Montgomery made his men fight, fight aggressively, and keep on fighting, and thus ensured the victory. Together with this, which was perhaps his greatest merit, lay his ability to recognize his own strengths and weaknesses, these last perhaps unconsciously, to fight within his limitations and to learn from his experiences. A victory was needed and a victory he won, and after El Alamein there was no threat to the Middle East from the west.

Chapter 21

Some Points for Further Consideration

Among all the many and varied lessons to be learnt from a study of the desert campaigns of 1940/42 the most interesting are those arising from the fundamental contrasts in style of the British and German commanders and of the tactics employed by both sides.

The Germans, with the experience of Poland, the Low Countries, and France behind them, arrived in the desert with a concept of the tactics of armoured warfare that was far superior to that of the British, and it was not until the arrival of Montgomery, who at Alam Haifa adopted tactics based on similar principles, that the British won a decisive victory over Rommel's panzer divisions.

German practice required that tanks, guns, and infantry should fight as fully integrated parts of a whole, and based their tactics on their ability to bring down a concentrated weight of fire on any chosen target, usually the enemy armour, whose destruction was the key to tactical success. Their tanks would advance and then halt and wait until the British armour attacked them, when they would retire to the protection of their anti-tank guns and fight what became in effect a tank *versus* gun battle in which the gun was usually the victor. They were fortunate in possessing in the Pak 38 50 mm anti-tank gun, the 88 mm dual purpose gun, and later the Russian 76 mm anti-tank gun, the three best anti-tank weapons in general use in the desert but they made full use of these advantages whereas until El Alamein the British consistently failed to make the best use of the numerical superiority in tanks which they normally enjoyed, certainly in the major battles. The Germans also provided their tank and anti-tank guns with High Explosive as well as Armour Piercing ammunition and it was the British failure to do likewise, combined with their bad armoured tactics, that contributed chiefly to the tactical defeats of 1941 and 1942.

The crucial factor was probably the inability of the British tanks and infantry formations to deal with the enemy's anti-tank guns, for apart from the German Specials the British tanks were not in general inferior to those of the enemy. The latter, however, because of their ability to neutralize the

British anti-tank batteries, were able to retain the tactical initiative and to draw the British armour into action in the way they wished, namely, against the concentrated fire of their tank and anti-tank guns. Because of their belief that tanks could and would be used to fight enemy tanks with little reference to other arms the British had neglected to provide their armoured regiments and anti-tank guns with anything other than armour-piercing shot, and it was not until the arrival of the 6-pounder anti-tank gun and the Grant tank, which was capable of firing high explosive, in the spring and summer of 1942, that the 8th Army had either a satisfactory anti-tank weapon or a tank capable of dealing with the enemy's anti-tank guns themselves.

The 2-pounder anti-tank gun, short of range and penetrating power and very vulnerable to enemy shell fire, was thus unable to fulfil its main task, and the 25-pounder field gun had to be pressed into service as a tank killer. In this role it was very successful but the army's artillery was unbalanced in consequence. This inefficiency of the 2-pounder meant that the British infantry formations were almost defenceless against enemy armour, and accentuated the divergence of views between infantry and armoured commanders. All too often the armour felt that it was diverted from its main task, and restricted in its ability to fight and manoeuvre by the need to protect the infantry, and the infantry that they had been deserted by the armour. Few seemed to realize that infantry, armour and artillery were fighting the same battle, and it is noticeable that when the British did fight with all arms in concert, as in O'Connor's and Montgomery's campaigns, they were successful.

For a comparison of the tanks and anti-tank guns used by the desert armies reference should be made to Appendix 8 of Volume III of the Official History, but it may be stated here that the ability of the Germans to up-armour their tanks in 1941 and after significantly increased their effectiveness. This strengthening of armour was followed by the mounting of long-barrelled 50 and 75 mm guns in some Pzkw Ills and IVs, and though these tanks, the Specials, were never present in quantity, only 33 fighting at Gazala, and 100 at Alam Haifa, they were nevertheless powerful enough to increase Rommel's armoured strength out of all proportion to their numbers. At the same time care should be taken not to over-emphasize the importance of the 88 mm, which though an excellent gun, each one being capable of fighting a tank squadron, was another weapon never present in large numbers, no more than 40 being in the desert at any one time before Alam Haifa. On the few occasions when it was used the 3.7in. AA gun showed that it could be as efficient a destroyer of tanks as the 88 mm, but the British High Command

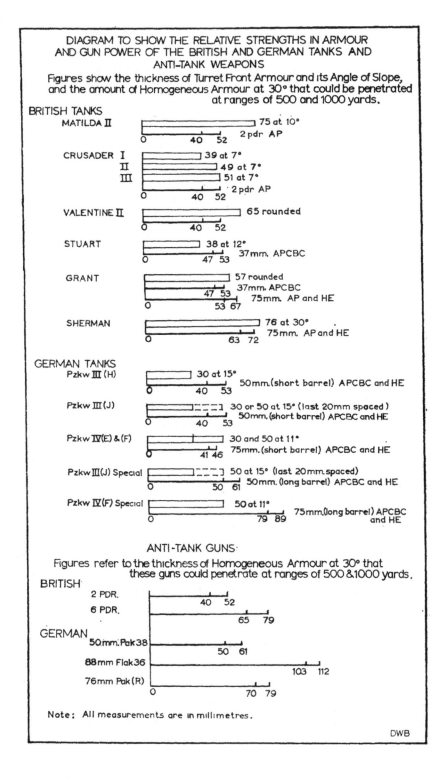

DIAGRAM TO SHOW THE RELATIVE STRENGTHS IN ARMOUR
AND GUN POWER OF THE BRITISH AND GERMAN TANKS AND
ANTI-TANK WEAPONS

Figures show the thickness of Turret Front Armour and its Angle of Slope,
and the amount of Homogeneous Armour at 30° that could be penetrated
at ranges of 500 and 1000 yards.

BRITISH TANKS

MATILDA II — 75 at 10° / 2 pdr AP — 0 40 52

CRUSADER I — 39 at 7°
II — 49 at 7°
III — 51 at 7° / 2 pdr AP — 0 40 52

VALENTINE II — 65 rounded — 0 40 52

STUART — 38 at 12° / 37mm. APCBC — 0 47 53

GRANT — 57 rounded / 37mm. APCBC 47 53 / 75mm. AP and HE 53 67 — 0

SHERMAN — 76 at 30° / 75mm. AP and HE 63 72 — 0

GERMAN TANKS

Pzkw III (H) — 30 at 15° / 50mm.(short barrel) APCBC and HE — 0 40 53

Pzkw III (J) — 30 or 50 at 15° (last 20mm spaced) / 50mm.(short barrel) APCBC and HE — 0 40 53

Pzkw IV(E) & (F) — 30 and 50 at 11° / 75mm.(short barrel) APCBC and HE — 0 41 46

Pzkw III(J) Special — 50 at 15° (last 20mm.spaced) / 50mm.(long barrel) APCBC and HE — 0 50 61

Pzkw IV(F) Special — 50 at 11° / 75mm.(long barrel) APCBC and HE — 0 79 89

ANTI-TANK GUNS

Figures refer to the thickness of Homogeneous Armour at 30° that
these guns could penetrate at ranges of 500 & 1000 yards.

BRITISH

2 PDR. — 40 52

6 PDR. — 65 79

GERMAN

50.mm. Pak 38 — 50 61

88mm Flak 36 — 103 112

76mm Pak (R) — 0 70 79

Note: All measurements are in millimetres.

DWB

decided that it was of more use in its primary role and kept the few that they had to defend vital base areas against air attack.

The real reasons for the German successes were their use, in the panzer divisions, of integrated forces of tanks, anti-tank guns and artillery; their correct appreciation of the importance of fire power; their system of training which enabled new troops to be introduced into the army without a serious loss of efficiency; and the British habits of fighting tanks with tanks, using them in "cavalry charges", and allowing their main armoured forces to be dispersed and then committed to battle in penny packets. The integration of all arms in the enemy formations also meant that tactical dispersion was less dangerous than in the British army where if the armour was drawn into battle the infantry were likely to be exposed to heavy attack without the means of defending themselves.

To a certain extent the need to protect the infantry can be made to account for the British armour being fought dispersed rather than concentrated but this was essentially the result of a weakness in command during the period of Auchinleck's term as Commander-in-Chief, which compares badly with that of the Germans during the same period.

Throughout the desert war Rommel fought with his army firmly under his personal control and he always insisted on the course of action he laid down being followed to the letter. As a result, although he made serious mistakes, notably in his dash to the frontier during "Crusader", he was usually able to recover and was never, until Alamein, defeated in detail, and even then not in the way that Ritchie and Norrie had been. O'Connor, Wavell, and Montgomery also fought with their forces under close control in sharp contrast to Cunningham, Ritchie, and Auchinleck, who on more than one occasion allowed their battles to degenerate into isolated actions by divisions and brigades without there being a coherent and all-embracing plan for the whole army. The situation was aggravated by the fact that while Rommel was a master of the opportunity battle and experienced in armoured warfare, Cunningham and Ritchie were not.

Auchinleck won a great victory in "Crusader", but though he subsequently came to recognize the need for the integration of the teeth arms of his army he failed to insist on battles being fought in accordance with these principles, and by allowing Ritchie to proceed with his own ideas contributed significantly to the defeats at Gazala and Matruh. Ritchie himself was also at fault in permitting his battles to be fought by his corps and divisional commanders, as it were in committee. Throughout his period of command of the 8th Army there is seldom any evidence of a battle being fought on a single design, and there is no doubt that this lack of firm direction and control at all levels contributed significantly to the defeats of the British and French infantry at Sidi Muftah and Bir Hacheim, and of our armour in the Cauldron and at Knightsbridge. This was in part Auchinleck's responsibility for he should never have allowed Ritchie to remain in a position where such a situation was likely to arise, but all three, Cunningham, Ritchie, and Auchinleck himself, were responsible at different times for fighting their armour in isolated brigades. By so doing they not only nullified the advantage of the numerical superiority which they frequently enjoyed, but created the conditions for its defeat in detail.

On the other hand both Montgomery and Rommel retained a firm grasp on the conduct of operations, and won great victories, and in the latter case prevented a heavy defeat from ending in a catastrophic rout.

Both sides overcame the difficulties of supplying and maintaining an army in the desert remarkably well, but the British system was far superior to that of the Germans, and the 8th Army was never seriously short of fuel or ammunition once battle had been joined. The FSDs of O'Connor's campaign were destined to be the forerunners of a base and supply network that covered the whole of the desert, and the greatest credit is due to the supply services of the army, for although they were fortunate in having in the Egyptian base a war economy in miniature, the transfer of the necessary stores and supplies to the desert involved the solution of problems of the greatest difficulty.

The RAF, too, evolved a system of supply and maintenance which in enabling the desert squadrons to advance or retire with the army was far superior to anything that the enemy could achieve. While Rommel's advances frequently left his air support far behind, this was never the case with the DAF which was always close to the army and able to give it some degree of support and air cover.

Inevitably in an area like the desert, the presence of bases and supply lines was bound to have a very important effect on the conduct of operations, and it is necessary to consider how far Rommel's failure to capture the Thalata base during "Crusader", and Ritchie's fears for the Belhamed base during the Gazala actions, affected the outcome of these battles.

In the air the functions of the opposing air forces were also sharply contrasted. The RAF for the most part concentrated on the strategic targets of enemy bases and lines of communication whereas the Luftwaffe and the Italian Air Force operated mainly in close support of their ground forces. For a long time the Germans were better than the DAF in close support operations, probably as a result of the fundamental difference in outlook of the two services, but one may ask whether Rommel might not have been better advised to have directed more of his air effort against the British base areas and communications and less against the army in the field.

Inter-service co-operation among the British services was good, even when Auchinleck reduced the effectiveness of the DAF's support for the army by removing his own headquarters from the vicinity of Coningham's, and final victory came as the culmination of a long period of combined and inter-related effort by all concerned.

Ultimately the British were successful in North Africa because theirs was the sounder strategy and because, with control of the sea, they were able to build up and supply a large army in the desert, and in Montgomery, to find a general capable of outfighting Rommel. The Germans lost because they were first unwilling, and then unable, thanks to the Royal Navy, to supply Rommel with the men and the material support he required for victory. It is against this background of contrasted strategic policies that the desert fighting, O'Connor's brilliant campaign, the remarkable victories of Rommel, the bravery and determination of Auchinleck and the 8th Army in "Crusader", the disasters of Gazala and Tobruk, and the decisive battles of Alam Haifa and El Alamein must be seen. And it is pertinent, finally, to ask whether any power can do as Hitler's Germany did, and neglect a theatre of operations which its main antagonist deems to be vital to its survival.

Bibliography

The following works are prescribed reading for candidates for the Staff/
Promotion Examination:—

The Mediterranean and the Middle East, Vols. I-III, by Major-General I. S. O.
Playfair (H.M.S.O.).
War Memoirs, Vol. II, *Their Finest Hour,* by W. S. Churchill (Cassell).
War Memoirs, Vol. Ill, *The Grand Alliance,* by W. S. Churchill (Cassell).
African Trilogy, by A. Moorehead (Hamish Hamilton).
Foxes of the Desert, by P. Carell (Macdonald).

In the opinion of the author the following books and articles should also be
read if a proper understanding of the desert campaigns is to be obtained:—

Crisis in the Desert, by J. A. I. Agar-Hamilton and L. C. F. Turner (O.U.P.).
The Sidi Resegh Battles, by J. A. I. Agar-Hamilton and L. C. F. Turner
(O.U.P.).
Against Great Odds, by Brigadier C. N. Barclay (Sifton Praed and Co.)
The Desert Generals, by Correlli Barnett (Wm. Kimber).
El Alamein, by Major-General R. M. P. Carver (Batsford).
Articles in the Royal Armoured Corps Journal, 1949–51, by Major-General R.
M. P. Carver (Batsford).
Auchinleck, by John Connell (Cassell).
The Rommel Papers, by Captain B. H. Liddell Hart (Collins).
The Tanks, Vol. II, by Captain B. H. Liddell Hart (Cassell).
El Alamein to the River Sangro by Field-Marshal Lord Montgomery
(Hutchinson).
The Memoirs, by Field-Marshal Lord Montgomery (Collins).
Armour, by R. M. Orgorkiewicz (Stevens & Sons).

Suggested Works for Further Reading

The Memoirs, by Field-Marshal Earl Alexander of Tunis (Cassell).
The Phantom Major, by Virginia Cowles (Collins).

A Sailors Odyssey, by Admiral of the Fleet Lord Cunningham of Hyndhope (Hutchinson).

Operation "Victory", by Major-General Sir F. de Guingand (Hodder and Stoughton).

The Business of War, by Major-General Sir John Kennedy (Hutchinson).

Infantry Brigadier, by Brigadier Sir H. Kippenberger (O.U.P.).

Panzer Battles, by Major-General F. von Mellenthin (Cassell).

Montgomery, by A. Moorehead (Hamish Hamilton).

Alamein, by C. E. L. Phillips (Heineman).

Approach to Battle, by Lieutenant-General Sir F. Tuker (Cassell).

Rommel, by Brigadier Desmond Young (Collins).

Notes on Abbreviations and Other Terms Used in the Text

Abbreviations:

RAF   Royal Air Force.

DAF   Desert Air Force. (An independent Command within the RAF in the Middle East designed for work with the Army.)

DAK   Deutsches Afrika Korps. (The German Africa Corps, the main armoured force of Rommel's command, consisting of the 15th and 21st Panzer Divisions.)

OKH   Oberkommando des Heeres. (The German Army High Command, used by Hitler to exercise personal control of all operations.)

Outline Divisional Organizations I

(a) *British Armoured Divisions*—The original intention was that an armoured division should consist of two armoured brigades, each having three regiments of light or medium tanks; and a Support Group of two motorized infantry battalions, and field and antitank regiments of the Royal Artillery. After the retreat to Gazala Auchinleck decided to reorganize the armoured divisions, experience having shown them to be overweighted with tanks and weak in infantry and support weapons. Thereafter the armoured divisions consisted of an Armoured Brigade Group of three tank regiments, a motorized infantry battalion, and a mixed regiment of field and anti-tank artillery; and an Infantry Brigade Group of three motorized battalions and a similar artillery component. Both Brigade Groups also had Light AA artillery, RE, and administrative units.

(b) *British Infantry Divisions*—These began by having three Infantry Brigades, each of three battalions, and as Divisional Troops under the command of the Divisional Commander, three field regiments and one anti-tank regiment of the Royal Artillery, and RE, Signals, and administrative units. This organization was also changed by Auchinleck before the Gazala battles into one of three Infantry Brigade Groups each with three infantry battalions, its own artillery component, and a proportion of support troops.

Montgomery accepted the changes in divisional composition but ended the semi-independence of Brigade Groups and insisted on the Divisions being fought as single formations.

"I" Tank Battalions and Army Tank Brigades were never intended to be divisional troops and except in "Battleaxe" were allotted according to circumstances.

(c) *German Panzer Divisions*—These consisted of two regiments of motorized infantry (i.e., four battalions); one tank regiment; one panzer artillery regiment; and five battalions of supporting troops; a total of approximately 14,000 men.

Comparative Chronology of the Desert Campaigns

by
Major H.C.H. MEAD, M.A.
(After the Official History)

1940	General	Mediterranean	Egypt and Desert
June	11th. Italy enters war	23rd. Force "H" to Gibraltar (Admiral Somerville)	Frontier action
July	1st. Rumania cancels Anglo-French agreement. Battle of Britain begins	3rd. Oran 4th. French Fleet immobilized at Alexandria	
August	French Equatorial Africa declares for De Gaulle	1st. Hurricanes to Malta (HMS *Argus*)	
September	23rd-25th. French expedition to Dakar fails 27th. Axis pact with Japan	5th. Naval reinforcements to Alexandria	13th-18th. Italians invade Egypt 20th. Takoradi reinforcement route opens
October	23rd. Hitler meets Franco		16th. Eden's tour of Middle East

1940	General	Mediterranean	Egypt and Desert
November	4th. Spain assumes control of Tangier	11th. Fleet Air Arm attack Taranto 17th. HMS *Argus* flies Hurricanes to Malta 27th. Action off Cape Spartivento (Sicily)	
December	11th. Hitler cancels attack on Gibraltar 18th. Hitler's directive for attack on USSR		9th. O'Connor's offensive begins 16th. Capture of Solium

Red Sea and East Africa	Balkans
Italian submarines sunk Italians invade Kenya and Sudan 5th–19th. Loss of British Somaliland. Sandford Mission to Ethiopia	
	Germans in Rumania 28th. Italians invade Greece 29th. British move into Crete
6th–9th Action at Gallabat	4th. RAF in Greece 8th. Italian offensive collapses and Greeks counter-attack (18th) British liaison Mission to Turkey

1941	General	Mediterranean	Egypt and Desert
January		11th. First attack by Luftwaffe from Sicily	4th. Capture of Bardia 11th. LRDG raids Murzuk 22nd. Capture of Tobruk 29th. Aerial mining of Suez Canal begins
February		9th. Bombardment of Genoa 17th. Attempted landing, Kaso, etc. 25th. Landing of Castelorizo	6th. Capture of Benghazi 5th–7th. Battle of Beda Fomm 12th. Rommel arrives in Tripoli
March	1st. Bulgaria joins Axis 11th. Roosevelt signs lease-lend Act. Gariboldi replaces Graziani	Air attacks on Malta 28th. Action off Cape Matapan	24th. Axis occupy El Agheila
April		Heavy air attacks on Malta, and two operations to reinforce with aircraft 21st. Bombardment of Tripoli	Axis advance— 1st. Mersa Brega, 3rd. Benghazi, 8th. Mechili (General O'Connor captured 7th) 10th–11th. Axis reach Berdia and Solium. Attacks on Tobruk
May	Fliegercorps X begins to leave Sicily 19th. Air Marshal Tedder replaces Longmore	Air attacks on Malta lessen Malta reinforced with aircraft 5th–12th. Passage of "Tiger" convoy (238 tanks, 43 Hurricanes)	4th. Attack on Tobruk fails 15th–17th. British attack Hafaya– Sollum–Capuzzo ("Brevity") 27th. Germans retake Halfaya

Red Sea and East Africa	Balkans	Levant and Middle East
British offensive begins 19th. Capture of Kassala 22nd. Capture of Moyale	13th. Greeks decline British help 29th. General Metexas dies 31st. Churchill's appeal to the Turks	
3rd. Battle of Keren begins 23rd. Emperor enters Ethiopia 25th. Mogadishu captured	22nd. Eden Mission in Athens 26th. Eden Mission in Ankara	
27th. Capture of Keren	5th. British troops sail for Greece 9th–16th. Italian offensive in Albania 27th. Coup d'etat in Yugoslavia	Iraq political situation grows worse
5th. Addis Ababa taken 11th. Red Sea open to US shipping	6th. German invade Greece and Yugoslavia 24th–30th. Evacuation 27th. Germans in Athens	3rd. Raschid Ali seizes power 30th. Siege of Habbaniya begins
5th. Emperor enters Addis Ababa 16th. Duke of Aosta surrenders Axis in Syria	20th. Germans attack Crete 28th–31st. Allies evacuate Crete	6th. Siege of Habbaniya lifted 31st. Armistice signed in Iraq Axis in Syria

1941	General	Mediterranean	Egypt and Desert
June	Begin regular flow of US supplies 22nd. Germans invade Russia	Four operations to reinforce Malta with aircraft	Tobruk besieged 15th–17th. "Battleaxe" attack Halfaya–Sollum–Capuzzo fails
July	5th. Auchinleck replaces Wavell. Bastico replaces Gariboldi 31st. Panzergruppe Africa formed	"Substance" and "Style" convoys to Malta. Italian EMBs attack Grand Harbour, Malta	Tobruk besieged 18th. Australians to leave Tobruk 29th. Auchinleck and Tedder to London to discuss offensive
August	14th. Atlantic Charter signed	2nd. "Style" convoy reaches Malta	Tobruk besieged 19th–29th. First stage of relief of Australians. Planning for "Crusader" begins
September		Operations to reinforce Malta with aircraft. German submarines in Mediterranean 20th. Italian human torpedo attack on Gibraltar 24th–28th. "Halberd" convoy to Malta	Tobruk besieged 2nd. Preliminary orders for "Crusader" 14th–15th. German raid on Sofafi fails 18th. 8th Army formed 19th–27th. Second stage of relief of Australians from Tobruk
October	2nd. Lease–Lend funds to Middle East 24th. Germans attack Kharkov	Force "K" arrives at Malta	Tobruk besieged 9th. Western Desert Air Force formed 12th–15th. Third stage of evacuation of Australians from Tobruk

Red Sea and East Africa	Balkans	Levant and Middle East
Capture of Jimma and Assab		8th. British and Free French enter Syria 20th. Damascus captured German intrigues in Persia 3rd. British occupy Mosul 29th. Command in Iraq reverts to India
Campaign in Ethiopia draws to close, and South African troops begin to leave for western desert		German intrigues in Persia 14th. End of hostilities in Syria
Nigerian troops return to West Africa Blockade of French Somaliland continued		25th. British forces enter Persia 28th. Persian resistance ceases, and government falls
25th. Italians at Wolchefit surrender Blockade of French Somaliland continues 15th. East African Command formed		17th. British and Russians enter Teheran Start of development supply route to Russia
Preparations to attack Gondar 21st. Red Sea transferred to Mediterranean station Blockade of French Somaliland		

1941	General	Mediterranean	Egypt and Desert
November	1st. 9th Army formed. US Mission in Cairo 22nd–28th. Heavy fighting at Rostov	9th. Force "K" sinks Duisburg convoy 13th. HMS *Ark Royal* lost. Mediterranean Fleet operations in support of "Crusader" 25th. HMS *Barham* sunk	Tobruk besieged "Crusader" begins
December	7th–8th. Japanese attack Pearl Harbour and land in Malaya 11th. Axis declare war on USA	13th. Action st Cape Bon 14th. HMS *Galatea* lost 17th. Battle of Sirte (1st) 19th. Disaster to Force "K". 19th. Italian human torpedoes damage *Queen Elizabeth* and *Valiant* at Alexandria (Fortunes in Mediterranean at lowest ebb)	1st. First attempt to relieve Tobruk fails 5th. British advance resumed 10th. Tobruk relieved 16th. Enemy withdraws from Gazala 25th. British take Benghazi
1942			
January	1st. United Nations Declaration	Three small convoys reach Malta	2nd. Bardia surrenders 17th. Solium and Halfaya surrender 21st. Axis advance from Mersa Brega 28th. British evacuate Benghazi and retire to Gazala
February	15th. Fall of Singapore	12th–15th. Convoy from Alexandria fails to reach Malta	2nd. 8th Army stabilizes line at Gazala-Bir Hachim

Red Sea and East Africa	Middle East and Levant	Persia and Iraq
End of East African campaign: General Nasi surrenders at Gondar Blockade of French Somaliland		US Military Mission in Baghdad
Blockade of French Somaliland		
Blockade of French Somaliland	12th. Command of troops in Iraq passes from India to Middle East	
Blockade of French Somaliland	16th. 10th Army formed	

1942	General	Mediterranean	Egypt and Desert
March	20th. Sir Stafford Cripps visits Middle East	Heavy air attacks on Malta 7th, 21st, 29th. Three operations to reinforce Malta with aircraft 22nd. Battle of Sirte (2nd) 23rd. Convoy reaches Malta to be sunk in harbour	Lull in desert
April	Admiral Cunningham leaves, succeeded by Vice-Admiral Pridham-Whippell (temporary)	Force "H" leaves Gibraltar for Madagascar Air attacks on Malta reach peak 10th. Submarine flotilla leaves Malta 20th. USS *Wasp* flies Spitfires to Malta	Both sides build up for major attack
May	5th. British take Madagascar 8th. Gort succeeds Dobbie at Malta 20th. Admiral Harwood C.-in-C. Mediterranean US strategic bomber force arrives	Air attacks on Malta gradually decrease 9th. *Wasp* and *Eagle* fly Spitfires to Malta 18th. *Eagle* flies Spitfires to Malta 14th–15th. Italian human torpedo attack on Alexandria fails	10th. Cabinet orders Auchinleck to attack in May 26th. Axis beats us to the punch with attack on Gazala- Bir Hachim position

1942	General	Mediterranean	Egypt and Desert
June	Peak sinkings in Atlantic 4th–6th. Japanese defeated at Midway Island Formation of US Army Command and US Middle East Airforce 27th. Eisenhower appointed C.-in-C. Allied Expeditionary Force	3rd, 9th. Two operations to reinforce Malta with Spitfires 12th–16th. "Harpoon" convoy reaches Malta from West "Vigorous" convoy from East turns back	5th–6th. Cauldron disaster 10th. Bir Hachim evacuated 11th–12th. Defeat of British armour. 14th. Decision to withdraw from Gazala positions. 21st. Fall of Tobruk. 25th. Auchinleck takes over command of 8th Army from Ritchie, at Matruh

Red Sea and East Africa	Middle East and Levant	Persia and Iraq
Blockade of French Somaliland		

1942	General	Mediterranean	Egypt and Desert
July	Anglo–US agreement on "Torch". 24th. Germans take Rostov. US Tactical Air Force starts to arrive in Middle East	1st–14th. Heavy air attacks on Malta renewed (pre-invasion) 15th–21st. Two operations to reinforce Malta with Spitfires 10th. Submarine flotilla returns to Malta	1st–5th. Rommel fails to breakthrough at El Alamein 10th–26th. Repeated British attacks end indecisively Both sides exhausted
August	4th–10th. Churchill in Cairo 12th. And attends first Moscow Conference 15th. Alexander succeeds Auchinleck as C.-in-C. 16th. Germans reach Maikop in Caucasus 24th. Allied H.Q. for "Torch" set up	10th–15th. "Pedestal" convoy to Malta 11th. *Eagle* sunk 11th–17th. Two operations to reinforce Malta with Spitfires	13th. Montgomery takes command of 8th Army 30th–31st. Axis offensive begins Battle of Alam Haifa
September	Peak of struggle for Stalingrad		2nd. Rommel begins to withdraw 7th. Battle over British prepare to take offensive (Battle of Alamein, 24th October– 4th November)

Red Sea and East Africa	Middle East and Levant	Persia and Iraq
		US Persian Gulf Service Command set up
		21st. Persia and Iraq Command set up under Maitland Wilson

Who's Who

Wavell of Cyrenaica and Winchester—1st Earl cr. 1947; Field-Marshal Archibald Percival Wavell, G.C.B., G.C.S.L, G.C.I.E., C.M.G., M.C.; born 1883; educated Winchester College; R.M.C. Sandhurst; Staff College Camberley; commissioned into the Black Watch, 1901; served in the South African War; India; 1914–16 France (M.C.); 1917 Russia; 1917–1920 Egyptian Expeditionary Force; Brevet Lieutenant-Colonel, 1917; B.G.S. XX Corps, 1918–1919; B.G.S. Egyptian Expeditionary Force, 1919–1920; Colonel, 1921; Major-General, 1933; Lieutenant-General, 1938; General, 1940; Field-Marshal, 1943; commanded 6th Infantry Brigade, 1930–34; 2nd Division, Aldershot, 1935–37; G.O.C. Palestine and Transjordan, 1937–38; G.O.C.-in-C. Southern Command, 1938–39; C.-in-C.Middle East, 1939–41; C.-in-C. India, 1941–43; Supreme Allied Commander south-west Pacific, January-March, 1943; Viceroy and Governor-General of India, 1943–47. Numerous honorary degrees; author of famous works on Military History, including "Allenby, Soldier and Statesman", and on poetry; President of the Classical Society; died 24th May, 1950.

O'Connor—General Sir Richard, G.C.B., D.S.O., M.C.; born 1889; commissioned into The Cameronians, c. 1909; 1914–1918 France and Italy (D.S.O. and Bar, M.C., 9 Mentions in Despatches); G.S.O.2 War Office, 1932–34; Imperial Defence College, 1935; commanded Peshawar Brigade, 1936–38; Military Governor of Jerusalem, 1938–39; commanded Western Desert Force and XIII Corps from 1940 until February, 1941; captured during first German offensive, April, 1941; escaped from PoW camp, 1943; Corps Commander in N.W. Europe, 1944; G.O.C.-in-C. Eastern Command and N.W. Army India, 1945–46; Adjutant-General, 1947; retired 1948.

Creagh—Major-General Sir Michael O'Moore, K.B.E., M.C.; born 1892; commissioned into 7th Hussars, 1911; 1914–18 Western Front (M.C. and Mention in Despatches); Brevet Lieutenant-Colonel, 1931; Colonel, 1938;

Major-General, 1941; commanded 7th Armoured Division in Egypt and Libya, 1940–41; retired 1944.

Beresford-Peirse—Lieutenant-General Sir Noel de la Poer, K.B.E., D.S.O.; born 1887; joined Royal Artillery from R.M.A. Woolwich, c. 1906; served on Western Front, 1914–18 (D.S.O.); filled various appointments during inter-war years and qualified at the Staff College Camberley; Lieutenant-Colonel, 1935; Colonel, 1937; Major-General, 1938; commanded 4th Indian Division, 1940–41, in Western Desert, and after December, 1941, in Eritrea; commanded Western Desert Force, April–September, 1941; G.O.C. Sudan, September, 1941–April, 1942; Commander XV Indian Corps, 1942; G.O.C.-in-C. Southern Army India, 1942–45; Welfare-General India, 1945–47; retired 1947; died January, 1953.

Morshead—Lieutenant-General Sir Leslie James, K.C.B., C.M.G., D.S.O.; born 1889 at Ballarat, Victoria; 1914–18 France and Gallipoli with Australian Imperial Forces (6 Mentions in Despatches); 1916–19 commanded 33rd Australian Battalion; in Australia commanded 14th Infantry Brigade, 1933; 15th Infantry Brigade, 1934–36; 5th Infantry Brigade, 1937–39; 1939–41 commanded 18th Australian Infantry Brigade in UK and Middle East; 1941–42 commanded 9th Australian Division, and Tobruk during the first siege; G.O.C. A.I.F. (Middle East), 1942–43, including 9th Australian Division at El Alamein, 1942; returned to Australia and commanded 2nd Australian Corps, 1943–44; G.O.C. New Guinea, 1944; 2nd Australian Army, 1944; G.O.C. 1 Australian Corps and Task Force for Borneo, 1945 (3 Mentions in Despatches); died 26th September, 1959.

Harding of Petherton—1st Baron cr. 1958; Field-Marshal John Harding, G.C.B., C.B.E., D.S.O., M.C.; born 1896; educated Ilminster Grammar School; served in T.A., and 1914–18 with Machine Gun Corps on Western Front (M.C.); regular commission in Somerset Light Infantry, 1920; *p.s.c.*, 1928; Brevet Major, 1935; Brevet Lieutenant-Colonel, 1938; B.G.S. Western Desert Force, 1940; D.C.G.S. Middle East, 1941–42; commanded 7th Armoured Division, 1942, including El Alamein; Lieutenant-General and Corps Commander in Italy, 1943; C.I.G.S., 1952–55; Governor of Cyprus, 1955–58.

Auchinleck—Field-Marshal Sir Claude J. E., G.C.B., G.C.I.E., C.S.I., D.S.O., O.B.E.; born 1884; educated at Wellington, and commissioned into 62nd Punjabis, 1904; served in Middle East, 1914–18 (D.S.O., O.B.E.,

Brevet Lieutenant-Colonel); Imperial Defence College, 1927; D.S. at Staff College Quetta, 1930–33; commanded Peshawar Brigade and Mohmand Operations, 1933–36; D.C.G.S. India, 1936–38; G.O.C. Northern Norway, 1940; G.O.C. Southern Command, 1940; C.-in-C. India, 1941; C.-in-C. Middle East, 1941–42; C.-in-C. India, 1943–47; Supreme Commander India and Pakistan, 1947.

Cunningham—General Sir Alan, G.C.M.G., K.C.B., D.S.O., M.C.; joined Royal Artillery from R.M.A. Woolwich, 1906; served in France, 1914–18 (Brigade Major and G.S.O.2, D.S.O., M.C., and 5 Mentions in Despatches); Naval Staff College, 1925; Brevet Lieutenant-Colonel, 1928; Imperial Defence College, 1937; C.R.A. I Division, 1937–38; Major-General, 1938; G.O.C. East Africa, 1940–41; Commander 8th Army, 1941; Commandant of Staff College Camberley, 1942; General, 1945. Younger brother of Admiral of the Fleet Lord Cunningham of Hyndhope *(see below)*.

Godwin Austen—General Sir Alfred Reade, K.C.S.I., C.B., O.B.E., M.C.; born 1889; joined South Wales Borderers from R.M.C., 1909; served on staff of 40th Infantry Brigade, 1914–18 in Gallipoli, Palestine, and Mesopotamia (O.B.E., M.C., 2 Mentions in Despatches, and a Brevet Majority); between the wars served on the staff in England, commanded the 2nd Battalion D.C.L.I., and commanded the 14th Infantry Brigade, and then the 8th Division during the Arab Rebellion in Palestine, 1938–39; August 1940, sent by Wavell to command in British Somaliland; returned to East Africa as a Divisional Commander under Cunningham, and played an important part in that campaign; July 1941, took over XIII Corps in 8th Army, again under Cunningham; February 1942, relieved of his command, at own request, by Auchinleck after a difference of opinion with Ritchie; Vice Q.M.G. during "Overlord" and N.W. Europe campaigns, 1944–45; 1945–47 Principal Administration Officer India; retired 1947; 1947–49 Chairman of S.W. Division of National Coal Board; died 1963.

Norrie—1st Baron cr. 1957; of Wellington, New Zealand, and Upton; Lieutenant-General Charles Willoughby Moke Norrie, G.C.M.G., G.C.V.O., C.B., D.S.O., M.C.; born 1893; educated Eton and Sandhurst; commissioned into 11th Hussars, 1913; 1914–18 served in France on staff, and with Tank Corps (D.S.O., M.C. and Bar, 2 Mentions in Despatches, 4 times wounded); Major, 1924; *p.s.c.* Camberley; 1926–30 Brigade Major 1st Cavalry Brigade; 1931–35 Lieutenant-Colonel commanding 10th Hussars;

Colonel, 1935; commanded 1st Cavalry Brigade, 1936–38; Commander 1st Armoured Brigade, 1938–40; Inspector Royal Armoured Corps, 1940; Commander 1st Armoured Division, 1940–41; G.O.C. XXX Corps, 1941–42 until after Gazala; Commander R.A.C., 1943; Governor of South Australia, 1944–52; Governor-General of New Zealand, 1952–57.

Ritchie—General Sir Neil, G.B.E. K.C.B., D.S.O., M.C.; born 1897; entered the Black Watch, 1914; 1914–18 served in France, Palestine, and Mesopotamia (D.S.O., M.C.); *p.s.c.*, 1930; G.S.O.2 India, 1933–37; Brevet Major, 1933; Brevet Lieutenant-Colonel, 1936; B.G.S., 1939; commanded 51st Highland Division, 1939–40; D.C.G.S. Middle East, 1941; commanded 8th Army, 1941–42; commanded 52nd Division, 1942–43; commanded XII Corps, N.W. Europe, 1944–45; C.-in-C. FARELF, 1947–49; retired 1951.

Freyberg—General Lord Freyberg, V.C., G.C.M.G., K.C.B., K.C.B., K.B.E., D.S.O.; born 1889; educated in New Zealand; commissioned as Sub-Lieutenant in the Naval Division, 1914; served at Antwerp, Gallipoli, and on Western Front, 1914–18 (V.C., D.S.O. and 2 Bars, 6 Mentions in Despatches, Croix de Guerre); took a regular commission in the Queen's Royal West Surrey Regiment, 1916; C.M.G., 1919; between the wars he served in various appointments and tried unsuccessfully to swim the Channel; Major-General, 1934; invalided out, 1937; 1939 recalled, and in November appointed to command the New Zealand Forces Overseas; commanded the New Zealand Division in Greece and Crete, 1941, and in Operation "Crusader" in the Western Desert; disagreed with Auchinleck and went with the Division to Syria; rejoined the 8th Army in June, 1942, still as Divisional Commander, and fought with it throughout the rest of the North African campaigns, and in Italy; played important parts in the Battles of El Alamein, the Sangro Crossing, and as Commander of the New Zealand Corps at Cassino; 3rd Bar to D.S.O., 1945; appointed Governor-General of New Zealand, 1946 and served until 1952; altogether he was wounded thirty times; died 4th July, 1963.

Alexander of Tunis—1st Earl cr. 1946; Field-Marshal Harold Alexander, K.G., P.C., G.C.B., O.M., G.C.M.G., C.S.I., D.S.O., M.C.; born 1891; commissioned in Irish Guards, 1910; 1914–18 Western Front (D.S.O., M.C., 5 Mentions in Despatches); *p.s.c.*, 1927; commanded Irish Guards, 1928–30; I.D.C., 1930; commanded Brigade in India, 1934–36; Major-General, 1937; commanded I Division, 1938–40; Commander I Corps, 1940; C.-in-C. Southern Command, 1940–42; G.O.C. Burma, 1942; C.-in-C. Middle

East, 1942–43; C.-in-C. Italy, 1943–44; Supreme Allied Commander Mediterranean, 1944–45;Governor-General of Canada, 1946–52; Minister of Defence, 1952–54

Montgomery of Alamein—1st Viscount cr. 1946; Field-Marshal Bernard Law Montgomery, K.G., G.C.B., C.B., D.S.O.; born 1887; joined Royal Warwickshire Regiment from R.M.C. Sandhurst, 1908; Lieutenant-Colonel, 1931; Colonel, 1934; Major-General, 1938; Lieutenant-General, 1942; General, 1942; Field-Marshal, 1944; 1914–18 Western Front (D.S.O., Mention in Despatches, Brevet Major); commanded 1st Battalion Royal Warwickshire Regiment, 1931–34; D.S. Staff College Quetta, 1934–37; commanded 9th Infantry Brigade, 1937–38; 3rd Division, 1938–40; V Corps, 1940; XII Corps, 1941; C.-in-C. South-East Command, 1942; commanded 8th Army, 1942– January, 1944; C.-in-C. Allied Armies Northern France, 1944; commanded 21st Army Group, 1944–45; B.A.O.R., 1945–46; C.I.G.S., 1946–48; Chairman of Western Europe Commanders-in-Chief Committee, 1948–51; Deputy Supreme Allied Commander Europe, 1951–58.

Tedder—1st Baron cr. 1946; Marshal of the Royal Air Force Arthur William Tedder, G.C.B.; born 1890; commissioned in Dorset Regiment, 1914; transferred to R.F.C., 1916; 1915–19 served in Egypt and France; transferred to R.A.F., 1919; commanded 207 Squadron Constantinople, 1922–23; Naval Staff College, 1923–24; Imperial Defence College, 1928; D.S. at R.A.F. Staff College, 1929–31; Director of Training Air Ministry, 1934–36; A.O.C. Far East, 1936–38; Director-General of Research and Development Air Ministry, 1938–40; Deputy A.O.C.-in-C. Middle East, 1940–41; A.O.C.-in-C. Middle East, 1941–43; Allied Air C.-in-C. Mediterranean, 1943; Deputy Supreme Commander under Eisenhower in N.W. Europe, 1943–45; Chief of the Air Staff, 1946–50.

Coningham—Air-Marshal Sir Arthur, K.C.B., K.B.E., D.S.O., M.C., D.F.C., A.F.C.; born in Brisbane, 1895; educated in New Zealand; 1914–18 served with New Zealand Forces in Samoa, Egypt, and on the Western Front (D.S.O., M.C., D.F.C., and Mention in Despatches); served in Kurdistan operations, 1923; 1939–41 Bomber Command; 1941–43 commanded the Desert Air Force in support of the 8th Army; formed the 1st Tactical Air Force in French North Africa, 1943; A.O.C.-in-C. 2nd Tactical Air Force, 1944–45; Air-Marshal, 1946; A.O.C.-in-C. Flying Training Command, 1945–47; retired 1947; died 30th January, 1948.

Cunningham of Hyndhope—1st Viscount cr. 1946; Admiral of the Fleet Andrew Browne Cunningham, K.T., G.C.B., O.M., D.S.O.; born 1883, elder brother of General Sir Alan Cunningham *(see above);* entered the Royal Navy from HMS *Britannia*, 1898; Rear-Admiral, 1933; Vice-Admiral, 1937; D.C.N.S., 1938–39; C.-in-C. Mediterranean Fleet, 1939–42; First Sea Lord, 1943–46; died 1963.

Who's Who—2

Rommel—Field-Marshal Erwin Eugen Johannes; born 1891; entered army, 1910; served as infantry officer on French, Russian, and Italian Fronts, 1914–18, awarded Pour le Mérite and Iron Cross 1st Class; D. S. Infantry School Dresden, 1929–33; 1933–35 commanded infantry battalion; Instructor War Academy Wiener Neustadt, 1938; commanded Hitler's Escort Battalion, 1939; Major-General, 1939; commanded 7th Panzer Division in France from February, 1940; commanded Panzer Group Africa, February, 1941; Field-Marshal, after capture of Tobruk, June, 1942; Commander Army Group Africa from March, 1943; Commander Army Group B in Italy, 1943; C.-in-C. Army Group B in N.W. Europe, January, 1944; wounded, July, 1944; murdered, 14th October, 1944.

Who's Who—3

Graziani—Marshal Rodolfo, Marquis of Neghelli cr. 1937; born 1882; professional soldier and colonial administrator, and ardent Fascist; fought in 1914–18 War; Governor of Cyrenaica, and Commander of punitive operations against the Senussi, 1930–34; commanded on Southern Front during Italian invasion of Ethiopia, 1935–36; ruthless and unpopular Viceroy of Ethiopia, 1936–37; made Chief of Italian Army Staff, November, 1939; succeeded Marshal Balbo as Governor-General and C.-in-C. of Libya, June, 1940; crushingly defeated by Wavell and O'Connor in winter of 1940–41; resigned February, 1941; emerged as head of Fascist resistance in Italy after fall of Mussolini, 1943; died 1955.

Questions

(Selected by Major-General H. Essame, C.B.E., D.S.O., M.C.)

1. The 12th of August, 1942, found the allied armies in the Western Desert on the defensive, yet in under a month, by the 7th September, the battle of Alam Haifa had been won and the way had been paved for an Allied Offensive.

    Describe the steps that were taken to set the stage for the battle of Alam Haifa and draw a sketch map showing the dispositions of both sides at the start, and the Allied moves which took place during the battle.

2. The first British offensive in the Western Desert, which began on 9th December, 1940, was the first campaign in which two modem armies with comparable air forces had met and fought over undeveloped country.

    Describe the planning of the campaign and the measures taken to ensure success.

3. "Administration is not the drab servant of the art of war unworthy of mention in the same breath as battle, but is rather of war's very essence."

    Discuss this statement referring only to the war in the Mediterranean and Middle East.

4. Ferdinand de Lesseps, by building the Suez Canal, "marked the site of a future great battlefield."

    What were the factors that made Egypt so important as a base area in 1939; what improvements had to be made and how were these carried out?

5. The success of Operation "Compass" depended largely on the air and administration plans. State briefly what these plans were, and how security was maintained.

6. The attacks on Nibeiwa and Tobruk were both made by infantry and armour. What were the differences between the two plans and what were the reasons that prompted them?

7. By the end of January, 1941, Marshal Graziani was contemplating a withdrawal of all his forces to Sirte, while General O'Connor was about to resume his advance to Benghazi.

   What factors influenced these opposing commanders in their appreciations?

8. Describe in outline the engagement at Beda Fomm in February, 1941. What reasons led to the Italian failure to breakthrough the British encircling force?

9. Contrast the reasons for the Italian failures and British successes in Libya and Cyrenaica from December, 1940, until March, 1941.

10. Field-Marshal Sir William Slim has written "The British Army in the last war spawned a surprising number of special units and formations. I have come to the conclusion that private armies are expensive, wasteful, and unnecessary."

    Discuss this statement with reference to the formation, training, and operations of the Long Range Desert Group until March, 1941.

11. Field-Marshal Montgomery has said he considers that morale is the most important factor in war.

    Discuss this statement in the light of the situation before the battle of El Alamein.

12. The operations in the period August–November 1942 fall into three broad phases, the defensive occupation of the El Alamein position; the offensive between 23rd October and 5th November 1942; and thirdly the preparations for the pursuit.

    Discuss the main administrative considerations which had to be taken into account during the whole period.

13. The Army Commander's original conception of the plan for the El Alamein offensive had been to attack the enemy simultaneously on both flanks—the main attack to be launched on the right flank by XXX Corps with a secondary attack on the southern flank by XIII Corps. It was planned that X Corps should pass through the gap made by XXX Corps and sit astride the enemy supply routes. In early October, the Army Commander made certain major changes in this plan.

    What were these changes and what were the reasons and motives which caused him to make these alterations?

14. The battle of El Alamein was won by 4th/5th November, 1942. Describe the main strategical and tactical considerations which affected the plan for the pursuit of the enemy after the successful outcome of the

offensive and give the plan made by the Army Commander to regroup his forces for this action.

15. What plans were made to deceive the enemy and to conceal the strength, dispositions and intentions of the 8th Army, before and during the battle of El Alamein?

    Comment generally on the effect of these plans.

16. There are two ways, among others, in which a commander can conduct the defensive battle, both of which may ultimately lead to victory. The first is the use of counter-attack. The second, broadly, is for the commander to position his forces so that the enemy is compelled to attack him on ground of his own choosing.

    Discuss these two ways of conducting the defensive battle, illustrating your answer by examples from the period you have studied.

17. The influence of ground has always been a major factor in the conduct of the land battle. The battle of El Alamein was no exception.

    Describe the ground over which the battle was fought and show how natural physical features influenced the plan for the battle.

18. The battle of El Alamein was the culmination of a series of subsidiary battles in which both sides were players for position.

    Describe any one of these preliminary battles and explain the reasons which caused it to be undertaken.

19. Generals Alexander and Montgomery arrived in the Western Desert in August, 1942, but it was not until October that they took up the offensive.

    Describe the administrative steps taken to prepare for the battle of El Alamein.

20. The first British attack in the Western Desert in December, 1940, resulted in the capture of Sidi Barrani, and opened up the way to the advance across Libya and Cyrenaica which culminated in the capture of Benghazi. Success was achieved in the face of numerically superior ground and air forces.

    Describe the preparations for this attack and state what werein your opinion, the principal factors which contributed to success.

21. "Balance on the battlefield implies the disposal of available forces in such a way that it is never necessary to react to the enemy's thrusts and moves; a balanced Army proceeds relentlessly with its plans in spite of what the enemy may do."

    Show how this doctrine was applied at (a) Alam Haifa, (b) El Alamein.

22. "Surprise is a most effective and powerful influence in war, and its moral effect can be very great" (High Command).

    Give an example of strategic and of tactical surprise being obtained in North Africa in the period May, 1941–July, 1942, and explain in both cases the methods used to achieve it.

23. Discuss the RAF's contribution in the battle of Gazala and the subsequent withdrawal to the El Alamein position in 1942.

24. "Rommel's success in North Africa must unfortunately be largely attributed to the mediocrity of all his opponents before Montgomery's arrival."

    Is this, in your opinion, a fair assessment of his performance in the period May, 1941–July, 1942?

25. "The lessons to be learnt from defeat are more than from victory" (Field-Marshal Slim).

    To what extent is the aphorism applicable to the battle of Gazala in June, 1942?

Index

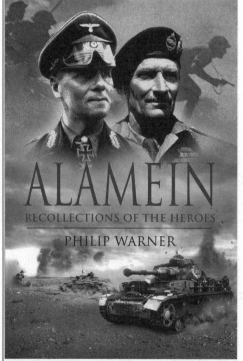